D1596653

Shakespeare
on the American
Yiddish Stage

STUDIES IN

THEATRE HISTORY & CULTURE

Edited by Thomas Postlewait

Shakespeare
on the American
Yiddish Stage

JOEL BERKOWITZ

University of Iowa Press ʊ Iowa City

University of Iowa Press, Iowa City 52242

Copyright © 2002 by the University of Iowa Press

All rights reserved

Printed in the United States of America

Design by Richard Hendel

http://www.uiowa.edu/~uipress

The publication of this book was generously supported
by the University of Iowa Foundation and the Koret Jewish Studies
Publications Program.

Printed on acid-free paper

Library of Congress Cataloging-in-Publication Data

Berkowitz, Joel, 1965–

Shakespeare on the American Yiddish stage / Joel Berkowitz.

p.   cm.—(Studies in theatre history and culture)

Includes bibliographical references (p.   ) and index.

ISBN 0-87745-800-6 (cloth)

1. Shakespeare, William, 1564–1616—Stage history—United
States.   2. Shakespeare, William, 1564–1616—Translations
into Yiddish—History and criticism.   3. Theater, Yiddish—
United States—History.   I. Title.   II. Series.

PR3105 .B47 2002

792.9'5'0973—dc21   2001057395

02 03 04 05 06 C 5 4 3 2 1

For my parents

Contents

Preface
Procedures, Methodology, Orthography

The history of each Shakespeare play performed in Yiddish has its own personality, the result of both nature and nurture. Certain works seem more likely to succeed with Yiddish audiences than others by virtue of the conflicts they depict: plays with a strong family component, for example — plays whose heroes, however superficially remote from an audience of working-class eastern European Jewish immigrants to the United States, struggle with emotions with which such an audience could identify. An Antony leading his legions between Egypt and Rome would offer little to interest them. A Lear, struggling to hold family and kingdom together, would and did.

Procedures and Methodology

The selection criteria for translating Shakespeare had a great deal to do with production trends as well. Some of the plays — such as *Hamlet*, to cite the most obvious example — seem ubiquitous from era to era and culture to culture. Still others never seem to have caught on; how often does one have the chance to see *King John* on stage? Yiddish actors and playwrights always had a keen sense of such patterns, following closely what their colleagues in other cultures were performing. They certainly would have realized that the great Shakespearean actors of their era wanted to play Hamlet, Othello, Falstaff, or Lady Macbeth, Cleopatra, or Rosalind. No one achieved Shakespearean immortality solely on the virtue of a memorable performance as Pericles or Henry VI.

The conditions that gave rise to the production of each play dictate, to a great extent, the sources I have relied upon to tell the story of its production history in Yiddish. Wherever possible, I have examined the text of the play. This is particularly helpful when extant manuscript versions can be found, for published versions of Yiddish dramas are notorious for being far from what the author originally wrote. In a few cases, a specific playscript can be identified with a specific production. A number of other extant manuscripts cannot be dated precisely, but were clearly used in production; many of these are labeled as having belonged to a particular actor's repertoire.

Complementing the scripts themselves are the Yiddish newspapers, which provide information from dates and places to minute production details. The period when any given production was mounted affects what sort of information the newspapers tend to provide. Only a smattering of Yiddish periodicals were published in the United States before 1900, and the microfilms that do exist of these publications often contain long gaps where weeks or months of the newspaper have been lost to the ages. Those that have survived tend to be fertile sources of theatre advertisements, whose evocative prolixity and boastfulness was, alas, tamed after a few years. But the diminished amount of information offered by the advertisements over time is more than compensated for by the increased attention the American Yiddish press pays to the theatre after 1900. Few of the early Yiddish reviewers were trained as theatre critics, so for the theatre historian, reading their reviews can often prove an exercise in frustration. They often spend most of their allotted space summarizing the plot, and then perhaps adding a few words about the performances and production values almost as an afterthought. This situation greatly improved over time, as the Yiddish dailies devoted regular columns — even whole pages — to the theatre and other arts, and assigned specialists to critique the cultural offerings of the Jewish quarter and beyond. In certain exceptional cases, the traffic flowed in the opposite direction, with English-language newspapers sending their critics to review Shakespeare in Yiddish, thus leaving us with important supplementary information about these performances.

The other most significant source of evidence about the productions can be found in the memoirs of Yiddish actors, playwrights, and composers who recorded their reminiscences about the production and reception of Shakespeare in Yiddish. The memoirs of many of the major and secondary participants in this story offer commentary on the phenomenon of Shakespeare in Yiddish, and often provide details of specific productions. Later scholarship — histories, lexicons, and a few scattered readings of the plays — provide supplementary information, but wherever possible, I have tried to build this story on a firsthand foundation by turning to the scripts, critics, and theatre personnel who had direct contact with the productions.

Just as the writers and theatre companies who created the tradition of American Yiddish Shakespeare productions had to make choices about which plays to produce and how, I have had to establish selection criteria as well. I have tried to set parameters that allow me to examine a wide range of material while avoiding the pitfall of examining any play with a vaguely Shakespearean resonance or turning up information on every American production of the plays I discuss. The mere resemblance of any Yiddish work to a Shakespeare play does not suffice to illustrate what Shakespeare meant to the American Yiddish theatre culture; two star-crossed lovers do not a *Romeo and Juliet* make, nor a jealous husband an *Othello*. This study focuses on Yiddish plays that, in one way or another, were advertised or otherwise publicly perceived as deriving from Shakespeare. Such a perception falls into four categories: first and most obvious, adaptations or translations that retain the original title; second, works whose altered titles give some obvious hint of a Shakespearean source (the most conspicuous examples being the many adaptations that bear the name *Shylock*); third, works whose main titles betray no hint of Shakespeare, but which advertise Shakespearean pedigrees in a subtitle or on the title page (e.g., Kobrin's *The Blind Musician, or, The Jewish Othello*); and, finally, plays that were described by contemporaries as deriving from a Shakespearean source even if they were not advertised as such (e.g., Gordin's *The Lithuanian Brothers Luria*, critiqued by Yiddish writer Y. L. Peretz as a Yiddish *Romeo and Juliet*).

Audience perception sometimes defines what is considered Yiddish theatre, for that category stretches beyond productions in which all or even most of the characters speak Yiddish. First of all, characters in plays from the first decades of the professional Yiddish theatre tended to speak in a stiffly elevated hybrid of German and Yiddish known as *daytshmerish* rather than in the everyday vernacular.[1] Furthermore, German Jewish guest stars such as Morris Morrison sometimes performed their roles in German with the supporting cast responding in Yiddish. Occasionally, Yiddish Shakespeare also traveled to non-Yiddish theatres, as when Jacob Adler played Shylock in Yiddish, accompanied by an English-speaking supporting cast, in 1903 and 1905. At other times, the Yiddish press published reviews and commentary on non-Yiddish productions, such as Maurice Moscovitch's Broadway run as Shylock in 1930.

While the pages that follow make forays into what American Yiddish actors called "the provinces" — that is, everywhere but New York — various historical factors conspire to keep the focus squarely on Manhattan's Bowery and Second Avenue. First and most obvious, New York was the capital of the American Yiddish theatre from start to near-finish. Corollary to that fact, most of the important American Yiddish interpreters of Shakespeare worked primarily in New York; the only major exception was Joseph Kessler, who performed for years in Chicago (his *Hamlet* is discussed in chapter 2). The New York Yiddish theaters also generated the plays that subsequently filtered out into the provinces. As an actor in Cleveland reported in 1903, "We get most of our plays and translations from New York. After they have outlived their usefulness there we can purchase them for from $25 to $40 each."[2]

The productions and publications discussed here span the period from the 1880s to the 1960s, but most appeared between 1890 and 1910. Shakespeare's plays entered the Yiddish repertoire at a time when theatre companies were hungry for new material, and there were not enough home-grown playwrights to provide original stories. These writers therefore turned to works that were not just "classics" — such a word is of limited value to a manager concerned about the health of the box office — but enjoying success among contemporary audiences, whether in English or in other European languages. The fact that Shakespeare's plays were considered classics served other needs as well, particularly the actors' desire to feel part of a great tradition, whereby they could — at least in theory — measure their talents against the leading players of their age.

Shakespeare's works seemed ubiquitous on American Yiddish stages in the 1890s, and nearly as prevalent in the subsequent decade or so. After World War I, however, they would take a far less prominent place in the Yiddish repertoire. The offerings of ensembles such as the Yiddish Art Theatre, founded in 1918, illustrate the very different place Shakespeare's work now occupied. One might expect that such a company, which declared in its mission statement that the theatre "must be a sort of holy place,"[3] would draw repeatedly upon the aesthetic sanctification that had come to be associated with Shakespeare, yet this rarely happened. In some three decades of activity, the Yiddish Art Theatre would stage but one translation of a Shakespeare play — *Othello*, in 1929 — as well as adaptations of *King Lear* (1919) and *The Merchant of Venice* (1947). When the company did translate plays from other languages, these tended to be contemporary or recent: works by such European — especially Russian — writers as Ibsen, Chekhov, Gorky, and Andreyev. Even more often, it staged original Yiddish works: classics by Goldfaden, Sholem Aleykhem, and Sholem Asch, or works by new talents such as H. Leyvik, Fishl Bimko, Osip Dimov, and Aaron Tseytlin. The very existence of a significant body of both established and new Yiddish plays helps account for the diminution of productions of works originally written in other languages; Yiddish now had its own modern stage tradition, which it sought to cultivate rather than to rely on outsiders for aesthetic sustenance.

Transliteration and Orthography

The transliteration of Yiddish words into the Latin alphabet generally follows the YIVO system of orthography throughout this book, providing a direct correspondence between Latin letters and the sounds of standard literary Yiddish. The sounds made by the letters in the left-hand column are pronounced as follows:

a	a as in father
ay	i as in wine
e	e as in bed
ey	a as in gate
i	i as in sit
o	similar to o in born
oy	oy as in boy
u	similar to oo in book
dzh	j as in jury
kh	ch as in Bach or chutzpah
tsh	ch as in cheer
zh	j as in the French je

I have made three exceptions to this rule: (1) No attempt has been made to standardize nonstandard Yiddish orthography; (2) When Yiddish names or words have a commonly accepted Latin transcription, I have used that: e.g., Thomashefsky rather than Tomashevski, *chutzpah* rather than *khutspe*; (3) I have tried to strike a balance between consistency of transcription and usefulness to researchers. Names more likely to be located elsewhere under a specific English spelling than by standard Yiddish transcription have been rendered according to the former: e.g., Zylbercweig rather than Zilbertsvayg, Hurwitz rather than Hurvits.

Acknowledgments

The support of many people and institutions has helped bring this book to fruition. To take last things first, the book has found a happy home with the University of Iowa Press, and I am grateful to its director, Holly Carver, and her staff. The editor of this series, Thomas Postlewait, has in many ways been the book's perfect reader and has ably shepherded it from manuscript to finished product.

This study began as a doctoral dissertation undertaken in the Ph.D. Program in Theatre at the City University of New York Graduate School. My supervisor, Marvin Carlson, as well as the rest of my committee — Walter Meserve, Judith Milhous, and Nahma Sandrow — offered valuable critiques of both methodology and style, and were unfailingly supportive throughout. Special thanks to my "shadow committee," Ed Dee, John Istel, and Paul Nadler, whose insights have added immeasurably to the quality of my work and the clarity of my thinking. Leonard Prager and Joseph Sherman also read complete drafts, to which they responded with challenging and constructive questions. Barbara Henry, Barbara Kirshenblatt-Gimblett, and Nina Warnke each read sections of the work as well, and made many valuable suggestions.

Generous institutional support at various stages of the project relieved financial burdens and allowed me time to research and write. A Roberts Fellowship from the CUNY Ph.D. Program in Theatre enabled me to expedite the final stages of the thesis, as did dissertation grants from the National Foundation for Jewish Culture and the Memorial Foundation for Jewish Culture. More recently, the Koret Foundation has generously subsidized the publication of the book.

The time spent researching this study was made productive and enjoyable by the availability of resources and assistance in several libraries and archives. The Billy Rose Theatre Collection of the New York Public Library provided helpful background information as well as material on important performers and productions. Peggy Pearlstein of the Library of Congress guided me to sources in the Hebrew Division. The extensive holdings of the YIVO Institute for Jewish Research provided much of the backbone of this study, and YIVO's archivists and librarians shared generously of their time and expertise; I am grateful to the late Dina Abramowicz, Zachary Baker, Marek Web, and their colleagues. The Jewish Division of the New York Public Library has been crucial to this research as well, and its friendly and capable librarians, formerly under Leonard Gold and now directed by Michael Terry, have made it a welcoming place to work.

Presenting my findings to wider audiences, in either oral or written form, proved invaluable for testing my ideas. My gratitude to Ed Burns, Eli Rozik, and Bernard Wasserstein for inviting me to lecture, and to Eli Rozik and Gary Williams for publishing sections of this study in their journals; an early version of chapter 1 was previously published in *Assaph: Studies in the Theatre*, and material from chapter 5 was previously published in *Theatre Survey*.

Thanks for questions, answers, comments, anecdotes, and other assistance to Neelum Ali, Nikolai Borodulin, Brad Sabin Hill, Eve Jochnowitz, George Jochnowitz, Jonathan Levine, Michael Morrison, Avrom Nowersztern, Ron Robboy, and Raymond Wemmlinger. Fellow CUNY theatre students created a collegial atmosphere throughout graduate school, just as my colleagues at the Oxford Centre for Hebrew and Jewish Studies have done during the final stages of the process. Of the latter, my special thanks to Dov-Ber Kerler, full of wisdom and friendship in equal measure.

Finally, undying thanks to my family: my siblings, Adam, Dana, and David; my son Ari Sholom for his boundless spirit; my wife, Esther, for her love, patience, and support; and my parents, Daniel and Judith Berkowitz, for everything.

Shakespeare
on the American
Yiddish Stage

Introduction

Eddie: English! English! Say it in English for Chris sakes!
Gusta's voice: You can't say it in English, Eddie, it don't do the job.
— *Herb Gardner,* Conversations with My Father

Fartaytsht un farbesert! Translated and improved! With an inimitable combination of nineteenth-century American puffery and Jewish ethnic pride (sometimes difficult to distinguish from a well-developed inferiority complex), Yiddish theatres promoted their productions of Shakespeare's plays as being better than the sources that inspired them.

Better than Shakespeare? How could anyone dare to make such a claim? And who could be so gullible as to believe it? Let us take the second question first, for it may help us set aside some preconceptions and biases that could hinder our appreciation of what it meant to translate or adapt Shakespeare's plays into Yiddish. The answer is simple, really: an audience of recent immigrants from eastern Europe who, when Yiddish theatre began to be performed in the United States in the early 1880s, by and large knew little of Shakespeare and the three centuries' worth of cultural baggage his name carried. On the other hand, they quickly learned of the regard in which American and European culture held him, and the star status his prestige conferred on the greatest interpreters of his roles. Perhaps it was inevitable that a culture trying to find its place on the Western world's theatrical map would turn to Shakespeare for help. Shakespeare's plays in production have never stayed pure, but have always had a remarkable adaptability to every possible sensibility: Elizabethan, Victorian, modern, postmodern; democratic, imperialist, Communist, Fascist; European, American, Indian, Japanese; proscenium, thrust stage, festival theatre; drama, opera, ballet, film.

As so many cultures have done, the American Yiddish theatre made Shakespeare its own; if it had not, the audience probably would not have taken much notice. Ever since the late seventeenth century, every culture and era that has turned to Shakespeare has reinvented him in its own image, and the American Yiddish theatre was no exception. Beginning in full force in the early 1890s — about a decade after the birth of the American Yiddish theatre — Yiddish playwrights began drawing upon Shakespeare as a source for theatrical productions. Some translated his plays with the original stories more or less intact, though not without making numerous cuts, changes, and even additions. Others went further afield by making the characters and settings Jewish; indeed, many of the most popular Yiddish versions of Shakespeare were "Judaized" in this way. This would not have surprised Boris Thomashefsky, matinée idol and Yiddish Shakespearean:

> In my opinion, the Yiddish theatre must be Jewish. It must present plays of Jewish life. The music must be authentically Jewish; the melodies must penetrate the hearts of the Jewish audience. I myself have often tried producing lovely plays that had been huge successes in Gentile theatres, but those same plays failed on the Yiddish stage. There were only a few plays from the world repertoire that Yiddish actors could not murder, such as *Hamlet*, *Romeo and Juliet*, and [Meyerbeer's] *The Huguenots*.[1]

A number of Shakespeare's plays, in both translations and Judaized adaptations, would ultimately occupy a substantial place in the American Yiddish theatre.

This book sets out to examine the history of Shakespeare's plays on American Yiddish stages. Because Yiddish adaptors were far more concerned with pleasing the masses than with appeasing the purists, their Shakespearean adaptations vividly illuminate the character of the American Yiddish theatre culture as a whole. As one historian has observed, Shakespeare yields "to the manipulation, the 'form and pressure' of each succeeding era, and, in the process turns himself into the most delicate barometer of social and cultural history."[2] Examining Yiddish versions of Shakespeare's plays in the United States provides a means of measuring developments in the audience expectations, theatrical conditions, aesthetics, and ideologies of the American Yiddish theatre. Along the way, we will also encounter a variety of related materials, including critical commentary, parodies, editorial cartoons, actors' memoirs, and playbills that further illustrate the place that Shakespeare and his work came to occupy in the minds of American Yiddish audiences.

Many of the changes made in Shakespeare's plots and characters for presentation to Yiddish audiences "are little short of startling and might vex the soul of a lover of the Bard of Avon," suggested a Cleveland journalist in 1903.[3] A Shakespeare lover might feel no less vexed coming across descriptions of these plays today, but the turn-of-the-century American Yiddish audience would have been little moved by any protests on aesthetic grounds. Without translators to make Shakespeare's characters speak their language, Yiddish audiences would have had no access to his plays. And without writers and theatre companies to tailor the original works to the expectations of the Yiddish audience, Shakespeare's plays would have meant little more than box-office poison at worst, an evening's diversion at best. They came to mean much more, however. Surely, a great deal was lost in translation. Now let us look at what was gained.

Exodus

In order to understand how it came to view Shakespeare, we need to know something about where the American Yiddish theatre and its audience came from, both geographically and culturally. The productions and related materials examined in this study span the period from the 1880s to the 1960s, but since most are concentrated in the period before World War I, we can focus initially on the eastern European Jewish immigrants who came to the United States during that time. Up to the 1870s, some 7,500 eastern European Jews had settled in the United States, joining other Jews who had previously emigrated from Spain, Portugal, and central Europe. Some 40,000 Jews left eastern Europe for the United States in the 1870s, but political unrest soon multiplied these numbers dramatically. In the wake of the assassination of relatively liberal Tsar Alexander II in 1881 and the accession to the throne of his reactionary son Alexander III, the Jews of Russia, Poland, and Romania faced a rising tide of poverty and persecution, and began questioning en masse whether they had a future in their homeland. For millions, the answer was no. Over 200,000 immigrated to the United States in the 1880s, another 300,000 in the 1890s, and 1,500,000 more between 1900 and the outbreak of World War I. To put the figures another way, over one-third of the Jews of eastern Europe left their homes in just over three decades. The migration "constituted a momentous — and for the most part, irreversible — decision of a whole people."[4]

The vast majority of the Jews who emigrated from eastern Europe to the United States landed in the Northeast, and most of those settled in New York City. After being processed through an immigration center like New York's Ellis Island or Castle Garden — often a harrowing experience that would leave a lasting impression — the immigrants might be met by family or friends who had already made the Atlantic crossing. In any case, they would seek out a Jewish area, whether in New York or in some other city where they may have had contacts. Those who stayed in New York tended to gravitate to the densely populated neighborhood in downtown Manhattan known as the Lower East Side, though other options included less crowded areas in the Bronx or Harlem, or the Brownsville section of Brooklyn.

Contrary to the widespread conception that every eastern European Jew came from a *shtetl* out of *Fiddler on the Roof*, Jews lived in areas ranging from tiny villages, to *shtetlekh* (towns), to large metropolises such as Warsaw and Odessa. Every village, town, and city had its local customs. Each wave of immigration was spurred by new catalysts. With these qualifications in mind, however, we can identify certain general traits the immigrants shared. To begin with, they were native Yiddish speakers. Their pronunciation and some of their vocabulary varied from region to region, but a Yiddish speaker from Romania could understand a Yiddish speaker from Lithuania — though the Romanian Jew might make fun of the "Litvak's" dialect. Most eastern European Jews had at least a rudimentary ability to speak the official language of their country of origin; many were fluent in one or more of these languages, especially since national borders frequently changed. In addition, most Jewish men had at least a basic familiarity with the prayer book and parts of the Bible, and thus basic literacy in Hebrew. Those who had the opportunity to continue studying into adulthood achieved a high level of Jewish scholarship, which in practical terms was often likely to prove as much a hindrance as a help in the New World.

By and large, these immigrants were poor; the richer one had been in Europe, the less incentive one had to look for greener pastures.⁵ Although the need to learn English initially proved a daunting obstacle to acclimatizing to their new surroundings, it did not rule out employment. Immigrants — women and men, children and the elderly — found jobs as pushcart peddlers, from which they often worked their way up the ladder to grocery stores and other establishments, or gravitated in large numbers to the garment industry, as tailors, pressers, finishers, and the like. It was arduous labor, with long hours that frequently went well beyond the opening and closing of sweatshop or factory, for many supplemented their wages by taking home piecework in the evening.

Economic opportunity was a primary motive for many of these Jews to immigrate to America, as it had been for countless other groups. Another motive was the promise of freedom from religious persecution, but that freedom often proved elusive. The last decades of the nineteenth century brought "the emergence of an antisemitic society"⁶ in the United States, fueled by such factors as a general increase in nativist sentiments, economic turbulence, and the massive influx of new immigrants. The immigrants would never find American anti-Semitism as pervasive or virulent as it had been in Europe, "but hatred of Jews was carried to America at the very birth of the nation, and it was nourished by myths that portray Jews as eternally alien to Christendom and as unscrupulous moneylenders."⁷

The new tide of immigrants was not always met with enthusiasm by the Jews who had preceded them to America either. Many of the Jews who had arrived from central Europe between the 1820s and the 1880s expressed deep concern that the masses of refugees would overwhelm them financially, and would threaten their precarious status as Americans. Historian Naomi Cohen explains, "The east Europeans sensed, and often with good reason, that many of the Germans regarded them as subhumans who lacked the rudiments of civilized behavior. The Germans never tired of preaching to them through their high-handed philanthropies on how to dress, behave, and even believe."⁸ While the "German" Jews would often display remarkable benevolence toward their "Russian" brethren, prejudices that each group harbored about the other bred frequent conflict between the two communities, though this dissipated in the wake of Russian pogroms in the early 1900s, which coincided with the peak years of Jewish immigration to America.⁹

Even when the immigrants' Jewishness was not being intentionally targeted by their adversaries, it was still not safe from the challenges of daily life. The countless promises that Jews leaving eastern Europe had made not to abandon their religious practices came under assault almost from the moment they stepped ashore in America. Men found that their *peyes* (sidelocks) and dress made them stand out in the factory and the street; married women felt the same about the *sheytls* (wigs) that Jewish laws of modesty prescribed for them. Observing the Sabbath, the most frequent as well as the most sacred of Jewish holidays, often limited or even jeopardized one's employment. Adhering to Jewish dietary laws could prove no less difficult. The issue of negotiating the delicate balance between maintaining the traditions of the Old World and succeeding in the new land engendered volumes of commentary in the American Jewish fiction, drama, memoirs, and newspapers of that era.

All of these challenges put a tremendous strain on the family. Many a Jewish husband or father, unable to afford ship tickets for his wife and children, emigrated alone and saved his wages until he could send for the loved ones awaiting him in eastern Europe. The process might last months, or even years. The passage of time brought with it differences that might make husband and wife, parent and child seem like strangers. Abraham Cahan, who we will meet in these pages in his capacity as theatre critic, had himself made the journey from Vilna to New York in 1882. By the following decade, he was publishing fiction in English, including this description of his character Yekl's reunion with his family at Ellis Island:

> The prospect of meeting his dear wife and child, and, incidentally, of showing off his swell attire to her, had thrown him into a fever of impatience. But on entering the big shed he had caught a distant glimpse of Gitl and Yosselé through the railing separating the detained immigrants from their visitors, and his heart had sunk at the sight of his wife's uncouth and un-American appearance. She was slovenly dressed in a brown jacket and skirt of grotesque cut, and her hair was concealed under a voluminous wig of a pitch-black hue. . . . Since Yekl had left home she had gained considerably in the measurement of her waist. The wig, however, made her seem stouter and shorter than she would have appeared without it. It also added at least five years to her looks. But she was aware nei-

ther of this nor of the fact that in New York even a Jewess of her station and orthodox breeding is accustomed to blink at the wickedness of displaying her natural hair, and that none but an elderly matron may wear a wig without being the occasional target for snowballs or stones.[10]

The abyss that has formed between Yekl and Gitl ultimately proves unbridgeable, but even in less extreme cases than theirs, varying rates and styles of adjustment created tension. Traditional parents were often dismayed by how quickly their children seemed to shed their Jewish identities, clothes, and language in the rush to Americanize, just as those same children were often embarrassed by the tenacity with which their parents held on to practices that now seemed out of place in the American context.

Immigrants struggling to survive in their newly adopted country may have cursed *amerike ganef* — America the thief — but for all the hardship their new lives brought, most Jewish immigrants saw the United States as *di goldene medine*, the golden land. Their rate of return to their countries of origin was lower than that of any other immigrant group of the period, a not entirely surprising statistic given that they had no national home to return to, unlike their Irish and Italian neighbors. The Jews immersed themselves in every aspect of life in America. When they managed to get away from their pushcarts and sewing machines, they attended lectures, concerts, and theatre; formed and ran mutual aid organizations; enrolled in night classes and universities; devoured books, journals, and newspapers; and played American sports and music. They would bring their tremendous adaptive capacity to absorbing much of American culture, including its boundless love of Shakespeare.

"We Were Slaves!": The Yiddish Repertoire

These immigrants brought to America a centuries-old theatrical tradition, but primarily an amateur and seasonal one. The roots of the Yiddish theatre developed in the Middle Ages, with performances of Purim plays, wedding entertainers, and minstrels.

Purim, celebrating the Jews' salvation from their enemies in ancient

Persia through the intervention of Queen Esther, is a time of inversion, like the Roman Saturnalia or the Christian Feast of Fools. Jews
are encouraged to get so drunk on Purim that they cannot distinguish
between the holiday's hero, Esther's uncle Mordkhe, and its villain,
Haman. Yiddish speakers thus say of a contrary person, *"a gants yor
shiker, Purim nikhter"*: drunk year-round, but sober on Purim. The
holiday's spirit of abandon brings with it a loosening of traditional
restrictions in Jewish law against theatrical performance, and while
Orthodox law prohibits women from performing in public for men
regardless of the occasion, Purim allowed male actors to play the roles
of women as well as men.

At first, the term *purimshpil* referred to a monologue, sometimes
performed in costume, usually consisting of a rhymed paraphrase of
the Book of Esther or a parody of other religious texts. The first
known *purimshpil* in its more mature form, as a scripted play with
multiple actors, dates back to 1598, when the *Shpil fun Tev Yeklein mit
zayn vayb Kendlein un mit tsvey zinlekh fayn* (Play about Tev Yeklein, his
wife Kendlein, and their two fine sons), apparently a satire targeting a
specific family, was performed in Tannhausen, Germany.

Purimshpiln were usually presented in the homes of the wealthiest
members of the community, and were usually kept fairly short in order to allow the players — typically students from religious schools
and seminaries — to make the rounds of these houses during the
course of the holiday. The subject matter included not just the Purim
story, but such favorites as the sacrifice of Isaac, the sale of Joseph
into slavery, and Samson and Delilah. The plays tended to share certain formulaic features, beginning with a prologue offering blessings
for the audience, an outline of the contents of the play, and an introduction of the actors. Like the German *Fastnachtspiel*, the proceedings
were introduced, conducted, and concluded by a narrator, and often
relied on profanity and erotic contents as prime sources of comedy.
An epilogue, bestowing blessings on the spectators and asking for
a reward for the actors, generally ended the performance. Initially
performed in either rudimentary costumes or masks, with no scene
changes, the *purimshpil* gradually grew more elaborate in cast size, costumes, and text. By the late sixteenth century, *purimshpiln* were performed in some places throughout the Hebrew month of Adar, two
weeks on either side of Purim itself.[11]

Aaron Halle Wolfssohn (1754–1835) loathed the *purimshpil*. To him, it was a dramatic medium that symbolized the superstition and benightedness of European Jewry, and he set out to write a new type of Jewish play that would supplant the old form. Wolfssohn belonged to the first generation of *maskilim* (singular, *maskil*), proponents of the Haskalah, or Jewish Enlightenment. The movement was launched in Berlin by Wolfssohn's mentor, Moses Mendelssohn (1729–1786), a brilliant philosopher and polemicist who exhorted his fellow Jews to become less parochial by learning from the cultural and intellectual achievements of western Europe and adopting its dress and manners. Starting with Wolfssohn, who also worked on Mendelssohn's famous translation of the Bible into German, the *maskilim* wrote plays attacking their archenemies, the Hasidim, whose grassroots movement began revolutionizing religious practice in the mid-eighteenth century. The two movements, along with traditional Orthodoxy, struggled bitterly for the soul of European Jewry, and throughout much of the nineteenth century, a small but important body of Yiddish plays — mostly satires — circulated among the intelligentsia of eastern Europe, advocating the *maskilic* agenda. The Haskalah, like Hasidism, dramatically altered Jewish life, but in almost the opposite direction: by making millions of Jews more accepting of non-Jewish ideas. Though no stable Yiddish theatre existed as the Haskalah arose, the movement would make such a theatre possible by creating a change of the communal mind set, and several Haskalah playwrights, such as Wolfssohn, Shloyme Etinger (Solomon Ettinger, 1800–56), and Yisroel Aksenfeld (1787–1866), would influence both the form and content of their successors' works.

Even before a full-fledged professional Yiddish theatre began developing in the 1870s, Yiddish speakers were entertained by at least two types of professional performers: the *batkhn* and the Broder singer. The primary function of the *batkhn*, or wedding jester, was to entertain the guests at Jewish weddings, a goal he achieved in part through impromptu rhymes and songs, sometimes with a touch of bawdiness that ruffled the feathers of religious authorities. He frequently served as master of ceremonies as well, and sometimes even assumed duties traditionally assigned to the rabbi, such as reminding the bride of her marital responsibilities.[12] Broder singers — named after the city of Brod in Galicia — as Nahma Sandrow explains, "were essentially secular *batkhonim*, who appeared at the lively wine gardens and inns which were proliferating in eastern Europe, instead of only in respectable Jewish households."[13]

An encounter between a Broder singer and a Yiddish writer led to the birth of the professional Yiddish theatre in 1876. On that fateful evening, a published Hebrew and Yiddish poet and sometime song-writer named Avrom Goldfaden (1840–1908) paid a visit to Shimen Mark's Green Tree café in Jassy, Romania, where Yisroel Grodner was performing an act that included some Goldfaden songs. Gold-faden was invited to perform as well, but he made the unfortunate choice of reciting solemn poetry rather than performing the comic ballads that Grodner had helped popularize. As Goldfaden continued, the crowd's initial silence turned to hissing, which subsided only when Grodner reappeared to cajole them with comic stories and songs. This scenario would resurface time and again in the Yiddish theatre: a powerful, vocal audience dictating the material on the program, chasing away a writer/performer who miscalculated its expectations, and finding satisfaction in a popular star entertainer with a better understanding of its tastes. The lively dialectic between artists and audiences would often have a strong influence on the way in which Shakespeare's plays were adapted into Yiddish.

Rather than discourage him, Goldfaden's initial failure simply focused his attention on coming up with more successful ways to reach such audiences. Looking back near the end of his life, he compared the first Yiddish audiences to a baby (which they were, in a manner of speaking):

> When the child outgrew its diapers, I knitted a little shirt for it . . . and when it grew to be 5–6 months old, I dressed it in a pair of breeches of my own making. You surely understand, my clever reader, that at the time I could not have dressed the child up in a frock, in trousers with suspenders. I had to put it in a pair of breeches with the seam buttoned up at the back![14]

What sort of entertainment did they want, then? Plays on a biblical theme? Something historical? (He would later write plays that fit into both of those categories.) Or perhaps he should have adapted the classics? After all, Goldfaden says, he had been a rabbinical student, had read "practically all of Russian literature," and had had the op-

portunity to see the Othello of the legendary African American actor Ira Aldridge (1807–1867), who toured Russia a number of times
in mid-century: [15] "*Nu?* Couldn't I have translated, even back then,
'Othello,' 'Hamlet,' [Karl Gutzkow's] 'Uriel Acosta,' or other Russian
and German dramas and comedies for the newborn Yiddish stage?" [16]
Of course, his answer is no. Why? "The reason is, '*avodim hoyinu*' —
'We were slaves!' I was a slave to the conditions of the time, to the
theatregoers and the unpolished performers." [17] Such an audience
would enjoy a farce like his *Shmendrik*, which he says was about all that
the first performers could handle; more sophisticated stuff would
have to wait.

Whether we prefer to read this assessment as an astute analysis of
audience expectations or as a self-serving apologia, the fact is that
he and his contemporaries did not immediately choose to translate
Shakespeare, though his influence on European dramaturgy and stage-
craft was too widespread for them to have avoided Shakespearean
elements completely even if they had wanted to. They did not want
to. Goldfaden and his early competition put each other under tremendous pressure to turn out a seemingly endless stream of new scripts
and music; and they borrowed stories, characters, and melodies from
European and American drama at every turn.

Becoming Professional

While the first years of the Yiddish theater have been chronicled elsewhere,[18] a few of the salient features of this era merit discussion here, for they have an important bearing on the adaptation of
Shakespeare's plays for Yiddish stages in the United States.

Like the Jewish people as a whole for much of their history, the
early Yiddish actors tended to be nomads. Most actors lead peripa-
tetic lives, but the first professional Yiddish actors had to travel for
political as well as professional reasons. When Tsar Alexander III
forced them off the stage and into exile by signing the punitive, anti-
Jewish May Laws of 1882, the demographics of world Yiddish theatre shifted with the westward flow of the eastern European Jewish
masses, from cities like Lemberg (present-day Lwów, Ukraine) and
Warsaw, to London, and on to North and South America. Meanwhile,

a great deal of Yiddish theatrical activity continued in Europe well into the twentieth century, most notably in Poland and the Soviet Union. (Yiddish theater became officially permissible again in Russia after the revolution of 1905, though various troupes had managed to find gaps in the enforcement of the ban on Yiddish theatre all along.)[19] American Yiddish stars sometimes revisited their European roots by touring the capitals of European Jewry for months at a time, and managers like Boris Thomashefsky and Jacob Adler took numerous summer trips across the Atlantic to recruit new stars for their theatres. Throughout their wanderings, actors and playwrights had to be chameleon-like in adapting to new surroundings, customs, and languages. They succeeded to a remarkable degree, and helped to cultivate their audiences as well.

Wherever they came from, Yiddish actors and playwrights initially tended to share a common background in their traditional Jewish education. Many of these figures — particularly the men, for whom such education was emphasized — were well versed in Hebrew, the Bible, and biblical commentary, however far away from traditional Judaism they might have drifted as adults. During the first decades of Yiddish theatre, even nonreligious Jews had some familiarity with Jewish religion, history, customs, and traditions, and this common source of knowledge emerges on almost every page of every Yiddish play, whether in plot, character, setting, allusion, or imagery. Shakespeare's Christian worldview did not immunize the adaptation of his plays from this influence any more than his Western stage practice prevents his plays from being performed by Kabuki troupes in Japan. Once a Yiddish playwright made the choice to adapt a Shakespearean play, it was only natural for the original to be recast, to a greater or lesser degree, in Jewish terms.

The religious upbringing of Yiddish theatre personnel directly affected the music of the Yiddish theatre as well. As musicologist Mark Slobin observes, the pioneers of the Yiddish theatre "began life as thinkers and teachers, not clowns and minstrels. The leading musical figures of the movement were all trained in the synagogues as upholders of liturgical music, not as street singers."[20] Enormously popular stars such as Sigmund Feinman, Boris Thomashefsky, and Sigmund Mogulesco — the latter two also prolific theatre composers — all received their first musical training as *meshoyrerim* (choirboys). A significant part of their musical imagination had its roots in the synagogue, which served as their first stage, and the professional Yiddish theatre would retain much of the ritual flavor of its genesis.

The ranks of the first Yiddish theatre companies in Romania and Russia were often well stocked with boys who had been stealthily hired away from synagogue choirs by enterprising managers in search of singers with beautiful voices. Competition for the best singers, as for every other element of production, was fierce, and would remain so. In such a small and intimate theatrical community, where actors and playwrights often moved in mid-season from one theatre to its rival down the road or across the street, everyone knew everyone else's business, and did their utmost to seize it for themselves. This rivalry meant that once a Yiddish Shakespearean repertoire developed, a Shakespeare production at Theatre A often triggered a competing one at Theatre B — occasionally even the same play at the same time.

European and American theatres, which tended to revolve around star actor/managers in the first half of the nineteenth century, saw a great deal of such competition. In the tightly knit Yiddish theatre, rivalries could get very personal. The Yiddish press devoted numerous articles to the phenomenon of *patriotn* (fans) of Yiddish stars, and the extremes to which their ardor sometimes carried them. Boaz Young (1870–1955), a character actor from the first generation of professional Yiddish performers, defines a *patriot* as "someone who used to attend the theatre at least two or three times a week, sit in the balcony with other *patriotn*, meet with them every night after work in a saloon on Hester Street (run by a certain Spivak, where for three cents one could get a liver steak with bread and drink a bit of beer), or just meet on Hester Street and discuss the plays and actors."[21] Encounters between *patriotn* — whom Young tells us were nicknamed after the actors they championed — were not always so peaceful: "People started to quarrel, get in fist fights until they drew blood — every *patriot* for his actor."[22] Yet this was a far cry from the sort of violence, often rooted in class-based animosities, that sometimes led to fatal clashes between groups of American theatregoers, as in the Astor Place Riot of 1849, the deadly culmination of years of squabbling between the fans of American actor Edwin Forrest and his English colleague William Macready. In the Yiddish theatre, a choice of one actor's interpretation of a character as opposed to another's was usually based not on any underlying ideology, but simply on the preference for one star's personality or theatrical style.

An etiquette manual published in 1910 decried the pervasiveness of applause in the Yiddish theatre, exhorting the actors "to wean their *patriotn* away from applauding in the middle of the act. Applause causes a rupture and disturbs the action." [23] The writer was probably wasting his breath, for Yiddish actors had come to rely on their claques as a measure of their greatness. "An actor without *patriotn*," wrote leading lady Bessie Thomashefsky, "was like a meat market with dogs: sha, quiet, no one to shout and clap." [24] The actors would have had to be made of strong stuff to resist letting such adoration go to their heads. It seems that they put up no struggle whatsoever. "The Yiddish actors . . . take themselves with peculiar seriousness," observed non-Jewish journalist Hutchins Hapgood,

justified by the enthusiasm, almost worship, with which they are regarded by the people. Many a poor Jew, man or girl, who makes no more than ten dollars a week in the sweatshop, will spend five dollars of it on the theatre, which is practically the only amusement of the ghetto Jew. He has not the loafing and sporting instincts of the poor Christian, and spends his money for the theatre rather than for drink. It is not only to see the play that the poor Jew goes to the theatre. It is to see his friends and the actors. With these latter he, and more frequently she, tries in every way to make acquaintance, but commonly is compelled to adore at a distance. They love the songs that are heard on the stage, and for these the demand is so great that a certain bookshop on the East Side makes a specialty of publishing them. [25]

As powerful as Yiddish actors would eventually become, the first decade of Yiddish theater in the United States (1882–1892) saw even the most famous performers deferring to two domineering playwrights, "Professor" Moyshe Hurwitz (1844–1910) and Joseph Lateiner (1853–1935). [26] In the first years of Yiddish theatre in New York, Hurwitz and Lateiner reigned as resident dramatists of various companies on the Lower East Side, where they turned out play after slapdash play, with a song here, a dance there, a tearful scene followed by a farcical one, and every convoluted turn of the plot bumping along towards the finale. The music was critical to a play's success. The plans for Professor Goldfaden's Dramatic School, as it was to be called, drawn up in 1888 but never brought to fruition, set out a curriculum consisting of four courses: acting and diction, sight reading, tuition on a musical instrument, and dance.[27] The emphasis on music suited the composition of the offerings on the Yiddish stage at the time, since "no Yiddish theatre production was without songs until Jacob Gordin's first Yiddish plays in 1891. Audiences at Turn Hall [another venue for Yiddish performances in the 1880s] either saw an 'historical opera,' such as *Uriel Acosta*; a 'comic operetta,' such as *The Sorceress*; or a 'melodrama with music,' such as *The Last Hour*. The most popular works during the Turn Hall stay were 'historical operas,' a genre more akin to 'operetta' than 'opera.'" The plays often ended happily, but the so-called historical operas, for all their poetic license, could not always avoid a catastrophic dénouement.[28]

The actors and managers who worked with Hurwitz and Lateiner defended their house playwrights with gusto. Leon Kobrin (1872–1946), who would eventually become one of the most prominent Yiddish playwrights of his generation, had trouble sparking interest in his first play when he brought it to the Windsor Theatre, where Hurwitz reigned as house playwright. When Kobrin confronted the manager after being all but ignored, the manager responded, "Here we don't perform plays by *yolds*" (simpletons), using the theatre lingo for an inexperienced playwright. The prejudice against newcomers created a Catch-22: in order to become an experienced playwright, one had to have prior experience as a playwright. When the *yold* did not go away after a simple dismissal, the actors relished the chance to humiliate him utterly and elaborately. One of many methods of doing so was for Hurwitz's company to express interest in a play, but to confess that they were scared to death of their playwright. After sufficiently establishing the fear Hurwitz inspired in his underlings, the company would make an appointment for the would-be playwright to read his new play to them (a common practice at the time), but insist that it had to be done in secret. Once the reading was under way and the playwright had the feigned interest of the actors gathered around him, another actor would start stomping towards them from backstage, prompting the onstage actors to look at each other with panic-stricken expressions and cry, "The Professor is coming!" They all raced to the nearest exit, their performance teaching their audience of one that he should find another way of making a living.[29]

The Lateiner/Hurwitz stranglehold during the 1880s was so powerful that even Goldfaden had trouble getting his new plays produced in New York, though several of his earlier works had become staples in the Yiddish theatre diet. Goldfaden was notoriously difficult to work with, but Marvin Seiger, the chief chronicler of the first decade of Yiddish theatre in New York, provides an additional explanation for the duration of the monopoly:

> As a carryover from the early Goldfadn [sic] period in Roumania and Russia, the company dramatist became the focal point of importance in a troupe. It was he who supplied the new repertory. Actors were dependent on him for survival, and they displayed their appreciation by protecting him from other writers who dared to challenge his supremacy. Such a situation explains why new dramatists had a difficult time getting their plays into production during the early seasons. Unless a playwright received the support of either Hurwitz or Lateiner, he had no opportunity to sell his work to a troupe.[30]

But Lateiner's and Hurwitz's grip slowly began to weaken in the late 1880s, with the occasional production of works by such playwrights as Rudolph Marks, Reuben Weissman, Nokhem-Meyer ("Shomer") Shaykevitsh, and Moyshe Zeifert. Finally, in the 1890–1891 season, works by new playwrights far outnumbered plays by Lateiner and Hurwitz in the New York theatres.[31]

The monopoly disintegrated for good after 6 March 1891, when Jacob P. Adler turned the mounting battle for audiences into a three-way war by opening the 1,200-seat Union Theatre, formerly known as Poole's Theatre, on Eighth Street, between Broadway and Fourth Avenue.[32] The opening heightened the need for new plays and quickened the pace at which playwrights had to provide them. Theatre historian Bernard Gorin describes how this phenomenon worked: "A writer who wanted to write for the stage had to be able to write plays at the drop of a hat. The writer in the new land had to stick to the American principle of 'hurry up'; he who did not understand how to do this was out of a job."[33] Adapting works from the Western dramatic repertoire sped up the output of plays much as the sewing machine accelerated the production of pants, and the 1890s consequently saw a flood of translations from the classics — especially Shakespeare, Goethe, and Schiller — and from contemporary European drama.

Nights at the Yiddish Theatre

The first major rivalry between Yiddish theatre troupes in the United States was fought in Lower Manhattan, where two theatres faced each other across the thoroughfare known as the Bowery: the Oriental Theatre, at 113–113½ Bowery, and the Romania Opera House at 104–106. The Oriental had previously been known as the Bowery Garden, "a long, narrow beer hall that had a little bit of a stage. . . . One could gain entrance to see a vaudeville there once he had drunk a glass of beer for a nickel." [34] When the Bowery Garden was converted to the Oriental, "all the beer tables were removed and replaced by theatre seats." [35] The Oriental housed the Karp-Silberman troupe in the early 1880s, where the performances

> were no longer restricted to Friday and Saturday evenings; Monday and Wednesday evenings were added to the schedule. A fifth performance was also added on Sunday evenings. The advertisements, however, never designated the title of the scheduled Sunday production. "Sacred Concerts" were announced instead, a ruse designed to circumvent the restrictive New York "Blue" laws. Friday and Saturday evenings remained the most popular performance dates for Yiddish theatregoers; week-day nights were reserved for "benefits" and special performances. . . . The first advertisements also inform the reader that the curtain was scheduled for eight P.M. Admission prices at the larger theatre were similar to those charged at Turn Hall [an earlier venue for Yiddish performances on the Lower East Side]: twenty-five, thirty-five, fifty, seventy-five cents, and one dollar for box seats. Sunday performances were less expensive, ranging from ten, fifteen, twenty-five, and thirty-five cents. [36]

However improved the facilities may have been over previous locations, not everyone was enthusiastic about the building. Actor Boaz Young, for example, recalls, "When I arrived at the Oriental Theatre on the Bowery (women who could not pronounce the word 'Oriental' called it the 'Yente' Theatre), the building did not impress me much. It was no larger than the Princess Street Club in London, although it looked more like a theatre."[37]

A reviewer attending an 1885 production of *Bar Kokhba* confirms Young's skepticism about the building while taking us inside for a closer look:

> In the Bowery not far from Hester street, and a few doors below Grand, is a miniature theatre which has had an eventful history. Devoted always to the cheapest and crudest entertainments, it has been, in turn, a museum, a menagerie, an aquarium, a variety theatre, and a lager-beer saloon. . . . The Oriental from without is not a very impressive structure; nor is it within particularly gorgeous in its appointments. The main entrance way is a short hall, flanked on one side by an apple stand and on the other by a candy vender's table. To the left is a bar, where so-called soft drinks — ginger ale, soda, and sarsaparilla — are retained. The auditorium is long and narrow; the stage is deep and wide. The main floor is nearly flat, and ordinary chairs bound in line by strips of pine are the substitutes for upholstered orchestra seats. There is nothing ornate about the establishment except the programme, which is printed in square Assyrian [*sic*] characters.[38]

Across the street at the Romania Opera House (formerly the National Theatre), the Mogulesco-Finkel troupe competed with the Karp-Silberman actors until the companies merged in 1891:

> An orchestra from the "Carl Sahm Club" was hired to play under "Professor" Finkelstein's leadership. . . . Advertisements in *Di yidishe gazeten* stipulate that the troupe played every night in the week, including "Sacred Concerts" on Sundays. For the first time, a Yiddish troupe was scheduled to perform on Saturday afternoon. A subsequent playbill for the season gives us the price range of tickets. "Private box seats" were $1.00 and $1.50. One paid $1.00 for "reserved orchestra seats," $1.00 and $.75 for "reserved parquet" chairs. "Dress circle chairs" and "reserved balcony chairs" were $.50 and $.35. "General admission" tickets were $.25.[39]

By the early 1890s, when Shakespeare's plays began entering the Yiddish repertoire, three theatres on the Lower East Side offered Yiddish plays: the People's, a 2,500-seat house located at 199–204 Bowery; the Thalia, a 3,000-seat theatre at 46–48 Bowery; and the Windsor, across the street from the Thalia at 45–47 Bowery, able to accommodate 3,500 in its capacious auditorium.[40] Being the largest house of the three, it is unsurprising that the Windsor, with Hurwitz as resident playwright, was known as the home of popular theater — and in that sense, very much in the mainstream of the American theatre, where

> in great measure tragedy as a dramatic form lost its voice and purpose in the nineteenth century, with the exception of Shakespearean performance. In the place of tragedy the American stage put melodramas, minstrel shows, comedies, farces, circuses, vaudevilles, burlesques, operas, operettas, musicals, musical revues, medicine shows, amusement arcades, and Wild West shows — the whole hieroglyphic world of popular culture. And, in turn, most of the entertainment in the twentieth century on stage, radio, and screen continued to be presented in these popular modes, to the satisfaction of the majority of spectators.[41]

Such spectators were the majority in the Yiddish theatre as well; no wonder that musical theatre, comedy, and vaudeville would thrive on the Lower East Side.

"The company at the Windsor is the weakest, so far as acting is concerned, of the three," observed one visitor. "Very few 'realistic' plays are given there, for Professor Horowitz [Hurwitz] is the lessee, and he prefers the historical Jewish opera and 'culture' plays. Besides, the company is not strong enough to undertake successfully many new productions, altho it includes some good actors."[42] Wandering into the Windsor on a Saturday afternoon in the early 1900s, Henry James marveled "to see the so domestic drama reach out to the so exotic audience and the so exotic audience reach out to the so domestic drama."[43] Scrutinizing the audience as much as the play, James could hardly believe it that these "exotics" partook of the same entertainments as the Americans he used to know, when "exotic" usually meant "Irish":

> There they all sat, the representatives of the races we have nothing "in common" with, as naturally, as comfortably, as munchingly, as

if the theatre were their constant practice — and, as regards the munching, I may add, I was struck with the appearance of quality and cost in the various confections pressed from moment to moment upon our notice by the little playhouse peddlers.[44]

So long had James been away from the United States that he had missed one crucial fact; by now, the theater was "their constant practice."

What the Thalia lacked in size compared to the Windsor, it made up for with *yikhes* — loosely translated, good pedigree — for German performers, with their refined language, prestigious repertoire, and respected acting tradition, had made this building their home throughout the 1880s. The very idea of that legacy was enough to excite any actor with a sense of history. Boris Thomashefsky, for example, found the Thalia "the most beautiful theatre in all of downtown. The stage was very large, as was the theatre itself. The greatest German artists played there. In the Thalia Theatre I had seen the world-famous German actor Ludwig Barnay in *Uriel Acosta*, when I had been in America for just a couple of days. And now I will act on the same stage! . . . What an honor! What a sensation!"[45] Thomashefsky's wife and leading lady, Bessie Thomashefsky, shared his enthusiasm about the building: "The stage was large, the largest we had been on until then. . . . The beautiful theatre, the large stage inspired us to act, and we opened the season in great splendor."[46] That splendor would still be in evidence to visitors to the theatre a decade later:

The old house . . . is different from the present-day theatres, both as regards outside and inside architecture and decorations. The pit has been removed . . . and the orchestra chairs now occupying that space sit so low that what is called the orchestra circle is almost as high as the balcony in some theatres. Unyielding iron back chairs of the 60's and 70's are still in use, and while comfortable enough, are vastly different from the modern marvels of the upholsterer's art.[47]

The third player among the theatres in the fin-de-siècle Yiddish rivalry in New York City was the People's Theatre, which would serve as principal home to most of Jacob Gordin's plays of the 1890s. Located up the road from its competitors, the People's served a slightly fancier clientele:

It panders to the "uptown" element of the Ghetto, to the down-town tradesman who is beginning to climb a little. The baleful influence in art of the *nouveaux riches* has at this house its Ghetto expression. There is a tendency there to imitate the showy qualities of the Broadway theatres — melodrama, farce, scenery, etc. No babies are admitted, and the house is exceedingly clean in comparison with the theatres farther down the Bowery. Three years ago this company were [*sic*] at the Windsor Theatre, and made so much money that they hired the People's, that old home of Irish-American melodrama, and this atmosphere seems slightly to have affected the Yiddish productions. Magnificent performances quite out of the line of the best Ghetto drama have been attempted, notably Yiddish dramatizations of successful up-town productions.[48]

These three venues would serve as the main homes of Yiddish theatre in New York City, the capital of the American Yiddish theatre, during the years when Shakespeare was most prominent on Yiddish stages. Shakespeare would be heard in Yiddish on many other stages as well, including New York theatres built expressly for Yiddish productions, such as the Grand and Yiddish Art Theatres; other venues housing resident Yiddish troupes, from the Bronx and Brooklyn to other major cities around the country, most notably Philadelphia, Boston, Chicago, Cleveland, and Detroit; vaudeville houses; and established mainstream venues such as the Academy of Music in New York, and its cousin of the same name in Philadelphia.

The Shakespearean Context

The adoption of Shakespeare's plays by Yiddish troupes and their audiences would be influenced by a complex interaction of factors from within and outside of the culture. Such factors were often based on assumptions and expectations that differed radically from the connotations that the name of Shakespeare tends to evoke today. Cultural historian Lawrence Levine offers this perspective:

If Shakespeare had been an integral part of mainstream culture in the nineteenth century, in the twentieth he had become part of "polite" culture — an essential ingredient in a complex we call, significantly, "legitimate" theater. He had become the possession of the educated portions of society who disseminated his plays for the enlightenment of the average folk who were to swallow him not for their entertainment but for their education, as a respite from — not as a normal part of — their usual cultural diet.[49]

This was a far cry from the prevailing cultural environment for much of the previous century; as Levine observes, "Shakespeare *was* popular entertainment in nineteenth-century America."[50] Speeches from his plays were quoted by heart by working-class fans, parodied in minstrel shows and burlesques, and mingled with an array of entertainment forms that were yet to be fixed into strict hierarchies and separated from one another on different bills, in different theatres, for distinct audiences.

Shakespeare, a consummate man of the theatre, skillfully addressed the political, social, cosmological, and metaphysical questions of his day in a form suited to the theatrical conditions of his time. The spare scenery of the Elizabethan stage allowed for frequent changes of scene. The thrust stage brought actors into the bosom of the audience, and Shakespeare's soliloquies and asides capitalized on the intimacy of the actor/audience relationship. Given the widely varying social composition of his audience, Shakespeare provided something for everyone: Petrarchan sonnets, social satire, political commentary, bawdy puns, physical humor. Yet there were limits. With a powerful queen with her own interest in the theatre, the treatment of political subject matter on stage could be a sensitive issue. Had Shakespeare gone too far in any of his frequent explorations of regicide, usurpation, and abdication, he might have joined the long list of his own characters sent to the Tower of London.

In short, Shakespeare's plays were a product of their time, and when times changed, so did the production, publication, and reception of the plays:

> Shakespeare's texts, written according to Elizabethan dramatic and theatrical conventions, are fundamentally incompatible with the conventions and conditions of later periods; the scripts must be "translated," adapted or willfully transformed in order to be presented on these later stages for later audiences. Consequently, the degree and nature of the translation of a play in production in a later period reveals the fundamental nature of the theatrical expe-

rience of that later period; a period writes its own theatre history through its productions of Shakespeare.[51]

This transformation began in the Restoration, after civil war had closed down the London theatres for eighteen years. In August 1660, the very month that Charles II became king, two theatrical entrepreneurs won licenses to produce theatre in London. Thomas Killigrew's company owned the rights to many of the most popular plays of the previous era, but William Davenant, with a less established company and repertoire, proved the more innovative of the two managers, making numerous small changes to the texts of *Hamlet*, *Romeo and Juliet*, *Twelfth Night*, and *Henry VIII*, and more extensively adapting *The Tempest* and *Macbeth*. "Although a lifelong devotee of Shakespeare," concludes one historian, "Davenant recognized that, to achieve popularity with Restoration playgoers, Shakespeare had to be made their contemporary."[52]

The alterations made by Davenant and others were dictated by a variety of factors, including political pressure, the period's aesthetic norms, and the ever evolving English language, which had already traveled a good distance from Elizabethan English by the late seventeenth century. Lest we find ourselves inclined to scoff at Yiddish translators' tendency to replace Shakespearean metaphor with the literal meaning, we would do well to keep in mind what Davenant did with the text of *Hamlet*:

> Many changes regularize the irregular grammar of Elizabethan English or normalize Shakespeare's often abnormal word order. Others curtail the physicality, particularity, unembarrassed vulgarity, and sheer cussed strangeness of the language, rendering Shakespeare immediately comprehensible, easily digestible. . . . [O]ur editorial glosses sometimes unwittingly echo Davenant's revisions. What later editors and commentators will put into the footnotes — paraphrases that explain Shakespeare's meaning — Davenant simply sticks into the dialogue itself. The gloss displaces the text.[53]

From Davenant's day until well into the nineteenth century, playwrights and managers had no qualms about making the Shakespearean text — to the extent they even knew what that was, given the amount of textual corruption that had occurred in the interim —

bend to the spirit of the times. Indeed, such emendations were often seen as a distinct improvement, heretical as that may sound to us today.

Whether the sensibility of any particular culture led it to reinvent Shakespeare because it felt that his plays needed improvement or simply because otherwise they would not be accessible, their transformation has taken place in every era, in theatres throughout the world. In the seventeenth and eighteenth centuries, English playwrights like John Dryden, Nahum Tate, and Colley Cibber made Shakespeare's characters and actions conform to neoclassical principles of verisimilitude and decorum — notions that had a profound effect on attitudes to Shakespeare elsewhere in Europe as well. Voltaire deemed Shakespeare brilliant but problematic, "a genius full of force and fecundity, nature and the sublime, without the slightest trace of good taste or the least knowledge of the rules."[54] Russian playwright Alexander Sumarokov worked from a French version of *Hamlet* to make his 1748 adaptation "a purely political tragedy that turned on the struggle of the lawful heir to a throne against a usurper and his accomplices."[55] Forty years later, Russian Tsarina Catherine II entertained her court by rewriting *The Merry Wives of Windsor*. Her 1786 adaptation *Vot Kakovo imet' Korzinu i bel'e* (A basketful of washing) set the play in St. Petersburg, with all the characters given Russian names and Falstaff rendered as a Frenchified Russian dandy decked out in Parisian clothing, coiffure, and perfumes, and peppering his language with French expressions such as "Chez nous à Paris" and "Parbleu!"[56]

Meanwhile, German and English critics establishing the foundations of Romantic aesthetic theory looked to Shakespeare as the quintessential romantic genius, whose frequent violation of such "rules" as the neoclassical unities of time, place, and action served the higher purpose of the organic unity of the work of art as a whole. Shakespeare inspired not only a significant body of German Romantic criticism, fiction, and drama, but also, beginning in the 1790s, the most ambitious translation project of his work to that point: the faithful but lively rendering of nearly all of his plays into German, led by August Wilhelm Schlegel and Ludwig Tieck. Their verse, "flexible, pleasant to hear, and rhythmically light," demonstrated that the German language "could achieve a range and expressiveness equal to

Shakespeare's English, [and] validated the advancement of German literature to European status."[57] While Shakespeare's plays would never be translated into Yiddish in nearly as ambitious an undertaking, we will see claims for the validation of Yiddish also based on its ability to handle Shakespearean language.

The Schlegel/Tieck translation was an auspicious end to the eighteenth century and a bright start for the nineteenth, which continued to see Shakespeare tailored to contemporary tastes. In France, while the neoclassical sensibility continued to hold sway in adaptations by Jean François Ducis, audiences at the Cirque du Monthabor in Paris could see J. G. A. Cuvelier de Trie's *Macbeth, ou les sorcières de la forêt* (1817), a spectacular pantomime featuring equestrian combat, Malcolm saved from Macbeth by a serpent and given a magic horn, the witches riding flying dragons, and Birnam Wood as "an enchanted forest which, at the end of the play, will part again to show Macbeth's castle being taken by assault and set on fire."[58] Productions in India could be no less spectacular, and perhaps more culturally specific. Songs and dances were frequently added, with vociferous audiences demanding that their favorite songs and scenes be repeated over and over. An 1894 adaptation of *All's Well That Ends Well* had Helena attribute her current predicament to misdeeds in a past life, while the soothsayer in Act V of *Cymbeline* "was replaced by a Brahmin astrologer, who promised a victory to Iachimo's side if he took care to feed the Brahmins."[59] One could, echoing the title of Goethe's essay *Shakespeare und kein Ende!* continue this list ad infinitum into the twentieth century, in countless translations and adaptations for page, stage, screen, and other media.

The Yiddish Shakespeare phenomenon is cousin to all these treatments, one culture's approach to a game that has been played for centuries. Casting an eye about them, the writers and performers in the Yiddish theatre would have seen both that Shakespeare seemed ubiquitous in America, and that he did not belong to the English language alone. Jewish intellectuals were familiar with many of the plays both by reading them in translation into other languages, and by seeing them on stage in eastern Europe. Besides, America in the late nineteenth century hosted a parade of foreign actors performing in Shakespeare, usually in tragedies. These included the Italian actors

Tommaso Salvini, Adelaide Ristori, Ernesto Rossi, and Ermete No-
velli; the Germans Ludwig Barnay, Ernst Possart, Adolph von Sonnenthal, and the Duke of Saxe-Meiningen's company; the Polish Bogu-
mil Dawison and Helena Modjeska; the Czech Fanny Janauschek;
the French Jean Mounet-Sully, Sarah Bernhardt, Constant Coquelin,
and Gabriele Réjane; the Anglo-French Charles Fechter; and the
English Adelaide Neilson, Henry Irving, Ellen Terry, Lillie Langtry,
Wilson Barrett, Johnston Forbes-Robertson, Mrs. Patrick Campbell,
and Herbert Beerbohm Tree. Collectively, these artists offered an international, multilingual tapestry of Shakespearean performance that
would serve as an inspiration, in direct and indirect ways, for their
Yiddish-speaking colleagues. An awareness of the Shakespearean
tradition in other cultures permeates Yiddish criticism and actors'
memoirs of the period, as in this 1901 commentary by critic B. Gorin:
"Almost all the names of the great actors of the world are connected with one or more characters from the great classic works. For
example: Betterton with Hamlet; John Philip Kemble with Coriolanus; Edmund Kean with Richard; Macklin with Shylock; Macready
with Macbeth; Rachel with Phèdre; Forrest with Lear; Salvini with
Othello, etc."[60]

Vilyam Shekspir

Once Shakespeare's plays began being produced in Yiddish,
it took little time for them to gain prominence on the American Yiddish stage. The Yiddish theatre of this period, like the European and
English-speaking American theatres during most of the nineteenth
century, was an actors' theatre, and Shakespeare provided star turns
(which could be enhanced with some judicious editing) for strong
leading actors. So just as such international stars as Kean (father and
son), Booth (father and sons), Kemble (the whole family), Macready,
Forrest, Cushman, Duse, and Salvini displayed their talents in Shakespeare's leading roles throughout the century, most of the leading
Yiddish actors in the United States would at some time or other test
their mettle in translations and adaptations of Shakespeare's plays.
After all, the professional Yiddish theatre was built on a foundation
of melodramatic leading roles, and as Levine has noted, many of

Shakespeare's plays were suited to this style, since "Shakespearean drama featured heroes and villains who communicated directly with the audience and left little doubt about the nature of their character or their intentions."[61] Moreover, a number of the most successful Yiddish playwrights, who were also accustomed to working in a melodramatic vein, would increase their fame and fortune by translating or adapting Shakespeare's work.

Yet all of these reasons combined — the need for new plots, powerful leading roles, Yiddish actors' quest for legitimacy and envy of their Gentile colleagues — only partially account for the important position Shakespeare's plays would attain in American Yiddish theatres and theatre lore. For reasons that changed with the rapidly altering circumstances of the American Jewish population, five of Shakespeare's plays took on special significance for Yiddish audiences. This book will focus on those five plays — *King Lear, Hamlet, Othello, Romeo and Juliet*, and *The Merchant of Venice* — devoting a chapter to the performance and reception of each.

Yiddish writers approached the adaptation of Shakespeare from various perspectives. Playwrights working essentially in the Goldfaden/Hurwitz/Lateiner vein combined a hodgepodge of melodramatic elements with a healthy dose of operetta. Later, when polemics over theatre heated up in the Yiddish press, critics would attach the word *shund* — literally, "trash" — to plays of this sort. Plots and characters taken from preexisting sources (as they so often were) were frequently Judaized; as Gorin explains, "It was customary for earlier playwrights to take a foreign play, squeeze every drop of juice out of it, change the Gentile names to Jewish ones, slap on manly beards and *peyes* and let them parade across the stage as Jews."[62] Sometimes such changes seemed gratuitous, an effective but superficial device to get the audience's attention, but at times they go far deeper.

Playwright Jacob Gordin (1853–1909) transformed the Yiddish theatre in many ways, including the manner of adapting Shakespeare. Gordin, a Russian-born Jew with a broad secular education and liberal political views, admired such reformers of the European drama as Ibsen, Hauptmann, and Gorky, and sought to emulate them in his work. Borrowing the broad outlines of Shakespeare plays but making the characters and situations Jewish, Gordin turned his Shakespearean sources into dramas that explored the challenges of contemporary Jewish life. Gordin established the paradigm for such adaptations with *The Jewish King Lear* (1892), to which he wrote a female counterpart several years later: *Mirele Efros* (subtitled "The Jewish Queen Lear"). Gordin would follow his own template to a lesser extent with an 1894 drama loosely based on *Romeo and Juliet*, and each of the five chapters that follow contains at least one example of Gordin and other playwrights Judaizing their Shakespearean sources.

Along with the new depth of seriousness which Gordin brought to the Yiddish stage came a new manner of performing the plays. According to critic Nokhem Bukhvald, Gordin not only changed the Yiddish theatre by moving away from the false heroics and romanticism in *shund* plays; he also "made a positive impact with his plays both by educating an audience and by developing in actors a spirit of respect for the role, a spirit of piety for the task of depicting a person on the stage."[63] Such actors as Jacob P. Adler (1855–1926) and Keni Liptzin (c. 1856–1918), who were instrumental in establishing Gordin's success, found subtleties in Gordin's characters that had been almost completely lacking in previous Yiddish drama, so the Yiddish theatre moved towards a style much closer to everyday speech and gesture than anyone could have imagined before Gordin.

Other Yiddish playwrights chose to stick closer to Shakespeare when producing Yiddish versions of his plays. While maintaining most of the original story, characters, and dialogue, these translations often make a number of cuts, sometimes for the sake of economy, sometimes for clarity, sometimes to censor bawdy or otherwise problematic language. Most of these versions, especially the earlier ones, disregard nuances of verse and metaphor; they tend to treat their sources as compelling dramas with juicy parts, not as sacred works of art. Occasionally, they even *add* dialogue: a new scene that summarizes several of Shakespeare's that have been removed, or passages that the playwright presumably thinks will heighten the play's success with the Yiddish audience (as in the remarkable additions to the dialogue of the tomb scene in *Romeo and Juliet*).

All of these changes indicate a culture that had little concern for the sanctity of the "original" text — that is, not some Platonic ideal of a pure original, but whatever was considered some sort of authoritative edition at the time. In fact, many Yiddish writers made their translations and adaptations from other translations, usually Russian or German. Even when these writers saw to it that their texts followed the general flow of the action and kept the same settings, they often cut entire scenes and eliminated or consolidated roles, just as many other adaptors of Shakespeare from the Restoration to the twentieth century have done. Yet there is a clear difference in spirit between such alterations and more sweeping changes of plot, character, and setting. Throughout the book, I will refer to Yiddish versions that essentially maintain the Shakespearean story and milieu as "translations," as opposed to the "adaptations" that refashion the Shakespearean source into a story of Jewish life.

Theatre That Mattered

The story that unfolds in these pages happened not very long ago in historical terms, but it belongs to a worldview that may seem to belong to the distant past. The American Jewish community has changed radically in the over one hundred years since the beginning of this story: it is more affluent, generally less religious, better educated in secular matters and less so in Jewish knowledge, and much further removed from its European heritage, including the Yiddish language itself. Details of those changes get chronicled as they are reflected in the plays discussed here. But perhaps more fundamental than any other difference between current theatregoers and the immigrants of one hundred years ago is their gut reaction to theatre. Today, theatre competes with countless other forms of entertainment, many of them cheaper and far more popular. For most of America, theatre has become marginal, a luxury. This was not the case with audiences who made the American Yiddish theatre a pulsating, vital entity of adoring fans, actors they treated like gods, magisterial playwrights, and fascinated visitors from uptown. In short, it mattered, and mattered deeply. Historian Henry Feingold has written,

Perhaps the most remarkable facet of the Yiddish culture generated in America was its consumers. They were people who toiled bone-wearying hours in the shops and then mustered the energy to drag themselves to the libraries, lectures, innumerable discussion groups, and theater to get culture and education. Few other groups in America, native or immigrant, [have] had such an appetite, such a desire to elevate [themselves].[64]

Those same sweatshop workers would skip lunch to save money for theatre tickets. The Yiddish theatre was not the icing on the cake; it was the cake itself.

chapter 1

'Gordin Is Greater Than Shakespeare'
The Jewish King and Queen Lear

It was Jacob Gordin (1853–1909), more than any other play-wright, who gave Shakespeare a Yiddish accent. A handful of Shakespeare's plays had been staged in Yiddish before, but Gordin translated far more than just the language of his source. Retelling the Lear story from the vantage point of a contemporary eastern European Jew in *The Jewish King Lear* (1892), Gordin taught audiences a little bit about Shakespeare and a great deal about what it meant to be Jewish in their newly adopted home, the United States. Six years later, Gordin topped the success of *The Jewish King Lear* with *The Jewish Queen Lear*. The latter play, which quickly came to be known simply by its subtitle, *Mirele Efros*, departed more freely from the structure of *King Lear* while conveying its message with greater subtlety. The two plays combined would, paradoxically, help popularize Shakespeare while preempting any more faithful version of *King Lear* from ever taking hold with American Yiddish audiences. After 1892, if you mentioned *King Lear* to an American Yiddish theatregoer, he would undoubtedly think not of Shakespeare, but of Jacob Gordin and the actors who played his King and Queen Lear. Most Yiddish audiences would have agreed with the theater manager who reportedly claimed, "Gordin is greater than Shakespeare, for besides having the same dramaturgical talents, he also has Jewish charm, Jewish humor and Jewish pathos — qualities that Shakespeare does not possess!"[1]

Gordin came late to playwriting. Born on 1 May 1853 in Mirgorod, Ukraine, he received both a traditional Jewish education and a broad exposure to Western culture. He married at age nineteen and was expected to settle into a business career, but quickly moved on to a series of other jobs while continuing his earlier work as a journalist and theatre critic and participating in a number of Jewish, socialist, and agrarian reform movements.

After immigrating to the United States in July 1891, Gordin quickly made a strong impression among New York's Yiddish writers and actors. What first caught their attention was not Gordin the writer but Gordin the man, whose majestic presence made actors like Bessie Thomashefsky take note: "His appearance impressed all of us. He was tall and thin, with a remarkably handsome, noble face; deep, intelligent eyes; a beautiful black beard, neatly trimmed; a great head of thick, black, curly hair, combed down to his nape; a large, soft black hat with a broad brim; a poor but clean suit that fit him well; and a walking stick in his hand."[2] The critic Shmuel Niger argued that in order to understand Gordin's influence, one must recognize Gordin's persona as an integral part of his creative output: "His appearance was an expression of the strength he exerted, an emanation from his soul."[3] The combination of Gordin's enormous charisma with a dramaturgic talent for placing the resources of the Yiddish theatre in the service of his didactic goals helped him become what Niger described as "the last of the American Yiddish enlighteners."[4]

The Reformer

Fellow socialists invited Gordin to write for their newspaper, *Di arbeter tsaytung*, but since his sketches did not pay well enough to feed his large family, he sought to supplement his income by writing for the Yiddish theatre. He was, however, appalled by what he saw there. Yiddish plays at the time shared certain basic ingredients: dialogue in a Germanized Yiddish known as *daytshmerish*; plot complications that would have sent an Aristotelian screaming for the exit; and songs, dances, jokes, and sword fights at every possible opportunity — and at some opportunities that might previously have been thought impossible. "Everything I heard and saw there was far from Jewish life," Gordin later wrote; "coarse, unaesthetic, false, mean, and vulgar."[5]

Ever the crusader (fig. 1), Gordin set out to change the situation himself — an undertaking he later described in characteristically inflated rhetoric:

I sat down to write my first drama, which at its circumcision was given the name "Siberia." I wrote my first play as a God-fearing

THE HEROES

OF

THE GHETTO

י. גאָרדין, צום פײַט.

1. Jacob Gordin, reformer of Yiddish drama, ready to do battle.
From the Archives of the YIVO Institute for Jewish Research.

scribe writes out a book of the Torah. Such a scribe, every time he writes God's name, immerses himself in the *mikve* [ritual bath]. Naturally, I did not go to the *mikve*, but I guarded my pen so that every word should be clean and every thought holy.[6]

Gordin launched his aesthetic campaign on two fronts: playwriting and criticism. A few months before the premiere of *The Jewish King Lear*, he published in *Di arbeter tsaytung* a 200-line poem in rhymed couplets entitled, "The Subject of My Future Drama." The poem describes a hypothetical, fantastical, five-act operetta, a blend of everything Gordin finds wrong with the Yiddish theatre. Lest his readers miss the point, Gordin follows with an explanation:

I just wanted to make all Yiddish actors aware that they are taking the wrong path: on the one hand . . . making fun of [the theatre-goer], on the other flattering him and letting themselves perform all sorts of idiocy to please him. They debase both the people and their own talents. I did not plan to become a Yiddish dramatist, but now that I am, I will do everything I can to clean the mud off of the Yiddish stage.[7]

Making such a declaration was simple enough, but in practice, the task would not be so straightforward. Working in the theatre is a collaborative process — not just between playwright and theatre company, but also between the producers and consumers of the theatrical event. What Gordin saw as the "wrong path" was the very path that had led dozens of actors from jobs in factories and behind pushcarts to careers on the stage. What he deemed "idiocy" delighted thousands of theatregoers every week. Gordin would have to balance his desire for reforming the Yiddish theatre with the practical need to keep both the other theatre personnel and their audiences satisfied — that is, to leave enough of their beloved "mud" behind while doing his cleaning.

That Gordin had some understanding of the pressures on theatre artists to compromise their aesthetic ambitions for the sake of commercial necessities come across in an early one-act sketch, *Yokl der opern-makher* [Yokl the opera maker]. The comic curtain raiser premiered along with another Gordin play, *Der yidisher galekh* [The Jewish priest], at a benefit for Gordin at Adler's Theatre on 3 May 1894. Publicity for the evening emphasized *Yokl*'s function as criticism:

"Whoever does not understand what Jacob Gordin has done for the Yiddish theatre and Yiddish literature, he . . . should go see the comedy "Yokl the Opera Maker." Then this critique of the Yiddish theatre will really make him begin to understand."[8] Gordin's sketch is billed as education as well as entertainment; the ellipsis appears in the original, as if the copywriter was so staggered by the thought of someone not appreciating Gordin's greatness that he had to pause to catch his breath.

In *Yokl* (a diminutive for Yankev, Gordin's first name in Yiddish), Gordin simultaneously airs his lofty ideas about art and pokes fun at his own seriousness, as the play makes clear that the Yiddish theatre has no place for such high-mindedness. Yokl, an idealistic composer, has been commissioned to write music for a historical operetta. Shlemiel Ox, the show's director, tries to teach Yokl the tricks of the trade:

> Take a look, I've brought some scissors, and in one hour I'll paste together a brand-new historical opera, with a scene from here, an act tacked on from over there, a couple of acts stolen from an old operetta, an epilogue pilfered from a French melodrama, a prologue from Barnum and Bailey's Circus with clever sayings for the comedians . . . and brother, there you have it: a new, stunningly successful, historical opera! And the morons pay their money and cry, "Bravo!" Yokl, don't be a yokel; write operas — that is, steal music and shut up.[9]

Gordin implies that Shlemiel carries out the standard operating procedure for writing Yiddish plays, brazenly stealing material from sources that have nothing in common except their potential entertainment value.

When Yokl naively tries to resist such cheap tactics, Shlemiel insists that the more outlandish the effect, the more the audience will applaud. "And Shakespeare? What will he get you? A bloody abscess and two ulcers!" (186). Yokl balks at the allusion:

> Oh, why is poor Shakespeare guilty, when you destroy him? Shakespeare and Professor Treytl Henfoot [a thinly veiled allusion to Yiddish playwright Moyshe Hurwitz] are all the same to you. You throw scenes out of Shakespeare's classic works and insert silly

couplets and stolen jokes and perform it so that the public doesn't understand what you say, and the actors don't understand what Shakespeare wants from them. I saw Shakespeare's "Antony and Cleopatra" on the Yiddish stage. Antony stands with the posture of a highwayman, gnashes his teeth, rolls his eyes, puckers his lips and cries, "*Gevald* [help], Cleopatra, I love you!" And Cleopatra moves about like a beast, contorts her mouth like a little boy who's been spanked, makes a sour face as if she had just bitten into a lemon, and screeches . . . (186)

Yokl's description suggests that Yiddish actors adopt a particular style for performing classic plays, making them lose whatever claim to naturalness their performances may achieve in other genres.

Gordin goes so far as to have Yokl quote some of the stilted lyrics from this imaginary performance. As the stars are shamelessly mugging for the audience, they move to a safe position behind the prompter's box and sing:

Gey nit fun mir!
Ay vey iz mir!
In hartsn a geshvir!
Es iz heys un ikh frir! (186)

[Do not leave me!
Oh woe is me!
An ulcer in my heart!
It is hot, and I am freezing!]

The chorus responds in non sequiturs and a mishmash of unconnected phrases from the Hebrew liturgy, ending improbably with "Hooray, hooray!" In this Shakespearean spectacle, music and lyrics contribute to the incongruity and falseness of the proceedings.

Initially, Shlemiel Ox plays the role of pragmatist, with Yokl resisting his boss's more outlandish proposals for the forthcoming production:

Today we need to read through a new play, then turn it into a historical opera, then stick a catchy name onto the opera, then rehearse it, and by Saturday we'll be putting it on stage with eye-catching scenery; stunning effects; Oriental music; African dances;

Arabian horses; Spanish sheep; authentic, historical Jewish goats; Turkish costumes; Chinese shoes; Russian nihilists; Italian melodies; Indian marches; German swords . . . (184)[10]

In an environment that lumps all these elements together so shamelessly, Shakespeare is but one more ingredient on a long list of attractions, a cheap cultural commodity to be exploited only so far as the audience applauds the effects his work provides. As passionately as Yokl excoriates the composers and lyricists who collaborate in this process, he joins their ranks once he realizes that he will never make a living as long as he insists on unrealistically high artistic standards. Even Shlemiel, it turns out, once had ideals, but he has learned from hard experience that the Yiddish audience wants something else: "Oh, how happy I would be if our audience would demand serious words, pure, true art, beautiful music! There are talented, capable people among us. But is it our fault if that's not what they demand? You ask us for second-rate American machine work, so that's what we have to produce!" (193). *Yokl* turns out to be a joke ending in an Aesopian moral rather than a punch line. If the audience will only get its act together, the Yiddish theatre, in Shlemiel's words, "can hold its own with any theatre in the world . . . serve truth, and campaign for lofty ideals as well as the richest languages in the civilized world!" (193).

If Gordin was to be the Moses to lead the Yiddish theatre out of its bondage to melodrama and operetta, he would need an Aaron to convey his message. He found his first spokesman in actor Jacob P. Adler (1855–1926), who had been among the first Yiddish actors in Russia, and was already a star by the time Gordin arrived in New York. After encouraging Gordin to write for the theatre, Adler took the starring role in Gordin's first play, *Siberia* (1891), a realistic drama that omitted many of the typical ingredients of the American Yiddish theatre at the time, and thus risked alienating both actors and audience. Critic Irving Howe helps account for how resistant Gordin's first audiences were to realistic drama:

> Realism seldom attracts uncultivated audiences: it is a sophisticated genre resting on the idea that a controlled exposure to a drab reality will yield pleasure. To the masses of early Jewish immigrants, most of whom had never before seen a professional stage production, realism seemed dry, redundant, without savor. What stirred

their hearts was a glimpse of something that might transcend the wretchedness of the week: a theatre bringing a touch of the Sabbath, even if a debased or vulgarized Sabbath.[11]

A tale of a refugee from Siberian prison camps who escapes and tries to start a new life elsewhere, only to be blackmailed by someone who knows the secret of his past, would hardly "transcend the wretchedness of the week" — particularly if unalleviated by songs, dances, and comic scenes.

During rehearsals, Adler urged his fellow performers to respect Gordin's dramaturgy, and had to cajole the audience into giving the play a fair hearing on opening night. The spectators reportedly grew increasingly restless during the first two acts, prompting Adler to make a tearful appeal to them after the Act II curtain: "I stand here embarrassed and humiliated, my head bowed in shame, that you, my friends, cannot understand such a masterpiece by the famous Russian writer Yakov Mikhailovitsh Gordin. My friends, my friends, if you understood what a great work we are performing for you today, you would not laugh and would not shout."[12] Adler's ploy worked. According to fellow cast member Leon Blank, the audience settled down for Act III, and burst into tears at the play's climax. Significantly, Adler couched his exhortation in terms extraneous to the merits of the play itself. His speech, as described by Blank, consisted of two parts Jewish guilt ("embarrassed and ashamed"), three parts intimacy ("my friends"), two parts condescension ("you cannot understand," "if you understood"), and a healthy dollop of cultural snobbery ("such a masterpiece by the famous *Russian* writer Yakov Mikhailovitsh Gordin"). Adler, in effect, browbeat his audience into appreciation, using both his relationship with the theatregoers, and *their* relationship with Russian high culture, as his weapons.

With *Siberia*, Gordin had scored a resounding critical success — if only a modest one commercially — and found in Adler his leading man par excellence: attentive enough to detail to create a rich subtext for his characters, but not so grounded in realism as to be unable to deliver a climactic speech in grand nineteenth-century fashion. Gordin followed *Siberia* with another drama of Russian life, *The Pogrom in Russia* (1892). He then adapted two plays by Avrom Goldfaden before, in the words of theatre historian Zalmen Zylbercweig,

"swimming in the great sea of the world repertoire" by turning to
Shakespeare.[13] But though Gordin's first plays had caused a sensation
among critics and the intelligentsia, the actors were harder to impress.
When the time came for Gordin to read his new play to them (standard practice in the Yiddish theatre at the time), one of the actors
launched into a sarcastic running commentary that theatre historian
B. Gorin reports was "so coarse that one cannot put it down on
paper."[14] Even Adler, who had championed Gordin so vigorously,
found enough fault with Gordin's dialogue to add some of his own —
something the playwright would not tolerate. But Adler, realizing how
much he could do with the role and knowing that he would lose it if
he crossed Gordin, backed down and played his part as written.

The Jewish King Lear

Shakespeare had undoubtedly influenced Yiddish drama before Gordin, particularly in indirect ways via his enormous impact on
other European and American drama. One can point to numerous
moments in Yiddish drama of the 1870s and 1880s that arguably seem
borrowed from Shakespeare, whether deliberately or not. Gordin
went much further, advertising his indebtedness to Shakespeare in the
very title of his play, *Der yidisher kenig Lir* — a practice that had a recent precedent in his countryman Ivan Turgenev's 1870 novella, "*Step-
noi korol' Lir*" (King Lear of the steppes). As a Russian intellectual,
Gordin undoubtedly would have known Turgenev's version, which
turned Lear into a contemporary Russian petty landowner, a powerful
giant whose two daughters' cruelty drives him to bring his own house
crashing down upon his head. Just as Turgenev carefully researched
Russian property law to recast Lear's transfer of his estate into an
authentically Russian context, Gordin drew upon Jewish ritual, tradition, and politics to connect Lear's situation more directly to the lives
of American Yiddish theatregoers.

The Jewish King Lear opened on 21 October 1892 at New York's
Union Theatre. Adler (fig. 2) created the role of Dovid Moysheles, a
wealthy Jewish businessman in Vilna who has decided to divide his
estate among his three grown daughters and move with his wife to
Palestine. As in Shakespeare, the two older daughters praise the idea,

יאקאב פ. אדלער, אלס דער יודישער קעניג ליאר.

2. Jacob Adler as Dovid Moysheles, the Jewish King Lear.
From the Archives of the YIVO Institute for Jewish Research.

the youngest resists it, and her father casts her out of the house. Dovid soon pays for his actions; the daughter and son in-law who now control the family finances cut him off with nothing, and Act II finds him back from Palestine and dependent upon what for them passes for hospitality. Like Shakespeare's Gloucester, he also pays with blindness — though Dovid's comes from a degenerative disease, not a moment of violence. Five years later, in Act III, the situation becomes so dire that Dovid and his faithful servant, Shamay, leave the house to go begging in the streets. The fourth and final act opens on the wedding day of Taybele, the youngest daughter. She has in the interim become a physician, and is marrying her former tutor, now also a doctor. Just before the wedding, Dovid and Shamay come knocking at the door, and not only is the family reconciled, but we learn that Dovid's blindness can be cured with a routine operation.

The action of the play begins with Dovid's wife Khane-Leye preparing for Purim, the holiday celebrating the Jews' victory over their enemies in ancient Persia. While the holiday is a joyous one, family gatherings often bring family anxieties. The first conflict in the play involves whether or not to invite the man who tutors Taybele, Dovid and Khane-Leye's youngest daughter, to the family's Purim feast. Trivial as it may seem, this question foreshadows much of the unhappiness that will follow, for at issue are the ideas the tutor represents. The more traditional members of the family — that is, everyone but Taybele — continually refer to the tutor Yaffe as *"der daytsh"* — that is, the German (Jew). The problem is not so much nationality as sensibility; in this context, German means modern and secular. As the locus of Moses Mendelssohn's Haskalah movement, Germany stands for the source of ideas that challenge traditional Jewish life.

The question of whether to invite Yaffe also allows Gordin to begin setting up the grand entrance of his protagonist. Khane-Leye worries about Yaffe's presence at the celebration not so much on her own account, but because she fears it will ignite the wrath of her husband, from whose stormy moods she clearly works hard to protect the rest of the family. Taybele's request to invite Yaffe is thus met with, "What do you need that poor German for? After all, you know what your father is like!" [15] But it does not take the presence of a potentially unwanted guest to set Dovid off, for a few moments later, Khane-Leye asks her daughter, "Taybele, my child! Just take a look with your young eyes — have we forgotten anything? I don't want your father to get angry during the meal, God forbid." Repeated references to Dovid's temper may have left Gordin's original audience anticipating, with delicious apprehension, the emotional fireworks soon to come from their larger-than-life Jacob Adler.

Yaffe has arrived by this point, and is soon followed by Taybele's older sisters, Etele and Gitele, and their husbands, Avrom Kharif and Moyshe Khosid, who enter squabbling with one another. Now that all the other characters are in place, Dovid can make his grand entrance, accompanied by a musical flourish from the orchestra. Fellow actor Boaz Young felt that the music sent a clear message, saying "'Here he comes, the great artist, take a look!' And the public did indeed applaud, and it became festive on the stage when he entered." [16] Dovid's expansive first speech contributes further to the festive mood:

Happy holiday, children, may you enjoy long life! Khane-Leye, get the old gold coins out of the dresser and give two to each of the children. I want everyone to remember this Purim. What I will share with you today will amaze all of you. . . . Now sit down, children! Have something to eat and drink.

The audience will soon see how abruptly this warmth can turn to fire, but for the time being, he is in great form, leading his family in song and even welcoming Yaffe.

On Purim, it is customary to give gifts — particularly food and wine — to family and friends — and food to the poor. Dovid elaborates on the gift-giving custom, bestowing jewels on each of his daughters as he moves successively, in fairy-tale like fashion, from oldest to youngest. The two eldest reply with formulaic expressions of thanks, while Taybele has to be pressed to respond at all. When she does, she gently expresses her lack of enthusiasm for the gift, finding natural human beauty more glorious than diamonds. Her response evokes a torrent of patronizing responses about a woman's place in society not just from all the men except Yaffe — with some of them quoting rabbinic texts to support their point — but from her sisters as well. Nevertheless, this crisis blows over quickly, with Dovid readily making peace with his youngest and favorite daughter, and expressing his appreciation of her teacher: "Nu, Reb Yaffe, come here and we'll drink another toast! I like a person who is intelligent and honorable, even if he is a heretic!" Yaffe similarly reveres his host: "And I like a person who is intelligent and honorable, even if he's Orthodox!"

These warm feelings turn out to be short-lived. After another brief moment of tension, when Taybele refuses to drink with her father, we finally reach the true moment of conflict, with larger principles at stake than gifts or drinks. He announces to all the guests that he has decided to divide up his estate among his children and move to the Land of Israel. Besides registering her annoyance at not having been consulted, Khane-Leye is the first to predict that the children in whose hands he is placing his fortune will prove ungrateful. The subsequent action of the play will show Dovid and Khane-Leye to be like many a set of parents in Yiddish fiction and drama — Sholem Aleykhem's Tevye and Golde being a perfect example. The father turns out to know far less about his children than he thinks, while it is the mother who has a less idealized, more realistic sense of who her children are.

Khane-Leye will not say another word for the rest of Act I, as her worst fears about her husband's temper are realized. Once again, Taybele, unlike her older sisters and their husbands, cannot or will not flatter her father. She is again silent until Dovid exhorts her to say something, at which point she expresses both her sadness that her father is going away and her worry that Kharif will prove an untrustworthy administrator of the estate. Finally, Dovid's wrath reaches full boil:

> What? You dare to be unhappy? You dare to give me advice? You dare to tell me to listen to you? And I, old fool that I am, thought she would gladden my heart with sweet words of thanks, that she would give me the strength to take the path that God demands of every person who understands that this world is vanity of vanities. I do as I see fit. Get out of my sight!

Thus Taybele, like Cordelia, is banished from her father's kingdom.

If we recognize that this situation has a precedent, we are not the only ones. Gordin not only models Dovid upon Lear, but makes the Jewish patriarch aware of his literary prototype in order to make explicit the connection between Gordin's play and Shakespeare's. Right after sending his daughter away, Dovid gets a free lesson in dramatic literature from her tutor:

> Reb Dovidl, please excuse me, but I do not know whether you have heard of the world-famous writer Shakespeare. I know a drama of his entitled *King Lear*. This king, at the same point in his life as you, divided his kingdom. Just as you have expelled your beloved daughter Taybele, so he expelled his beloved daughter Cordelia, who told him the truth. Ach, how dearly that old man paid for what he did. And you are the Jewish King Lear. May God protect you from the fate that befell King Lear.

Yaffe's précis of Shakespeare's play serves a threefold purpose: to acquaint the audience with the name of a "world-famous writer" and with that of one of his masterpieces while explaining the title's connection to the story. Yiddish play titles before Gordin's time tended simply to identify the protagonist, a central event, or some other straightforward feature of the play. A theatregoer unfamiliar with Shakespeare's *King Lear*, however, would need an explanation of the epithet "The Jewish King Lear."

By transplanting *King Lear* rather than simply translating it, Gordin makes the play Jewish — or more precisely, makes it correspond to his vision of Judaism. His extensive use of Jewish imagery and symbolism continually remind us that we are watching the Jewish *King Lear*, and it is undoubtedly the play's Jewish flavor that gave it such lasting power over Yiddish audiences. The play abounds in Jewish references, creating a shorthand that guides the audience to the moral awaiting it at the end of the evening.

Gordin's Jewish politics dictate the course of the action. Upon Shakespeare's framework of two evil daughters and one virtuous one, Gordin superimposes the three main branches of nineteenth-century Judaism: traditional Orthodoxy, Hasidism, and the Haskalah, or Jewish Enlightenment. The eldest daughter and her husband are *misnagdim* (anti-Hasidic Orthodox Jews); the middle daughter and her husband, Hasidim. As much as these two couples despise each other, they find common ground in their contempt for the *maskilim* (adherents of the Haskalah) Taybele and Yaffe, whom they consider heretics.[17]

Gordin's agenda makes for a number of two-dimensional characters — precisely his intention, it seems. The older daughters and their husbands, with the emblematic names of Avrom Kharif (sharp, shrewd) and Moyshe Hasid, are usually cartoonish in their nastiness; for example, the first time we see them, the two husbands quarrel over who gets to sit next to Dovid at the table, then descend further to name-calling. All the daughters and their husbands represent abstract ideas; the human element of the play is left to Dovid and his servant Shamay.

Shakespeare's Cordelia, the one daughter who rejects superficial formulas of respect, is the one who truly loves and respects her father. Gordin creates a parallel irony: Taybele (whose name means "little dove"), the daughter who turns her back on traditional Judaism, proves truest to Jewish ethics. The religious sons and daughters follow the letter of Jewish law but betray its spirit, while the play's so-called heretics prove to be the most moral characters by virtue of their honesty, learning, and compassion. Yaffe (from the Hebrew for "beautiful") uses imagery from Purim, the holiday with which the play begins, to sum up Gordin's preference for good deeds over good words: "*Koylitsh* [a large *khale*, or coiled white bread] and *megile* [the book of *Esther*]," he announces, "are Jewish history in its entirety. *Megile* is Jewry's blind faith and fanaticism, *koylitsh* its practical life. Ach, little Jews, the less *megile* and the more *koylitsh*, the healthier you'll be!" In a sense, the rest of the play is a footnote to Yaffe's remark.

Recent eastern European Jewish immigrants struggling to strike an acceptable balance between their religious traditions and the customs of their new home may have found comfort in Gordin's secular approach to Jewish values. Historian Arthur Hertzberg writes that these immigrants "knew that they had to learn American manners, and that the observances of the Jewish religion, and especially of the Sabbath, were obstacles to success. . . . And yet, Jews continued to believe, into the second generation and beyond, that 'Jewish values,' the specific heritage that the immigrants had brought with them from Eastern Europe, had to be preserved." [18] Gordin, accordingly, advocates a Jewishness vaguely connected to religious values and traditions, but flexible enough to bend to what he considers the best of Western values and learning.

Since his audience is more familiar with Jewish than with non-Jewish references, Gordin relies upon Jewish terminology to convey the need for a departure from parochial thinking. This technique begins with the holiday preparations as the play opens. Purim is a time of festivity and plenty, with the family enjoying the feast provided by the generous Dovid Moysheles. But Purim also inverts the traditional order, which is exactly what Dovid has done by turning his estate over to such unreliable caretakers. Thus, when we see the household at the beginning of Act II, the feast has turned to famine. Dovid's servant Shamay complains, "The world is a *dreydl*. Here, just a year ago, I was a commissioner for Reb Dovidl. He gave me good tobacco, *kharoyses* for *Peysekh* [Passover], vegetables for *Shvues* and an *esreg* and a *lulav* for *Sukes*, wax for *havdole*, a carp for the Sabbath . . . and now I'm nothing more than a simple servant-*shikse*."[19] As Leonard Prager observes, "The central theme of the play is throughout symbolized in terms of food; the prevailing emotional state is one of oral anxiety; at the moment of greatest discord, the most violent act committed is the breaking of dishes."[20]

Audiences reportedly took the play's "oral anxiety" to heart. Jacob Adler's daughter Celia recalled that during a performance of the play in Montreal, one audience member ultimately could not suppress his agitation over the mistreatment of Dovid Moysheles:

> In that scene, my father would very vividly illustrate his hunger pangs. His big, impressive eyes broke the audience's hearts. One man in the audience could endure it no longer. He suddenly stood up and walked toward the stage, and as he walked he said at the top of his lungs: "My dear Yankl, that daughter of yours, that evil woman . . . you see now, that you won't get anything to eat from her today. She truly has a stone instead of a heart. Spit on her, Yankl, and come to me! My wife will give you a wonderful dinner. Come, Yankl! Let her choke, that awful woman, your daughter. Come to me!"[21]

This anecdote, enhanced in the telling, resembles many tales of so-called "unsophisticated" audiences.

A reviewer for *Harper's Weekly*, seeing Adler perform the play in 1899, appreciated the intense impact of "this primitive Shakspere" upon the audiences for which Gordin wrote:

> I have much consolation in Shakspere *à la Yid*. It lacks the colossal grandeur of the true Shaksperean play, the splendor of Shakspere's

diction, and the infinite wisdom of Shakspere's characterization. Yet this primitive "Lear" of the Ghetto has a certain Shaksperean quality that no one would dare to hope for in a Broadway theatre. Its costume and scenery are as simple and unobtrusive as were those of the original play as presented at the Globe; and the audience of Jewish tailors and shopkeepers is as wholehearted, and no doubt quite as keen and imaginative, as an audience in the little world of Elizabethan London. If any one wants to know what our best plays seemed like to the people for whom they were written, he will find much satisfaction at the Windsor.[22]

During this period (particularly until about World War I), critics writing in the Yiddish press regularly mocked American Yiddish audiences for their lack of worldliness and their taste for cheap entertainments. Critics for the English-language press, on the other hand, tended to write from a distance that gave them an appreciation for the sincerity such audiences brought to the auditorium, and their respect for the close bond between play and onlooker would become a frequent feature in outsiders' accounts of attending Yiddish performances.

Gordin, like other Russian Jewish intellectuals who dominated the rosters of Yiddish theatre critics, also scoffed at his audience in many of his writings, but his condescension was mixed with enough respect to allow him to try to convey at least some of Shakespeare's imagery to them — again in Jewish terms. The central metaphor for Dovid's fall and rise is his descent into, and promised redemption from, blindness. In Act II, Shamay reports that Dovid "cannot see any more. A curtain has been drawn over his eyes as over the Holy Ark." Dovid's literal blindness parallels the stunted moral vision that keeps him from distinguishing truth from flattery. The metaphorical curtain that covers Dovid's eyes figuratively conceals the Torah — and by extension, the understanding of what is right — from him.

Characters develop when they learn about themselves. In this case, a character adapted from Shakespeare learns about himself when he comes to appreciate his own Shakespearean-ness. Yaffe has periodically continued to lecture Dovid as the father has clung to his initial, misguided sense of his children: "Intelligent Reb Dovidl, you still do not want to open your eyes and see who is really true to you? You still play the role of King Lear and don't see what a true friend you drive away from you?" And again, some time later: "Oh Lear! Lear! Jewish King Lear! It's not for nothing that you come from a nation long known as a stiff-necked people." But only when his situation reaches its nadir does Dovid see his predicament in Yaffe's terms. In his final speech of Act III, in a moment that would enter the theatrical memory of a people, Dovid finally assumes the mantle Yaffe has placed on him: "Yaffe the teacher calls me the Jewish King Lear. Ha, ha! Respect for the king! Make way for the king! *Vivat* for the new blind beggar! Give alms to the Jewish King Lear! Alms! Alms!" In the eyes of author and protagonist, type and prototype have merged. Once Dovid learns his lesson, Gordin will allow the play's events to take a turn for the better.

In the end, it is the Haskalah that removes both the moral and the physical blindness. Dovid comes to realize that superficial gestures of religious piety sometimes mask ugly deeds, and that those who have moved away from traditional religion may still carry on its deepest values. It is Dovid's recognition of the characteristics he shares with Shakespeare's King Lear — a parallel repeatedly pointed out to him by the *maskil* Yaffe — that makes him see that his older daughters were false and the youngest one true. And it is Yaffe, trained in Western medical techniques, who also prescribes the cure for Dovid's physical loss of vision.

Gordin's happy ending departs radically from the bleakness of Shakespeare's dénouement — though not so drastically from the way *King Lear* was most often performed well into the nineteenth century, in Nahum Tate's 1681 adaptation, *The History of King Lear*. Tate's version did what countless other reworkings of Shakespeare's plays have done: it sought to bring the play into line with the audience's world view. Gordin provided the same service for his audience, and Leonard Prager suggests a strong communal need for the happy ending in Gordin's version:

Many [immigrants] faced difficulties in observing rituals and following precepts which had been second-nature in the Old World. In many families children initiated their parents into American ways and were, in effect, their parents' teachers and guides. This reversal of roles must have stimulated considerable anxiety, increasing fears of dependency which economic uncertainty further aggravated. Gordin's *The Jewish King Lear* symbolically sanctions the new pattern of dependency and reassures the parents that the most modernist of their children will prove the most reliable. The children who have availed themselves of the new dispensation will be their parents' eyes in the confusing transition world. There will be an abundance of *koylitsh* for those parents who accept the new *megile*.[23]

Thus Dovid's fortunate fate promises a similar outcome for the audience: they may be uprooted, poor, and struggling to understand their new surroundings, but — Gordin suggests — if they cast off the worst of the old ways and embrace the best of the new, they will succeed in the New World.

The message may not have differed greatly from what the audience could have heard at many a lecture on the Lower East Side at the time, and indeed, sometimes the play reads like a lecture, with the components of the plot marching in lockstep towards an ending manufactured to satisfy both Gordin's audience and the moral of the story. But if we suspend our own theatrical sensibilities for a moment, we might understand why one critic predicted that the play would "stay in the Yiddish repertoire forever."[24] First of all, unlike most Yiddish drama at the time, *The Jewish King Lear* had a strong social message; it dealt with issues facing its audience and addressed them articulately. Second, its use of colloquial Yiddish demonstrated that a Yiddish play did not have to mimic German to succeed at the box office. And third, at the center of the play stood Dovid and Shamay, two human characters in the midst of a whirl of ideologies. Gordin, who strove so hard to teach his audience, touched their emotions in the process.

Furthermore, Gordin was blessed with a group of actors, and particularly a leading man, capable of presenting his work at a high level. Like Shakespeare, Gordin knew for whom he was writing, and the *Harper's* reviewer was one of many who enjoyed the fruits of their partnership:

Adler dominated our minds quite as fully when softly chanting the Talmud to himself as when soaring in a frenzy of madness. The strongest effect of all was when, spent by their own fury, his forces were shattered and one saw the blight of old age descend on him.

His audience was one palpable mass of sympathy. If he merely stroked his daughter's hair, graspingly like a blind man, the women in the audience sobbed and the men blew their noses. And he is not only an actor of great temperamental force; he is technically a master. His voice has richness and sonority, and he husbands it well. He makes the slightest gesture count, and his frequent moments of quiet, one is tempted to say, count most of all. His costumes and make-up were as simple and unobtrusive as the setting of his stage; yet, as his clothes grew older and more worn from act to act, and his hair and beard thinner and more thin, the unconscious effect was stupendous.[25]

Whatever may have seemed programmatic in Gordin's writing — and it may not have seemed that way at all to most of his audience — might easily be overlooked in the face of Adler's performance.

The play's combination of moral lesson and emotional catharsis apparently produced practical results. According to actor Boaz Young, "Fathers brought their children to the theatre so they could take example; hundreds of thank-you letters came to Adler from Jewish mothers: their Shloymes and Moyshes had become better children since they saw the play."[26] And years after the play's debut, composer Joseph Rumshinsky found that it still held its moral sway over Yiddish audiences. Entering a bank on the Lower East Side one Monday morning, Rumshinsky was told by an employee that because Adler had performed *The Jewish King Lear* over the weekend, the bank was filled with young people sending money to their parents back in Europe.[27]

The play influenced Gordin's fellow playwrights as well, prompting them to turn to Shakespeare as a source for Yiddish plays. Before *The Jewish King Lear*, Shakespeare's name got little attention in the American Yiddish theatre and press. After 1892, though, it would sometimes seem as if Shakespeare had become one of the more prolific American Yiddish playwrights. As we will see in the next chapter, productions of *Hamlet* and *Othello* at two neighboring theatres on New York's Bowery competed fiercely with each other in the fall of 1893. In the next three years, Yiddish versions of at least six different Shakespeare plays would premiere in New York. Curiously, though, almost all of them translated Shakespeare into Yiddish without making his characters Jewish, as Gordin had. His colleagues apparently concluded from the success of *The Jewish King Lear* that, on the one hand, Shakespeare could bring both respectability and respectable ticket sales, but on the other, that they should not try to compete head-on with Gordin. Not until after several years of un-Judaized translations of Shakespeare — most of them box-office failures — and another Gordin adaptation of *Lear*, would other Yiddish playwrights begin adapting Shakespeare in something resembling the Gordin vein.

That Other King Lear

While the production pattern provides a strong suggestion as to why Boris Thomashefsky went on a hiatus from new Shakespeare translations in the second half of the 1890s, the reasons for his return to commissioning Shakespeare translations in the first decade of the twentieth century are less clear. The most likely impetus seems to have been the enormous success of *The Yeshiva Boy* in 1899. Perhaps that play, promoted as a Yiddish *Hamlet*, led Thomashefsky back to attempting straight translations of Shakespeare in the hope that his audience's taste for Shakespeare had been whetted anew.

Thomashefsky returned to such translations with Mikhl Goldberg's rendering of *King Lear* at the People's Theatre on 23 October 1903. *King Lear* was by then a staple in the theatrical diet of Yiddish audiences, but with a distinctly Jewish flavor. They knew Dovid Moysheles as the "Jewish King Lear" and Mirele Efros as the "Jewish Queen Lear" without having seen their pagan prototype before.

An advertisement for *King Lear* announced

a holiday for art, a holiday for drama, a holiday for all art-loving people. Magnificent equipment, brilliant stage effects for this play have been worked on for weeks. . . . At the beautiful, noble People's Theatre will appear for the first time a work by the greatest poet of all times and all nations: Shakespeare's *King Lear*, translated by M. Goldberg. Directed by Mr. Boris Thomashefsky. Mr. Thomashefsky as King Lear. Mrs. Lobel as Cordelia, Mrs. Gudinski as Goneril, Mr. Rosenthal as Edgar and Mr. Tornberg as the Fool, Mr. Young as Gloucester, Mr. Kessler as Bastard, Mr. Conrad as Kent. — Mr. Thomashefsky will exert all his energy, effort and know-how to make this play a success." [28]

The advertisement extols Shakespeare in a manner that has by this point become commonplace in the Yiddish theatre culture, but it by no means depends solely on Shakespeare's prestige to attract audiences; it simultaneously embraces lovers of "art" and of "stage effects," fans of the "greatest poet of all times" and of one of the greatest Yiddish stars of his time.

Goldberg's *King Lear* puts Thomashefsky even more prominently at the center of the action than in the original by paring down the roles of the supporting characters. The roles of Goneril, Regan, and even Edmund are so drastically cut as to make them mere ciphers, and Albany and Cornwall become all but invisible. Furthermore, Goldberg takes every opportunity to give Lear the last word; Lear has the exit speech in Acts I, II, and IV of the Yiddish version. Shakespeare did not give Lear the last line of any act of the play except in the Quarto versions,[29] where Lear delivers the final words of Act IV: "Pray you now, forget and forgive: I am old and foolish" (IV.vii.84).

The most curious cut in Goldberg's adaptation is the near disappearance of Edmund. He does retain his soliloquy questioning the notion of illegitimacy, though without the wordplay of the original: "Why bastard? Wherefore base? . . . Why brand they us / With base? with baseness? bastardy? base, base?" (I.ii.6–10). The puns simply do not come across in Yiddish. In Shakespeare, this soliloquy sets up Edmund's intrigue against his legitimate half-brother Edgar. In Goldberg's translation, Edmund shows us a letter that he says will undo Edgar, but the scenes that follow up on his scheme have been cut. The Yiddish version ultimately gives Edmund the same comeuppance as the English, but the cuts make it a scarcely motivated punishment.

What makes the abridgment of Edmund's role most curious also helps explain a possible reason for it. Edmund was played by David Kessler, who rivaled Jacob Adler and Boris Thomashefsky in his popularity as a leading man. The tall, swarthy, and stocky Kessler made his strongest mark as a Gordin actor, creating such roles as Apolon Zonenshayn in *Sappho* (1900) and Hershele Dubrovner in *God, Man, and Devil* (1900), Gordin's reworking of *Faust*. Why deprive such a star of a chance to shine in such a richly villainous role? Because he might shine too brightly and thereby eclipse some of Thomashefsky's sun.

Yet despite Goldberg's introducing the Edmund subplot only to obscure it, his translation shows a great deal of thought, perhaps most

clearly illustrated by the storm on the heath. Goldberg's text provides detailed stage directions marking each use of thunder, lightning,
wind, and rain. A conflation of Shakespeare's text from the beginning
of the scene — with the cuts Goldberg has made — and Goldberg's
stage directions, should give a sense of the care that the translator has
taken to match the stage effects to the speeches:

Lear: Blow, winds, and crack your cheeks! rage! blow! (*strong light-
ning rain wind*)
You cataracts and hurricanoes, spout
Till you have drench'd our steeples, drown'd the cocks!
(*lightning*)
You sulph'rous and thought-executing fires,
Vaunt-couriers of oak-cleaving thunderbolts,
Singe my white head! And thou, all-shaking thunder,
Strike flat the thick rotundity o'th'world!
Crack Nature's moulds, all germains spill at once
That makes ingrateful man! (*strong rain*)
Fool: Good nuncle, in, ask thy daughters blessing (*lightning and
thunder very strong*); here's a night pities neither wise men
nor fools.
Lear: Rumble thy bellyful! Spit, fire! Spout, rain!
Nor rain, wind, thunder, fire, are my daughters.
I tax you not, you elements . . .
I never gave you kingdom, call'd you children,
You owe me no subscription. Then let fall
Your horrible pleasure. Here I stand your slave,
A poor, infirm, weak, and despis'd old man . . . (*much light-
ning*) (III.ii.1–20)[30]

Goldberg has clearly taken care to match each occurrence of special
effects to both the meaning of the dialogue and the emotional intensity of the scene.

The subsequent action moves quickly toward the end, cutting most
of the rest of Act III and almost all of Act IV except for Lear's re-
unions with Gloucester and Cordelia. Unlike in Shakespeare, the bodies of Goneril and Regan are not brought in at the end. This choice
may seem curious in light of the fact that three years earlier, translator
B. Vilenski had Ophelia's drowned body brought onstage in Bertha
Kalish's *Hamlet,* despite a lack of indication for doing so in Shake-

speare's text. Yet such divergences make sense in the context of other signs of what worked with Yiddish audiences. The audience might appreciate the poetic justice of the deaths of Lear's evil daughters, but seeing their corpses would not add to the spectators' sense of satisfaction. Showing the drowned Ophelia, on the other hand, capitalizes on the Yiddish love of sentiment presented as grandly as possible, and thus makes eminent theatrical sense.

Goldberg resolves the rest of the action essentially according to Shakespeare, though he simplifies the language and cuts the last few speeches. The Yiddish version thus ends with Edgar saying of Lear, "O, virklekh tot,"[31] an equivalent of "He is gone, indeed." Shakespeare, on the other hand, closes the action with two elegant couplets:

The weight of this sad time we must obey,
Speak what we feel, not what we ought to say:
The oldest hath borne most; we that are young
Shall never see so much, nor live so long. (V.iii.324–8)

Goldberg's ending feels abrupt in comparison. Like most of Thomashefsky's Shakespearean endeavors of the 1890s, this version of *King Lear* did not last long on the stage, managing just one performance beyond the weekend of its premiere. Thomashefsky may have been drawn to the role by the great prestige it represented, especially by its tradition in German. But he seems to have been less suited to the role than his rivals Adler and Kessler, both of whom were far more renowned for exploring humanity's darker side than was Thomashefsky. Furthermore, within the parameters of American Yiddish culture, perhaps Gordin was once more proving "greater" than Shakespeare. With the Jewish idiom for *King Lear* firmly established by this point, the original may have seemed something of an anticlimax.[32]

The Jewish Queen Lear

On 13 and 14 June 1898, audiences attending a Gordin version of a Greek tragedy in Philadelphia were treated to scenes from his latest adaptation of a Shakespearean tragedy. The featured play at the Arch Street Theatre that weekend was *The Wild Princess, or, Medea's Youth*; the excerpts, from a work then billed as *The Jewish Queen Lear*. Gordin wrote the title roles of both plays for Keni Liptzin (c. 1856–

1918), one of the outstanding actresses of the Yiddish theatre of her day, and every bit as fervent a Gordin disciple as Jacob Adler. The excerpts that closed the season in Philadelphia then traveled to New York's Thalia Theatre, where *The Jewish Queen Lear, or Mirele Efros*, opened on 19 August 1898. Before long, the main title and subtitle would trade places, and the name Mirele Efros would become a household word in Yiddish-speaking homes. The change in nomenclature attested to both the power of Keni Liptzin's star performance and the fact that this time around, Gordin was well enough established, and had moved far enough away from his source, for the title to stand alone without leaning on Shakespeare for support.

If it was mere coincidence that *Mirele Efros* first appeared in previews during performances of a Gordin adaptation of *Medea*, it was a telling coincidence. Gordin had translated Franz Grillparzer's *Medea* for Liptzin the previous year, and while both versions fared well commercially and critically, their success was modest next to that of the most popular roles of the three most important American Yiddish leading men: Adler, David Kessler, and Boris Thomashefsky. Zalmen Zylbercweig suggests that what the two Medeas lacked, and what the chief roles of Liptzin's male counterparts had, was a connection to Jewish life.[33] If Gordin was to create a breakthrough role for Liptzin, it would have to be not only strong, but Jewish as well.

In that case, returning to *King Lear* would be as logical a choice as any. For one thing, his previous adaptation of it had been an enormous success — indeed, it was still a staple in the repertoires of Adler and of any number of Adler imitators — and Zylbercweig goes so far as to call the title *The Jewish Queen Lear* a "trick" to capitalize on the success of its predecessor.[34] That is undoubtedly true, but perhaps Gordin also saw in the enterprise a chance to improve on his own work, for as striking a contrast between the two versions as the sex of the protagonists is how differently the stories develop. Where the action of *The Jewish King Lear* often seems to follow the whimsies of fate rather than the motivations of its characters, every plot development in *Mirele Efros* is dictated by the will of the heroine herself.

Mirele Efros opens with preparations for the wedding of Yosele Efros, the older of two sons of the wealthy widow Mirele Efros, and Sheyndele, a beauty from a poor family. Though the generous Mirele savors the idea of using the match to raise another family's station in life, the crudeness and pettiness of her future daughter-in-law's parents leads her to break off the wedding. Yosele has become infatuated with the photograph of his betrothed, however, and tearfully begs his mother to allow the marriage. The end of Act I finds the couple under the wedding canopy. Act II picks up three years later, with a now shrewish Sheyndele and her self-serving parents having the run of Mirele's beautiful house in Grodno. Sheyndele, Yosele, and his brother Donye insist on taking control of the family finances, which they proceed to run into the ground. Mirele's sons grow increasingly assimilated as the play progresses, and Sheyndele's rule over the household grows stronger, until her behavior becomes so unbearable that Mirele moves out of the house. Mirele boycotts her children for a full decade, until the bar mitzvah of her grandson finally brings her back for the reconciliation that ends the play.

In a sense, Act I of *Mirele Efros* seems to bring us back to Act IV of *The Jewish King Lear*. We are again preparing for the wedding, on a stormy day, of one of the protagonist's children. These parallels underscore some momentous differences, however; the dethroned, blind, wandering patriarch has been replaced by a powerful, sharp-eyed matriarch, so in control of the situation that she can unflinchingly call off the wedding and then not only call it on again, but have it take place immediately (thus making the bride and groom forego their customary wedding-day fast), and in her own lodgings: "I will not go to Slutsk; Slutsk must come to me." [35]

Gordin provided his male Lear figure with a living spouse, though Khane-Leye tends to be under her husband's thumb. How different is Mirele Efros! She literally carries a big stick (fig. 3), which she bangs to punctuate her commands, and she manages her own finances; we even learn in Act II that it was she, not her late husband, whose business savvy built the family fortune. All of this leads one of her servants to marvel, "And she has a clear head and common sense. It's hard to believe that she's just a woman" (13). Mirele as combined matriarch and businesswoman reflects an economic reality among Jewish immigrants to the United States that perhaps Gordin himself, as a recent immigrant back in 1892, did not fully appreciate: the man's religious learning is at a far lower premium than it was in eastern Europe, and now more than ever, the woman's ability to provide for the family often spells the difference between survival and starvation.

Gordin has departed from Shakespeare's family dynamic in other

3. Keni Liptzin as Mirele Efros.
From the Archives of the YIVO Institute for Jewish Research.

ways as well. For one thing, he adds in-laws to the equation. Theatrically speaking, they primarily provide comic relief — especially
Sheyndele's bumbling father. But they also contribute subtly to Gordin's message. He has foresworn the central event of Shakespeare's
first scene and his own previous first act: the conflict with, and even-
tual banishment of, the youngest daughter. Here, there is initially no
conflict whatsoever between Mirele and any of her children. Indeed,
in contrast to Cordelia/Taybele, none of the children here is particularly admirable, and Sheyndele's model behavior gives no hint of the
tyranny she will later display. But what gives Mirele pause about the
wedding is the conduct of Sheyndele's parents, who try desperately
and crudely to get as much money as possible out of Mirele before
the wedding. Whether the problem is nature, nurture, or both, Mirele
fears that Sheyndele will not escape the taint of her vulgar parents:
"They say that the apple does not fall far from the tree, and on such
a tree can grow a terrible apple" (10). Sheyndele's greed, when it
emerges in the next act, will simply be a magnified version of her
parents' pettiness. Thus, the parents in Gordin's audience who behave
decently are given reason to hope for a better outcome from their
children.

Mirele, though, has Sheyndele for a daughter in-law, and Mirele
suffers, though both the source of her suffering and its consequences
are less obvious and extreme than their counterparts in *The Jewish King
Lear*. Dovid Moysheles's children all but starved him. Mirele leaves
upon less blatant provocation, but she suffers stoically for a long time
before going. When Makhele asks her mistress why she allows Sheyndele so much power, Mirele explains, "Makhele, strength comes not
from forcing others to do one's will. It also takes strength to make
oneself do what others want" (17). Gordin takes seriously a figure
who will later own her own chapter in many a joke book:

> Q: How many Jewish mothers does it take to change a light bulb?
> A: None; "Don't worry about me, I'll sit in the dark."

She has not yet become the stuff of caricature, though. At this point,
she is often holding the family together, and by making Mirele directly
responsible for everything that happens to her, Gordin signals to his
audience that they can, and must, take similar responsibility. If they
make mistakes, they should do so actively like Mirele, not passively
like Dovid.

Perhaps a less abrupt happy ending this time around signals not only a more experienced playwright, but one who has spent enough time in America to learn that his own utopian dreams are not so easily realized. Now, Gordin makes *Lear* not an allegory of Jewish ideology, but a family drama reflecting the struggles its audience faces daily — the sort of drama that will come to dominate American drama in English as well. Yet Gordin has not abandoned his didacticism so thoroughly as to leave us in doubt of the play's ultimate message. As in *The Jewish King Lear*, it is twofold: one for parents and one for children.

A strikingly different Mirele appears at the end of the play: bent over, using her stick as a crutch rather than a scepter. At one point she faints when recalling aloud all the memories the house brings back for her. The scene is calculated to bring tears to everyone's eyes — which it clearly did — and Mirele spells out the lesson to be learned from her years in self-imposed exile: "It is just as they say: the poor man is happy when he finds what he has lost. (*Bangs with her stick.*) Ah, foolish world, wouldn't it be better if everyone could appreciate his little piece of luck before he loses it? Wouldn't we be healthier if we did not . . . poison the sources of our life and happiness? Instead, one learns when it is too late . . ." (48).

By staying away all these years, Mirele irrevocably lost something — unlike Dovid's sight, which he will recover. Her tale is thus a cautionary one: the audience must not let the same thing happen to them. The more prominent message, however, puts the burden on the children to respect their parents — a moral with sociohistorical implications as well as religious ones:

> In some deep way *Mirele Efros* spoke to the common Jewish perception, grounded in a sufficiency of historical experience, that the survival of a persecuted minority required an iron adherence to traditional patterns of family life. Mirele represents the conserving strength of the past, which alone has enabled the Jews to hold together in time. And audiences grasped this intuitively, just as Gordin had projected it intuitively.[36]

Gordin also had a talent for summing up such messages in the pithiest of expressions; as Mirele's servant points out, "A Mama, brothers, is no small thing" (48).

Critics responded to *Mirele Efros* with an enthusiasm verging on disbelief; was this actually *Yiddish* theatre? To playwright and critic Leon Kobrin, the audience's rowdiness and the play's artistry belonged to two different worlds:

> To tell you the truth, as I sat in the Thalia Theatre yesterday, I forgot that I was sitting in a Yiddish theatre in America. It seemed to me that I was in Russia, in a Russian theatre, and that legitimate actors were performing a legitimate play for me. From time to time I was brought back to reality by the whining of a child or the pop of a seltzer-bottle stopper . . . but that was soon forgotten because of the interesting contents of the play and the natural performances of the actors.[37]

With *Mirele Efros*, Gordin was emerging more clearly than ever as the Yiddish theatre's highbrow playwright, whose work seemed out of place before such boisterous audience behavior. Critics found the acting so natural, in fact, that melodramatic touches commonplace in other Yiddish plays at the time could be jarring in this one. "It is a shame," complained Moyshe Katz, "that the music accompanies [Mirele's] recitation of a verse of the Psalms with a melodramatic fiddling that does not make the moment more moving at all; quite the contrary: it reminds you that you are in a theatre."[38]

The critics found in the production a greater degree of realism and a greater unity between the actors and the other components of the production than they had ever seen before on the Yiddish stage. Yiddish audiences had come to expect bravura performances from their stars, but B. Feygenboym reported that "this is the first time that I have seen such acting in the Yiddish theatre."[39] Katz illustrated why, describing Keni Liptzin as a performer so immersed in her character that she manages to reveal "what is happening in Mirele's soul. . . . Throughout almost her whole performance, I did not see her as an actress on the stage, but as Mirele Efros."[40]

The high praise for Liptzin and her supporting cast underscored the scarcity of such naturalism in the American Yiddish theatre at the time. Katz, for example, concluded that Maurice Moscovitch (Shalmon) was "not theatrical even for half a second," and never looked directly at the audience — suggesting that the opposite was commonplace.[41] Even the famously robust David Kessler (Yosele), according to Kobrin, "spoke so quietly that one could hardly hear him."[42] Yet even this production was not immune from moments of broader acting; Dina Feinman (Sheyndele), for instance, came across as "so theatrical in many places," often raising her hand to emphasize a point and falling into the "declamatory art of ending a monologue." Katz thought Mary Epstein's performance as Makhele even more jarring: "It would be better if Makhele did not speak . . . to the audience. How could Makhele, sitting in Mirele's house, know that there is an audience in the theatre? Her awareness of the audience reminds us that someone is playing the role of Makhele, but it would be better for us to see Makhele herself."[43] Ironically, acting that would have drawn no complaints in a lesser production now seemed woefully inadequate — a fact that suggested Gordin's potential for bringing about at least a certain measure of the aesthetic reforms he had been demanding.

The production's achievements led critics to see it as something far more than an enjoyable night in the theatre; perhaps, they hoped, the play would help Yiddish audiences rise to the demands of a higher level of artistry. Kobrin waxed evangelical, declaring, "*The Jewish Queen Lear* is truly a happy event for our impoverished stage, and I think that it is the duty of every intelligent person interested in the Yiddish theatre . . . to express his opinion about [the play]."[44] B. Feygenboym of the *Abend-blat* echoed Kobrin's opinion by declaring, "It is the duty of everyone who is serious about the spiritual development of the Jewish masses to 'push' this play as strongly as possible."[45] Feygenboym even dared to express his hope that non-Jewish audiences would soon discover Gordin, just as English-speaking readers had expressed an interest in Morris Rosenfeld's poetry, as translated into English by Sol Liptzin, and fiction written in English by Abraham Cahan.

Particularly heartening to the critics was how the audience seemed to appreciate the drama in spite of the cries of babies and the fizzle of seltzer bottles. Feygenboym felt that *Mirele Efros* could "delight even the simple theatregoer, who does not yet understand its art, since the plot alone is quite suspenseful."[46] And given the "enthusiasm with which the audience greeted the play," *Forverts* critic Moyshe Katz dared to dream that Gordin might be the playwright who could single-handedly drive melodramas and operettas from the Yiddish stage.[47]

Parody, Flattery, and Film

When the 1890s began, Gordin had yet to write his first play. Before the decade ended, his only rival for the mantle of the most important Yiddish playwright was Avrom Goldfaden. One measure of Gordin's growing importance was the extent to which, even off stage, his plays and what they represented were becoming enmeshed in the fabric of American Yiddish culture — a phenomenon in which his *Lear* adaptations would figure prominently.

In 1897, Dovid Moysheles found a strange bedfellow in Kuni Leml, the antihero of Goldfaden's wildly popular farce, *The Two Kuni Lemls*. The protagonists of the two plays all but come to blows in a satirical dialogue from the pen of poet Morris Rosenfeld, which appeared in a newspaper published by novelist and playwright Nokhem-Meyer ("Shomer") Shaykevitsh. "Kuni Leml and the Jewish King Lear" consists, à la Aristophanes' *The Frogs*, of an argument over which character's creator is superior. Kuni Leml insists that he is the greater character, since the Jewish King Lear "descends from *goyim*"[48] — thus turning the tables on Sholem Aleykhem's charge, in his 1888 essay "The Judgment of Shomer," that Shomer's novels borrowed excessively from non-Jewish sources. In Rosenfeld's poem, Shomer comes out the winner of the argument between the Goldfaden and Gordin characters, for the poet points out that both characters derive from Gentile sources, and only Shomer knows how to "show you a full-fledged Jew. . . . Bravo, bravo, Nokhem-Meyer," cries the poet in his ecstasy.[49]

But Gordin had other bards to sing his praises, as the popular "sweat-shop poet" Morris Vintshevski would do in a new prologue for *Mirele Efros* written for a 1901 performance commemorating Gordin's first decade as a playwright.[50] By then, fans of Gordin would hardly have argued with Vintshevski's assertion that

"Mirele Efros" badarf keyn prolog nit
Rikhtik tsu shatsn ir vert, ir gevikht,
Punkt vi men darf far dem likhtikn tog nit
Kinstlekhe flamen tsu vayzn zayn likht.[51]

[*Mirele Efros* needs no prologue
In order to extol its value and weight properly,

Just as we do not need artificial lights
To illuminate the light of day for us.]

Similarly, the prologue finds it unnecessary to dwell on the fact of
Gordin's talent, which it finds as self-evident as the power of the
ocean.

Indeed, the whole point of the prologue seems to be that it has
nothing new to tell us: the play's merit speaks for itself, as does Gordin's talent, and indeed, it is assumed that we already know the play:
"You will *once again* see" the world depicted in the play (emphasis
mine).[52] Most of the prologue simply reminds us of what we already
know: the personalities of each character, the other plays Gordin has
written, the moral of *Mirele Efros*, which is, according to the prologue,
"a mother's heart triumphing over a mighty woman."[53] By mentioning the too-obvious-to-mention, the prologue tells us something else
indirectly: that at three years old, *Mirele Efros* had already become a
classic.[54]

Such was its status, in fact, that another writer saw fit to borrow its
title, just as Gordin had twice borrowed Shakespeare's title. Zalmen
Libin's sketch "The Jewish Queen Lear" retells the Jewish Lear legend
in prose, this time setting the action in America. Where Gordin had
made the behavior of both the children and the parent less extreme
the second time around, Libin softens the edges even further, empha-
sizing early on that the children are "God-fearing Jews, and even here
in the land of wantonness, they did not abandon their Jewishness."[55]
And the three sons' and one daughter's treatment of their mother
Hinde is exemplary, at least for a while. The youngest son brings
Hinde to America, and they live as boarders in the married daughter's
house. When the son marries, he brings the mother to live with him
in his own home, but his wife soon balks at his taking all the responsibility for Hinde upon himself, setting off a process of passing the
mother from one child's house to another's. Like Mirele, Hinde suffers silently as the children's quarrel breaks into a "bitter war," in the
midst of which the daughter's buffoon of a husband dubs his mother
in-law "The Jewish Queen Lear." The children reach an agreement to
rent an apartment for her, with each contributing equally to the rent.
Eventually, though, one or the other starts "forgetting" payments, and
Hinde is ultimately forced either to get the money or move out. She

sets out in search of help, but a few blocks from her apartment, Hinde stops: "The old mother did not know to which of her children she should go."[56] Free of the pressure of turn-of-the-century American Yiddish theatre audience's expectations of high drama and a happy ending, Libin is at liberty to describe matter-of-factly the gradual disintegration of filial bonds, thus undoubtedly bringing the story even closer than Gordin had to the reality facing many of his readers.

Where Libin turned to the general theme of filial ingratitude that Gordin had exploited so effectively, A. Hart relied upon his audience's specific knowledge of *The Jewish King Lear* for the central joke of his vaudeville sketch, *King Lear as Boarder*. In the process of supplementing the income of many a Jewish immigrant family by renting their spare room, the boarder also became a staple in American Jewish folklore, song, and literature. Here, "He" is a Yiddish actor none too quick to pay his rent, and "She" the landlady who lets him get away with it because she harbors the hope that soon he will set up house with her rather than just rent a room. His prospects for paying the rent improve considerably when he receives a telegram inviting him to play the role of Dovid Moysheles, but when he begins rehearsing his lines in the presence of the landlady, what she hears causes her considerable anguish. The unsophisticated landlady takes the rehearsed dialogue about ungrateful daughters literally, exclaiming, "Oy! And he told me that he was a single man."[57] The boarder narrowly escapes a fate akin to that of Dovid Moysheles: this time, getting thrown out by the landlady rather than by the children. But when he assures her that his ideas belonged only to the character he was rehearsing, she softens her position, and they end by performing a duet together: naturally, the chorus from the end of Act I of *The Jewish King Lear*.

The same play figures prominently in an outing undertaken by a recent immigrant in playwright and critic B. Gorin's 1897 sketch, "Zelda Goes to the Theatre." Back in her *shtetl*, her only encounters with Yiddish theatre were the street performances of itinerant clowns and jugglers. She realizes that the Yiddish theatre in America is a far more elaborate affair, but although she has been eager to experience it, two years have gone by without her finding the right opportunity to do so. During the first year, it was out of the question; she needed to get acclimated to her new surroundings, and simply earning enough to survive was all she and her husband could handle. Even during the second year, she did not manage to buy tickets; although she and her husband are both employed and the money from three boarders helps pay the bills, more fundamental expenses than theatre constantly come due: the rent, the gas bill, mending a torn shoe or shirt. Besides, what would they do with the two children — one of them an infant — were they to spend an evening at the theatre? "The neighbors even try to convince that she can take the children along, but what do they know? She found it hard to believe that she could take the children to the theatre — it didn't make sense!"[58] Finally, even more daunting than money or babysitting are the theatre's many unfamiliar rules and customs. "It seemed to her that one should know something about how to behave there: how to enter, how to sit, how to stand. She was anxious not to be taken for a provincial, visiting the theatre for the first time" (179).

Given all these obstacles, Zelda's first visit to the theatre can only come when a number of favorable conditions are met, which finally happens when one of her boarders offers her a ticket to *The Jewish King Lear*, the upcoming benefit performance for his fraternal lodge. Not only is the ticket a gift, but the boarder, an experienced theatre-goer, will be able to guide her through the frightening social demands of excursion. Still, Zelda must undertake elaborate preparations in the intervening weeks. She makes her own dress and has the waist fitted, and a neighbor offers to curl her hair before the big night. All of these efforts meet with rave reviews from both neighbors and boarders, and after giving her husband a bottle for the baby, Zelda heads to the theatre.

Zelda's response to the play itself is hardly what its author would have intended. From the moment the curtain goes up, she spends the evening in a state of almost constant confusion. The very idea of the theatrical illusion being foreign to her, Zelda can only ask of the characters on stage at the beginning, "How did they get there? What are they doing there?" (182). Intimidated by the seasoned spectators around her, Zelda smiles when they smile, but has no idea what they find so amusing. Only once, we are told, does she react independently, smiling at the old bearded gentleman on stage who rocks a baby's cradle (though she does recognize that this same man was on stage as the play began). Yet while at first glance she seems not to appreciate the pathos inherent in Shamay's dilemma, perhaps this moment in the

play colors her reaction to her husband's complaints when she arrives home:

> "What is it? What's the matter?"
>
> "What is it! Don't you hear?" answers her husband, a little angry.
> "The baby is screaming."
>
> "So can't you calm him down?" she asks as she runs to the child.
>
> "I'm not a nurse, I can't nurse the child all night long."
>
> "What can you do? You can eat, can't you?" she asks angrily.
>
> "You don't feed me, so don't talk to me about my eating."
>
> "And do you feed me? I work like a dog, slave away, and in the
> end this is the thanks I get." (183)

Especially since such rancor between them seems uncharacteristic, we
may get the sense that the play has gotten under Zelda's skin more than
she realizes. Perhaps she is subconsciously thinking, "If the old man
with the goatee could take care of a baby, why can't my husband?"

The couple settle their differences before going to bed, and in the
renewed calm, he asks her for her impressions of the evening. Besides
telling him about the cradle that "someone rocked so nicely," all Zelda
can come up with is that "they made *kidesh* [the blessing over the
wine], just like Daddy used to do at home" (184). Her husband is
unimpressed: "You see, I don't envy you such pleasures. I enjoyed
myself like that here at home, and it didn't cost a penny" (184). Never
having been to the theatre himself, he cannot appreciate its power to
make the familiar unfamiliar. Zelda herself seems frustrated that she
cannot come up with more to say about the experience, but Gorin
leaves us with one final, tantalizing detail: when she sits down the next
day to describe it to her parents, she manages to fill four pages.
Whether this is dominated by a discussion of dressmaking and hair-
curling, or whether she manages to articulate something more sub-
stantive about the theatre itself, Gorin does not say. This silence itself
has a certain eloquence, reminding us how elusive is the effort to
recapture any one individual's experience of a theatrical event —
much less to try to characterize how hundreds or thousands of theatregoers may have perceived any given production.

While the reader does not need to know *The Jewish King Lear* to
enjoy the comedy of Zelda's preparations for, and intimidation by,
the theatre, Gorin clearly has her attend that play for a reason. He
also could have been confident, five years after the play's premiere,

„א מואוינג-פיקטשור"

יאקאב פ. אדלער (אלם הענינ ליער) : „שמאי, שמאי, פיהר מיך ! — מיט א פאאר הונדערט טויזענד דאלאר און מיט די הילפע פון נוטע מענשען, וועלען מיר מאכען א לעבען, וואו מיר וועלען קומען !"...

4. Jacob Adler, exiled from the Grand Theatre, *tells his servant, "Shamay, Shamay, lead me! With a few hundred thousand dollars and the help of good people, we will make a living wherever we go!" From* Der groyser kundes, *15 September 1909.*

that most of his readers would have seen it. The same would soon be true of *Mirele Efros*. Images from the texts and the original productions of both plays quickly became instantly recognizable, and thus ripe for satire. Years after the plays premiered, the satirical journal *Der groyser kundes* printed cartoons based on scenes from each play in order to comment on contemporary situations involving the actors who first brought Dovid Moysheles and Mirele Efros to life. In 1909, when the management of the Grand Theatre terminated Jacob Adler's lease in order to convert the building into a movie house, the *Kundes* pointed out the parallel to Dovid Moysheles' exile in a cartoon entitled, "A Moving Picture" (fig. 4). With the Grand Theatre in the background advertising "moving pictures" in Yiddish, Adler as the blind and barefoot Dovid Moysheles goes into exile. The caption has Adler "as King Lear" tell his servant, "Shamay, Shamay, lead me! With a few hundred thousand dollars and with the help of good people, we will make a living wherever we go!"[59] The cartoon acknowledges the aptness of its own analogy only up to a point; part of the humor lies in how far the prosperous manager Adler is from Dovid Moysheles' severe state of poverty.

In 1911, the *Kundes* similarly caricatured *Mirele Efros*, this time in a situation involving a revival of the play (fig. 5). The occasion was the American tour of Esther-Rokhl Kaminska, perhaps the foremost actress of the Polish Yiddish theatre at the time. Kaminska had performed in the United States before, but never as Mirele, a role that won her acclaim in Warsaw. Finally, in the autumn of 1911, she dared to bring her Mirele to the country where Keni Liptzin had held a monopoly on the part ever since the play's premiere in 1898. The cartoon shows Liptzin as Mirele, stick in hand, pointing to a similarly costumed Kaminska and complaining, "Shalmon, Shalmon! Look who is coming to take my place!"[60]

Regardless of Kaminska's talent, Liptzin's place as Mirele was not about to be threatened after thirteen years in a role that she would ultimately claim to have performed over fifteen hundred times.[61] *Forverts* editor Abraham Cahan admired the touches of realism Kaminska added to the role, but found that the "so-called classical" Mirele of Keni Liptzin "made a stronger impression" than the Mirele of Kaminska's "more modern, more realistic school." Mrs. Liptzin's Mirele is not a Jewish woman. Her pride, her good-natured humor, her dominant spirit, her practical intellect — all of that smacks not of Lithuania, but of Shakespeare. She is not proud like one of our Jewish women, but with the pride of a King Lear.[62] When *Mirele Efros* premiered, B. Feygenboym praised it for being "a Jewish play in the fullest sense of the word. Everything in it, every detail, is specifically Jewish, and relates to Jewish life and conditions in Russia."[63] One generation later, Cahan was downplaying the play's Jewishness in order to hail its universal appeal. The audience's taste, however, would run in the opposite direction: the more Jewish a Shakespearean adaptation was, the more enthusiastically the American Yiddish audience would tend to embrace it.

מירעלע אפרת (מאדאם ק. ליפצין) : — שלמון, שלמון! זעהסט וער סגעהט פערנעהמען מיין פלאץ ?

5. Keni Liptzin (seated), pointing to Esther-Rokhl Kaminska, her rival as Mirele Efros, cries, "Shalmon, Shalmon! Look who is coming to take my place!" From Der groyser kundes, *17 November 1911.*

Despite Kaminska's talent and celebrity, neither she nor anyone else would supplant Liptzin as *the* Mirele Efros for a generation of American Yiddish theatregoers. But new generations would applaud new Mireles, gaining the play a durability enshrined in a multi-Mirele extravaganza in 1936. The talent of the four actresses who played Mirele — Anna Appel, Berta Gersten, Dora Vaysman, and Bina Abramovitsh, each appearing in one act — prompted one reviewer to warn audiences against excessive nostalgia for the previous generation of actors, which he called a disservice to those currently performing.[64] And critic Alexander Mukdoyni summed up the ultimate significance of the evening: it showed *Mirele Efros* to be "*the* play for Yiddish Sarah

Bernhardts and Eleonora Duses."[65] Nevertheless, concluded Mukdoyni sadly, the four Mireles played to a tiny audience. "The Yiddish public should be ashamed," he chided.[66]

Elsewhere, though, Gordin's Lears kept going strong. Maurice Schwartz's *Legend of the Jewish King Lear*, produced at the Yiddish Art Theatre in 1932, featured a caricatured version of Gordin's play interwoven with a comedy of life behind the curtains. Mukdoyni applauded Schwartz for the concept: "this work by Jacob Gordin is very naive and the melodramatic element in it is so thick that the smallest caricature can make it ludicrously exaggerated in both tone and movement."[67] But Schwartz and his company, in Mukdoyni's view, failed to take full advantage of the opportunity provided by Gordin's play to parody the Yiddish theatre style of a previous generation: "Because of poor execution, out of Maurice Schwartz's wonderful idea comes a badly botched piece of theatrical frolicking. . . . Maurice Schwartz's production of *The Jewish King Lear* is only intermittently a parody; on the whole, it is nearer to imitation."[68]

Film versions of both plays, also produced during the 1930s,[69] would prove more admiring of the "first Golden Age" of Yiddish theatre than did Schwartz's production. When the New York Yiddish-language troupe of the Federal Theatre Project staged *The Jewish King Lear* in 1935, film director Joseph Seiden brought a crew to document the production, on which he served as technical supervisor. The directing credit went to Harry Thomashefsky (son of star Yiddish actors Boris and Bessie Thomashefsky), with Gordin's script being adapted for the screen by Abraham Armband. Thomashefsky's film indicates his reverence for the theatrical world of his parents' generation on the one hand, and a marked change in theatrical style on the other. The opening credits, introducing the film as "The immortal Jacob Gordin's classic The Yiddish King Lear," present each actor in character, holding a stock pose within a picture frame, as if exhibiting the gestures of an earlier theatrical generation in a museum gallery. Yet Maurice Krohner is a surprisingly gentle Dovid Moysheles, as if the naturalism that has come to dominate 1930s American theatre has crept into Yiddish culture, forbidding him to reach the levels of emotional turbulence that seemed so natural for Adler.

While historians of the Yiddish cinema have dismissed Thomashefsky's effort as "dull" and "static,"[70] the film version of *The Jewish*

King Lear does take the viewer into the streets of Vilna, and even to the crowded alleyways of Jerusalem to show us Dovid and Khane-Leye's experience in Palestine. By comparison, Joseph Berne's 1939 film version of *Mirele Efros*, featuring Berta Gersten in the title role and a screenplay by Yiddish playwright Osip Dimov, is far more static; indeed, film historian Eric Goldman deems it "little more than a well directed recording of the stage play." [71] At the time of the film's release, however, its modernization of the play's language, costumes, and acting style was a relief to the critics, one of whom deduced from the changes that "our good taste and our aesthetic feelings have come a long way." [72] Yet the film left Gordin's text sufficiently intact for critic Nokhem Bukhvald to find it necessary to prepare his readers. He explained that Gordin's contemporaries went to the theatre with a different sensibility from that of current viewers, who would have to suspend some of their expectations if they were to enjoy the film. "Go see 'Mirele Efros,'" he urged them. "If you judge the film with the appropriate measure of tradition and historical perspective, you will enjoy it. But if you go to 'Mirele Efros' as you go to a modern movie — this is not the right movie." [73]

How ironic, and also how natural. In 1892, Gordin expected Shakespeare to be so foreign to his audience that he had one of his characters give a lesson about the man and his work. Less than half a century later, many of the grandchildren of people who had wept rivers of tears watching Adler and Liptzin probably knew the English original better than the Yiddish adaptations. American Jewish life had been transformed so extensively and so quickly that changes had to be made in the early Yiddish plays in order to make them commercially viable. Even then, audience members would often have to make an effort to conjure up the world of their mothers and fathers in order to appreciate what they were seeing.

In his day, Gordin and his adaptations of *King Lear* contributed to that process of Americanization, helping the Yiddish theatre grow up and the Yiddish audience come to terms with the shock of beginning life again in a new and very different place. *The Jewish King Lear* and *Mirele Efros* became so deeply ingrained as to create a thousand ripples in the American Yiddish cultural waters — ripples that emanated from three large concentric circles.

First was the purely theatrical realm: the impact of these and another half dozen of Gordin's best plays on dramatic and theatrical technique. While not without contrived situations and stock characters, Gordin's *Lear* variations offered audiences scenes and characters that moved the action forward at all times, and offered actors leading roles they could flesh out to larger-than-life size.

Second was the culture at large. Gordin was not the first Yiddish playwright to derive source material from other cultures, but he was the first to make the very act of appropriation part of his goal: to help Yiddish theatre break out of its often stifling parochialism and connect it to the broader Western dramatic tradition.

In doing so, the plays resonated beyond the field of entertainment and into the wider social realm. They did even more than help change the way Yiddish dramas were written and performed, and build bridges carrying two-way traffic between Yiddish culture and the world beyond. They crept into the very soul of generations of audiences, making them see the world in ways it was never perceived before *King Lear* made its way into the Yiddish theatre.

Classical Influenza, or, Hamlet Learns Yiddish

Jacob Gordin had found a successful strategy for using Shakespearean sources by pointedly adapting them to the sensibility and circumstances of his audience. In retrospect, it seems curious at first glance that his fellow American Yiddish playwrights did not quickly take the same path, especially given their proven agility when it came to jumping on bandwagons. *The Jewish King Lear*, however, was not the phenomenon that *Mirele Efros* would come to be, and indeed, it did not take Gordin's colleagues long after *Mirele* premiered to produce Judaized Shakespeare plays of their own. Earlier in the 1890s, the merits of making Shakespeare Jewish would not have been as apparent; besides, the case of *Hamlet* in particular would make clear that *not* making Shakespeare Jewish had its advantages too.

Many of Shakespeare's plays go in and out of fashion, seeming to speak more eloquently to a certain era or culture than to others. *Hamlet* is a different story. As drama, it is that most familiar of texts to which readers continually return, for its poetry, its philosophy, its psychology — and, no doubt, for its enduring status as heavyweight of heavyweights. In production, it has been molded to suit as many directors' visions as there have been directors, and is ever present as the utmost test of an actor's ability. For Boris Thomashefsky, producing and starring in the first Yiddish version of the play was "actually a daring idea. I, a young Jewish actor reared on the plays of Goldfaden, Lateiner, Zeifert, Jacob Ter — I would appear in the world-famous work *Hamlet*?" [1] It would not take long for the idea of a Yiddish *Hamlet* to lose its novelty, but Yiddish translators and performers would repeatedly reinvent the play in versions that ranged from hack translation to serious artistic endeavor, from Danish to Jewish, from stage to page.

The Plague of the Classics

The American Yiddish theatre first turned to *Hamlet* out of a combination of the need for new material and the prestige the actors felt could be gained by appearing in Shakespeare. In his 1897 essay, "The History of the Yiddish Theatre," playwright Moyshe Zeifert (1851–1922) pokes fun at the pretensions of the Yiddish theatre to the classical repertoire beginning in the early 1890s — a phenomenon in which Zeifert himself had played no small role:

> All of a sudden, a horrible plague broke out in the theatre world, trampling on everything that had been planted with such energy and at such expense. This plague was called the Plague of the Classics. Our Yiddish actors, who went to sleep one night feeling fresh and healthy in every limb, woke up the next morning deathly ill. They had all suddenly caught Classical Influenza. They were all feverish, and fever made them babble things so wild that they would have been ashamed even to think them when healthy. "We are stars!" — they fantasized in the grip of the fever — "and because we are stars, the Yiddish repertoire is worthless! Enough of making fools of ourselves! From now on we will adopt Shakespeare, Schiller, Goethe, even Grillparzer! 'Moyshe' [in theatre jargon, the disparaging name for the Yiddish audience] should see who we are and what we can do! That which Salvini, Ludwig Barnay, Adolph Sonnenthal, Possart, Edwin Booth, Joseph Kainz, Sarah Bernhardt, Eleanora Duse and Fanny Davenport can do, we can do as well! We can certainly do that!!"
>
> And for such an influenza, there was nothing any doctor could do![2]

Tongue-in-cheek though he is, Zeifert articulates several key reasons for Shakespeare's entry into Yiddish, starting with the combined envy of and admiration for more famous colleagues (all of whom have earned their fame at least in part for their Shakespearean interpretations) who star in other languages.

Not only could performers in English, French, German, and Italian attract larger audiences than Yiddish actors could; their languages also had cultural prestige, in stark contrast to Yiddish, which was, in the words of literary critic Dan Miron, decidedly and vehemently rejected by almost all eighteenth- and nineteenth-century *maskilim* (proponents of the Enlightenment), including most of the important writers who used it for propagandistic as well as artistic purposes. It was generally regarded as a linguistic and cultural aberration; its speakers were constantly referred to as "stammerers," and their speech was often compared to meaningless noises produced by animals.[3]

While there were more exceptions to this characterization than Miron acknowledges, it is nevertheless true that a number of the very writers who helped establish Yiddish as a literary language wrote in Yiddish reluctantly, as if it were the only medium available until the masses would be ready for more sophisticated offerings.

This same ambivalence carried over to the stage, where the Yiddish repertoire (as Zeifert illustrates) is denigrated by the very actors who perform it. This attitude manifested itself in the language the characters spoke, for *daytshmerish* reigned as the onstage lingua franca in the early decades of professional Yiddish theatre. It was no wonder that Yiddish actors, who borrowed both the linguistic and dramaturgic clothes of their European and American counterparts in order to enable the Yiddish theatre to stand on its own, eyed their American and European colleagues enviously until ultimately resolving to prove to their audiences — and themselves — that they could master the classics.

Another 1897 essay made explicit the connection between Shakespeare and respectability. The inaugural issue of the Yiddish theatre journal *Di fraye yidishe folksbine* contained a piece entitled, "Is Yiddish a Language for Drama?" in which linguist Alexander Harkavy sets out to rebut arguments used by critics who asserted that Yiddish could not sustain serious dramatic literature. Skeptics, Harkavy writes, have remarked that Yiddish is too young, too lacking in words to express the range and complexity of emotion and experience required for dramatic literature. In response, Harkavy asserts that if a language needs a new word, it can either forge one from its own roots or borrow it from another language, especially Greek or Latin. After examining some of the implications of his claim, Harkavy provides a Yiddish translation of *Hamlet*'s entire "To Be or Not to Be" soliloquy, which is worth transcribing in part here:

Zayn oder *nit* zayn — dos iz di frage:
Tsi iz eydeler far dem gemit tsu laydn
Di shtekh un di fayln fun dem beyzn mazl
Oder aroysgeyn mit gever kegn a yam fun tsores
Un makhn fun zey an end? Shtarbn — shlofn —
Vayter gornisht! [4]

Harkavy goes on to provide the rest of the soliloquy in Yiddish, then concludes: "This little piece of Shakespeare in Yiddish says more than any other evidence that Yiddish *is* a language for drama, that our mother tongue *is* a language for the stage — not just for simple dramas but also for sophisticated ones; let good writers get to work, and there will be no obstacle to what our language can do!" [5] Earlier in the journal's pages, its editor, Joel Entin, had established its platform; third in his list of six goals was to raise the level of the Yiddish theatre repertoire in order to give it the "character of a true literature." [6] Entin enlisted Harkavy, a leading Yiddish linguist, to assure readers that Yiddish was sufficiently rich to attain such a character. In turn, Harkavy enlisted Shakespeare, the world's most respected playwright, to proclaim the suitability of Yiddish for drama. *Res ipsa loquitur:* a Yiddish rendering of the most famous passage in dramatic literature speaks for itself. [7]

Shakespeare could confer upon Yiddish actors the same measure of respectability that Harkavy sought to gain for the Yiddish language. Like their counterparts in other cultures, Yiddish actors were often viewed as ruffians and miscreants, and believed that Shakespeare could act as a useful agent in their quest for social and artistic legitimacy.

From as early as the 1890s, that quest found expression in countless articles in the Yiddish press on the history of Yiddish theatre, the state of Yiddish theatre, the future of Yiddish theatre. Actors still in the first half of their careers wrote about "How I Became a Yiddish Actor" or "The First Years of Yiddish Theatre." The Yiddish theatre waxed nostalgic about its beginnings almost as soon as it got under way, like a kindergartner introducing a memory of nursery school with the words, "When I was little. . . ." It does not occur to the child to take such a backward glance until he perceives a change in himself.

To the Yiddish actors, the first adaptations of Shakespeare were a stamp of legitimacy, a sign that they had moved from the swaddling clothes of their own repertoire to the grown-up attire of the world theatre.

In This Corner, In Black: Hamlet, Prince of Denmark

Moyshe Zeifert's translation of *Othello* premiered on 20 October 1893 at the Windsor Theatre in New York. It was no coincidence that one month later, another Zeifert translation, this time of *Hamlet*, was produced at the rival Thalia Theatre. Boris Thomashefsky was then performing at the Thalia, with Joseph Lateiner as playwright in residence. Thomashefsky's chief rivals, David Kessler and Jacob Adler, worked across the street at the Windsor, where Moyshe Hurwitz served as house dramatist. Thomashefsky would later recall, with no small degree of satisfaction, that the decision to stage *Othello* at the Windsor came about after Adler and Kessler unsuccessfully attempted to perform a Hurwitz operetta — a form that Thomashefsky dominated, and Adler and Kessler claimed to despise. After the Hurwitz play bombed, they commissioned Zeifert, a prolific journalist who had already written a few plays of his own, to adapt *Othello*.

Thomashefsky wrote two accounts of how this episode in the Thalia/Windsor rivalry came about. In a 1908 article, he recalls that the Windsor company was forced to produce more plays than he did at the time, for his appearance in Lateiner's *Alexander, the Crown Prince of Jerusalem*, was enjoying a long run. Thomashefsky attributes the success of the play to his legs, which he says were shown to great advantage in the silk-stockinged title role. In the midst of Thomashefsky's triumph as Alexander, the Windsor company launched an attack in the form of a poster that read: "Next week, we — true, realistic artists — will present *Othello*, the greatest tragedy in the world . . . Such a work can only be performed by great actors; boys with their legs will not dare to touch the greatest work in the world."[8] Thomashefsky, stung as well as stunned, quickly commissioned Zeifert to adapt *Hamlet* (fig. 6), and then issued what he called a "counter-poster" announcing, "Next week, Thomashefsky will present the

6. Advertisement for Boris Thomashefsky as Hamlet, 1901. From the Dorot Jewish Division, the New York Public Library, Astor, Lenox, and Tilden Foundations.

greatest tragedy, which William Shakespeare wrote especially for Tho-mashefsky — *Hamlet, the Prince of Denmark*, music by Arele Gral, dances arranged by Baraban."[9]

Thomashefsky offered another version of these events — similar in spirit but vastly different in the details — in his memoirs, published in 1937:

> One evening, my fans came running to me, all worked up: "You know, Mr. Thomashefsky, Adler just announced from the stage that soon he will stage the world-famous, sensational tragedy by William Shakespeare, the greatest work in all of world literature, *Othello*. He said in his speech that he will play *Othello*, and Kessler will play Iago, and they will switch off in the roles . . ."
>
> The fans also told me that Adler insulted me from the stage. He said that with a play like *Othello*, no one would be able to emulate him; that one must be an actor to be able to play *Othello*. *Othello* is not *Alexander, the Crown Prince of Jerusalem*. . . .
>
> I impatiently waited for that act of the performance to end. When I finished, I went out in front of the curtain and an-nounced to the public that . . . I would soon present William Shake-speare's greatest tragedy, *Hamlet*. I would play the role of Hamlet, Prince of Denmark. The theatre was packed with Jewish men, women, and young ladies. Most of them knew as much about *Hamlet, Prince of Denmark,* as an Orthodox Jew knew of Gentile cooking. They figured that this was some kind of new operetta. The little fans applauded, clapping their hands and feet and bang-ing sticks together.[10]

To the Thalia's audience, the title *Hamlet, Prince of Denmark* probably sounded like a Scandinavian transplant of *Alexander, Crown Prince of Jerusalem*. Given the latter's success, no wonder they applauded so enthusiastically.

The spontaneity with which Thomashefsky says he announced his *Hamlet* was commonplace in the Yiddish theatre, where the slightest hint that Troupe A had a potentially successful idea for a play would lead Troupe B to attempt to outdo it, preferably at or before the time Troupe A produced it. At times, plays with identical or nearly identi-cal titles premiered on the same day, such as competing versions of

Gasn kinder (Children of the streets) at the Thalia and Windsor Theatres on 28 October 1898, or *Uncle Tom's Cabin* at both the People's and Thalia Theatres on 3 May 1901.

Thomashefsky's accounts also illustrate how territorial these rivalries were. Typical of nineteenth-century European and American theatre, actors became known for certain "lines of business," a custom on which Adler tries to capitalize by insisting that Thomashefsky has overstepped the boundaries of his artistry. According to Thomashefsky, this insistence grew after he announced his *Hamlet*:

> was fuming: such *chutzpah*, Thomashefsky is going to perform *Hamlet* at the same time that Adler plays *Othello*. Every evening, Adler would make a speech to his audience about his *Othello*. Just think; while he, Jacob P. Adler, the king of the Yiddish drama, plays Shakespeare's *Othello*, someone else should dare to play *Hamlet*! And he sought to convince the audience that they should come to his *Othello*, which he and Kessler were entitled to perform. But the other one, the actor from across the street, had no right to perform Shakespeare's work![11]

The descriptions of the stars' announcements from the stage reflect divergent views of their audiences' understanding of what it meant to stage a play by Shakespeare. Thomashefsky condescendingly emphasizes their overall ignorance of *Hamlet* — a perception supported by a story related by his wife Bessie in her memoirs:

> We performed the play for several weeks and did brisk business, but one problem was that the audience clapped, cried, and called for the author, Shakespeare, to come and take a curtain call. My good servant, Becky, even suggested that we make up one of the actors and send him out as Shakespeare. But we begged the audience's pardon that Shakespeare did not take a curtain call. He could not come, since he lived so far away, in London.[12]

Adler, on the other hand (at least according to Thomashefsky's report), relies on unquestioning belief in both his and Shakespeare's greatness to assert that he has the talent to perform Shakespeare's roles, and that Thomashefsky's success in a lower theatrical form bars him from playing in the Shakespearean sandbox.

For all his outward bluster, Thomashefsky privately feared that he might be out of his depth, so he hired a director from the Irving Place Theatre, then a bastion of German drama:

> He simply put every word in my mouth, pointed out the meaning of the most important lines, clarified the ideas that Shakespeare wanted to bring out in his work. I studied my role day and night. Seven o'clock in the morning, when all the other actors were still sleeping, I was in the theatre shortly after breakfast, studying with Herr Walter. He measured every step that I had to take, showed me the tone of every word, every passage. He taught me where to remain calm, and on the other hand, where I should be tempestuous, enraged, etc.
>
> Walter also helped me order the necessary clothes, wigs, and other appropriate things. My colleagues, the actors, had a hell of a time learning their roles. Not one of them understood a single line. They complained, 'What does Shakespeare want from us?'
>
> Every rehearsal of *Hamlet* lasted three or four hours longer than our usual rehearsals.[13]

Hiring a director from outside was an unusual step. The extra precautions show that even though, according to Thomashefsky, Zeifert translated the play literally overnight, the actor was sufficiently impressed by the magnitude of performing Shakespeare — or even the shadow of Shakespeare — to throw a great deal of extra time and effort into the task. Nevertheless, it is difficult to escape the conclusion that Thomashefsky protests too much. One of the salient features of Yiddish translations of Shakespeare was their tendency to simplify language, spell out metaphors, and streamline the plot and characters — so much so, in fact, that the results are often clearer than the convoluted plots of many an original Yiddish melodrama or operetta. Nearly half a century after his debut as Hamlet, Thomashefsky recalls the production in a manner that emphasizes his seriousness as a performer, which perhaps he feels has been overshadowed by his popular success.

Even with that qualification in mind, the steps Thomashefsky claims to have taken to make himself worthy of a Shakespearean role provide an example of direct influence of the German-American theatre on the American Yiddish theatre — a relationship we will revisit in coming chapters via the remarkable careers of Morris Morrison and Rudolph Schildkraut. In the process of hiring a German director, Thomashefsky imports a production style that he assiduously tries to reproduce for his *Hamlet*. Rather than calming his nerves, the actor's extraordinary preparations seemed to have the opposite effect:

> At the last rehearsal, I really felt that I was falling apart. The thought that tonight I would have to appear as *Hamlet* completely unglued me. In my mind appeared all the *Hamlet*s I had seen on various stages. Especially engraved on my memory was the *Hamlet* of Edwin Booth. . . . The night before I appeared as *Hamlet*, I went to Booth's Theatre and saw his *Hamlet*. That was perhaps the fiftieth time I had seen him in the role. I recall how I once traveled from Baltimore to Washington to see him play *Hamlet*. I simply idolized Booth. . . .
>
> And tonight I myself have to appear in *Hamlet*! The first time in the history of the Yiddish theatre that Shakespeare's tragedy will be performed in Yiddish, and I have the luck to be the first Yiddish actor to play the starring role.[14]

Although already a major star by this point, Thomashefsky senses that playing *Hamlet* will change his status. It connects him to a tradition older than the professional Yiddish theatre and broader than the streets that border the Jewish neighborhoods of New York, Chicago, and Philadelphia. In short, it connects him to the greatest heights to which an actor can aspire, even if it does not alter the composition of his audience by a single viewer.

Where Thomashefsky showed awed reverence for Shakespeare, Moyshe Zeifert's respect for the poet was tempered by more practical concerns. In 1897, Zeifert described a dream from the night his *Othello* premiered. He has died and gone to his final judgment, where the prosecuting angel insists that Zeifert's plays "twisted the truth, crushed aesthetics underfoot and corrupted the public taste." The Chairman of the court sentences Zeifert to twenty years in hell, after which he will go to Pittsburgh to work as a Reform rabbi:

> "Halt! He is innocent!" cried out my defending angel in the nick of time. "He did not do it out of unscrupulousness, God forbid; the poor man was just terribly needy, with a large family, a wife and children. . . . There are men of the theatre with us here in Paradise who have sinned far more than he, but nevertheless they now eat

the nectar and drink the sacred wine. For example, take William Shakespeare! . . ."

"Shakespeare?" asked the Chairman with astonishment. "How has he sinned?"

"He wrote the play *Shylock* (*The Merchant of Venice*) and with it made a mockery and a disgrace of the best people on the face of the earth, the whole Jewish nation. In a word, he is simply a major anti-Semite."

"Bring Shakespeare to me," the Chairman demanded. Shakespeare came in riding on two adders. "Why did you insult the Jews with your *Shylock*?" the Chairman asked him.

"Your honor," Shakespeare answered proudly, "I was a poet, and we poets dream with our eyes open."

"That is a lame excuse, my dear sir," the Chairman answered. "You must be punished! . . . Go right now to the Windsor Theatre and see how the Yiddish actors mangle your *Othello*. . . ."

Shakespeare disappeared, and returned half an hour later. I hardly recognized him. He looked a hundred years older, a cloud of sorrow shading his fine, high forehead. "I have sinned, I have lusted, I have rebelled,"[15] he cried, and threw himself on one knee before the Chairman. "Punish me as you see fit, but not with that! Leave me be! I'll burn my plays up, I'll sell them as wrapping paper!"

"Aha!" exclaimed the Chairman. "Now you see the trouble it gets you when you trifle with the Chosen People? Go straight to Gehenna!" And so Shakespeare departed, sobbing and whimpering.

Now the Chairman turned to me: "You, Moyshe Zeifert, go back to the world below, take on Shakespeare's *Hamlet*, but remember: butcher it so thoroughly that not a scrap of it remains! And tell all your dramatist friends to chop the classics into sauerkraut. Go!"

A shiver ran through my body. I turned over, came to, and looked around. And that was my dream.[16]

In the cosmic battle between economic need and artistic integrity, Zeifert leaves no doubt as to which one had the upper hand when the Yiddish theatre was involved. Zeifert spins out a self-effacing fantasy here, but also a fantasy of Jewish writers deconstructing (or perhaps a better coinage would be destructing) the works of a Gentile poet.

At the same time, Zeifert's account of the aftermath of his dream shows his acknowledgment of Shakespeare's status as a great poet, and of the care that Shakespeare's plays require if they are to be adapted properly — indeed, more care than Zeifert and his colleagues can afford to give them:

> A few days after my terrible dream, I was called to the Thalia Theatre, and the company ordered me "to make *Hamlet!*" All complaints and protests were to no avail. I protested against the impudence of the company, but my *stomach* protested against *my* impudence. "Robber!" rang the voice of my stomach in my ears, "you get fifty dollars for this . . . Don't you know that with fifty dollars you'd be as rich as Wanamaker?"
>
> I undertook the "work." Woe unto me! What I didn't make from that *Hamlet*! Everything: an unsexed creature, an androgyne, everything in the world, but no *Hamlet*!! I exacted a high price from the play.
>
> From the gorgeous building, I took out the foundation, the walls, and the roof. I left not a single pane intact in the beautiful palace. I did it partly out of patriotism — I wanted to take revenge on the 'anti-Semite' Shakespeare — and partly, indeed, for the fifty dollars . . . The company was very happy with Shakespeare (? ? ?) and I believe that up there in seventh heaven, the Chairman was also happy with my "work," but Shakespeare, poor thing, could only bang his head against the walls of Hell.[17]

Zeifert struggles, albeit playfully, with mixed allegiances here. As a Jew, he relishes the chance to retaliate against an enemy. But as an artist — even one of modest talents — he has some pity for his doubly damned colleague/antagonist.

Whatever Zeifert's artistic sins, his *Hamlet*, according to both Boris and Bessie Thomashefsky, was a modest success. The editors of *Di arbeter tsaytung* viewed the fact that Zeifert's *Hamlet* was selling out in advance after two weeks as a sign that the Yiddish public was not so unsophisticated after all,

> and that it is not satisfied when the actor goes "pa" with his feet and sings "put — put — put." And we are sure that it will suffice

for the public to demand that the theatre directors produce plays that are really instructive and true to nature. . . . We only regret that the translation of such a serious play was not undertaken by someone in the position to understand the original well. "Doctor" Zeifert, as we know, cannot be suspected of doing so.[18]

A reviewer for *Di yidishe gazeten* echoed some of these reactions to the play that he described as a tragedy about "a big *shlimazl*," or chronically unlucky person. While also pleased that such a masterpiece has been performed for Yiddish audiences, the reviewer speculates that the translation may have been written "faster than the actors perform it."[19]

Elaborating on the translation's shortcomings, the *Yidishe gazeten* complains, "All of the characters besides Hamlet have almost nothing to say, and just hover over the stage like shadows." Claudius should come across as both a king and a murderer, but Zeifert has eliminated everything regal about him and reduces him to a common killer. Ophelia is appropriately "quiet and fine," but too much so for us to get to know her. The scene with the players drags, and the "To be or not to be" soliloquy is translated "so weakly, that [Thomashefsky] gets completely lost." Nevertheless, Thomashefsky performs the role of Hamlet with feeling and understanding, and Messrs. Conrad, Marks, and Bernstein "are as good as one can expect from them in such a play." The audience gets even higher marks: "Everyone in the audience listened attentively and followed the entire action with interest."[20]

Both the *Arbeter tsaytung* editorial and the *Yidishe gazeten* point to a dichotomy between the artistic merit of the play and the mediocrity of the translator. Jacob Gordin had averted such criticism by reworking his Shakespearean source in Jewish terms. The difference between Zeifert and Gordin as adaptors of Shakespeare goes a step further. Looking back on this period, Thomashefsky wondered, "without me, who knows how many years would have gone by until Shakespeare would have been performed on the Yiddish stage?"[21] This question conveniently overlooks not only the fact that Adler's company staged Shakespeare first, but also the existence of another previous Yiddish Shakespearean adaptation: Gordin's *The Jewish King Lear*. Yet Thomashefsky does not appear to see the need to distinguish Gordin's play from his own activity. If the attitude Thomashefsky expresses here was at all typical of the Yiddish theatre community, then *The Jewish King Lear* was seen not as the Shakespearean adaptation that broke the cultural ice for future adaptations, but as a Gordin play that happened to be inspired by Shakespeare.[22]

Such reasoning may help account for the fact that other Yiddish playwrights did not immediately follow Gordin's precedent of Judaizing Shakespeare, for while anyone could adapt Shakespeare, there was only one Gordin. This has nothing to do with which playwright was the greater artist, but with which one was still working. One could take great liberties with the dead, but to take on the most acclaimed living Yiddish playwright could prove commercially and artistically fatal.

Hamlet, Prince of Illusion

Zeifert's *Hamlet* continued to be performed for the rest of the season.[23] In the meantime, the Thalia mounted a Shakespearean spectacle of a different sort. A newspaper advertisement of 26 January 1894 shows what at first glance appears to be a stereoscopic illustration of Edwin Booth, the most famous American tragedian of his day, posing as Hamlet (fig. 7). Closer inspection shows the two images to differ in subtle details. While the two men are dressed and posed identically, the one on the right has his hair parted differently, a slightly broader nose than the purely aquiline one of his counterpart, and rounder eyes. The accompanying Yiddish text will at first play coyly with, and then explain, the near-twin illustrations.

The text identifies the man on the right as Edwin Booth and his counterpart as William Booth. Running vertically next to Edwin's picture runs the question in Yiddish, "Who among you wants to see a dead man come to life?" Next to William's portrait runs the question, "Who among you wants to say that he has seen the greatest tragedian and artist in the world?" The wording continues horizontally below the pictures:

Then come en masse on Sunday evening, the 28th of January, to that temple of art, the Thalia Theatre, where you will see the greatest artist in the world, Herr Edwin Booth, after his death repre-

7. *An Edwin Booth look-alike at the Thalia Theatre, January 1894.*
From Yidishe gazeten, *26 January 1894.*

sented by William Booth, in the two classic art roles by Shake-speare, Hamlet and Richard III. Besides that, nearly all of the Thalia Theatre company will take part in this sacred concert, such as Herr Thomashefsky, Marks, Bernstein, Conrad, Madam Thoma-shefsky, Fraulein Sabina Weinblatt, and many other Yiddish and English singers and dancers engaged especially for this great festi-val this Sunday evening, the 28th of January, 1894.[24]

Edwin Booth's death six months earlier, on 7 June 1893, had been front-page news. A public ceremony in his memory on 13 November 1893, where such colleagues as Henry Irving, Tommaso Salvini, and Joseph Jefferson III paid tribute to him, was just one instance of post-humous attention to the Booth name.

Edwin Booth left behind a number of legacies: a subdued, intellec-tual approach to acting that ultimately supplanted the athletic, bom-bastic style of the previous generation; The Players, the distinguished theatrical club Booth helped create in 1888, and to which he be-queathed the Gramercy Park building that remains its home; and a daughter Edwina by his wife Mary Devlin. But notably absent from Booth's literal or figurative offspring, or from anywhere in his family's genealogy, was anyone who went by the name of William.[25]

The Yiddish theatres in New York were in the midst of a Shake-speare boom when the Thalia Theatre presented its Booth imitation, advertised as an occasion to deposit Booth's memory in one's cultural bank account so that one will not only have "seen" Edwin Booth, but also be able to "say that one has seen" him — that is, to own the experience of having done so. The scholarship on Edwin Booth does not mention a parallel phenomenon in English-speaking American theatres, perhaps because it could not have happened among audi-ences more familiar with Booth's acting, and thus less willing to tol-erate a lesser imitation.

The promotion of "William Booth," spuriously suggesting a family connection to the great tragedian, recalls the episode in Mark Twain's *Huckleberry Finn* when the hero meets the two colorful charlatans who present themselves as the "Duke of Bridgewater" and the dauphin of France, who would have been Louis XVII had not a revolution inter-rupted his career. One of their various schemes to defraud the folks living along the Mississippi involves the duke's combined experiences at printing handbills and performing soliloquies, scenes, and sword fights from Shakespeare. The handbill announcing the duke's and dauphin's performance in a small town in Arkansas treats the towns-folk to a feast of outrageous claims that begins:

> Shakesperean Revival! ! !
> Wonderful Attraction
> For One Night Only!
> The world renowned tragedians,
> David Garrick the younger, of Drury Lane Theatre, London,
> and
> Edmund Kean the elder, of the Royal Haymarket Theatre,
> Whitechapel, Pudding Lane, Piccadilly, London, and the
> Royal Continental Theatres, in their sublime
> Shaksperean Spectacle entitled
> The Balcony Scene
> in
> Romeo and Juliet! ! ![26]

The Thalia's alleged William Booth probably had as intimate an ac-quaintance with Edwin Booth as the duke and the dauphin had with David Garrick and Edmund Kean. The duke counted on the lack of sophistication of "these Arkansaw lunkheads"[27] for his scheme to work. (It did, but only because he had the foresight to leave town immediately after collecting the ticket money for the third night's performance.) The Thalia management seems to have counted on Yiddish-speaking lunkheads to pay to see William Booth.

That the Yiddish theatres were not above carrying out other Barn-umesque ruses is illustrated by a 1909 Zeifert sketch entitled, "Anything for a Living, "which describes a sojourn in the American South, where the writer had gone to start a new Yiddish newspaper. Exploring the city upon his arrival, Zeifert comes across an astonishing Yiddish theatre poster announcing

> All the greatest Yiddish stars in America together. Friday evening for the first time in the Criterion Theatre, *Hamlet, or the Prince of Denmark*. The Jewish Kainz, Boris Thomashefsky, in the title role; the Jewish Salvini, the Great Eagle, Jacob Adler, as King Claudius[28]; the Jewish Coquelin, David Kessler, as Polonius; Madam Sara Adler as Queen Gertrude and Madam Bessie Thomashefsky as Ophelia, with the participation of the best actors from New York.[29]

Not unlike the duke and dauphin's handbill, the poster implausibly crowds a number of evocative names into a small space. Where Twain's charlatans borrow the names of the leading English Shakespeareans of the late eighteenth and early nineteenth centuries, the Yiddish poster cuts a wider cultural swath, explicitly comparing its leading men to the great figures of the Austrian, Italian, and French stages. Even setting such rhetoric aside, Zeifert is amazed to find these rival talents assembled in a provincial city. Was this a dream? Had the Messiah come?

Neither, actually. When Zeifert goes to see the show only to behold the entrance of one character after another bearing no resemblance whatsoever to the stars named on the poster, he storms backstage to demand an explanation. The stage manager, turning yellow upon learning that Zeifert hails from New York, begs him to hold his tongue out of pity for the poor troupe, who have wives and children to feed. As in the nightmare Zeifert had described a dozen years earlier, business takes precedence over artistic integrity. A disheartened Zeifert decides to return to New York, unwilling to provide a Yiddish newspaper for a town that turns nobodies into stars.

Back to Reality

Several years after he first appeared as Hamlet — probably in the late 1890s — Thomashefsky returned to the role in a translation by Mikhl Goldberg, who would translate a number of other Shakespeare plays into Yiddish around the turn of the twentieth century.[30] Goldberg's *Hamlet* opens in the castle rather than on the ramparts, and places the ghost scenes together, thus cutting down on the number of scene changes required — a rearrangement common in Shakesperean staging ever since the English Restoration. Instead of cutting whole scenes, Goldberg tends to cut long speeches so that the action moves along quickly. Because of this technique, Goldberg reduces the role of Polonius from a "foolish prating knave" to little more than a fencing dummy. This economy carries over to consolidating certain roles. Tom Stoppard might be sorry to learn that Guildenstern is worse than dead in this version; he never appears at all. Rosencrantz does, though, and takes over his absent schoolmate's lines.

While many of Goldberg's cuts simply advance the action, he also consistently eliminates material with any sexual overtones, thus preventing Hamlet from speaking of "country matters" with either Ophelia or Gertrude. Hamlet does confront his mother in her chamber, but without mentioning anything as explicit as the "rank sweat of an enseamed bed" (III.iv.92). The Yiddish theatre tended to be conservative about such matters. Sexually explicit language and double entendres, even from the pen of a great Gentile poet, tended to be taboo.

Goldberg's script provides occasional stage directions designed to bring the emotion of certain scenes to the surface. Nowhere does this occur more strongly than when Hamlet first sees his father's ghost, at which point the prince falls into Horatio's arms and loses his hat. Thunder and lightning underscore the Ghost's commands to "Swear!" Where Shakespeare has the three friends exit together at the end of the scene, Goldberg sends Horatio and Marcellus off before Hamlet, who then has a short soliloquy:

Fridn zay tsu dayner ashe in dayn kaltn grab! Fridn tsu dayn unruikn gayst. Her mikh! Dayn rekher lebt! Un er vet far dir kemfn, kemfn biz in zayn letstn otemtsug, zo helf mir der himl![31]

[Peace unto your body in your cold grave, unhappy son of the earth; peace to your restless spirit. In Heaven hear me: your avenger lives and will fight for you, fight until his last breath.]

As he finishes this speech, Hamlet raises his sword to Heaven. His enthusiastic tone here is just the opposite of that of the speech that Goldberg has cut, which concludes with the memorable couplet, "The time is out of joint — O cursed spite, / That ever I was born to set it right!" (I.v.188–9). Typical of Yiddish adaptors, Goldberg replaces an emotionally ambivalent ending to the act with a stirring one; he directs the audience's moral compass, rather than leaving them to figure out where things stand.

For someone who finds it so difficult to bring himself to kill his father's murderer, Shakespeare's Hamlet appears remarkably dispassionate after he accidentally kills Polonius. Again, Goldberg alters Hamlet's reaction and brings the character's emotions to the surface. Shakespeare ends Act III by having Hamlet "lug [Polonius'] guts into the neighbor room" (III.iv.212). In the Yiddish version, Hamlet "draws his dagger, runs to his mother, she cries out. He throws away his sword, falls to her feet." And he cries, "O mother! Mother!" The Yiddish Hamlet's behavior after killing Polonius may be no less strange than in the original, but at least it is not detached — an attitude that does not seem to have been in Thomashefsky's theatrical vocabulary.

The final moments of the play, in typical Goldberg fashion, focus on the death of the hero rather than on a closing speech that promises the restoration of order. Just as he did with the Prince's speech at the end of *Romeo and Juliet*, Goldberg cuts Fortinbras's final speech in *Hamlet*; indeed, he has cut the Fortinbras subplot out of the play altogether. The play closes with Hamlet's dying words:

> Horatio, I am dying. The black veil of death is spreading over my eyes. The poison is working. Everything is swimming in a sea of fire. The flames are rustling. Adieu, friend. I am going where eternal silence reigns. Now you are freed of your oath. Tell everything you have seen this terrible night. (*Dies. All kneel. Bells are heard ringing. Curtain.*) [32]

This ending exploits the sentimentality of the scene, an emphasis that ethnomusicologist Mark Slobin finds in American Yiddish song as well. For example, a popular song written in response to the devastating Triangle Fire of 1913 sees the incident "not as a step to politicize the proletariat, but as an event that created orphans and caused bereaved mothers to bewail their daughters 'lying in shrouds instead of wedding gowns.'"[33] Goldberg's trimming of the end of *Hamlet* similarly foregrounds the personal over the political. Where Shakespeare's dénouement broadens the perspective to the larger significance of the corruption in the Danish court, Goldberg's stays with the death of the hero, for whom the audience has time to cry as the death knells ring.

A Jewish Hamlet

In a sort of coda to his performances in Zeifert's and Goldberg's translations, Thomashefsky also starred in a popular adaptation of *Hamlet* into a Jewish milieu. Isidore Zolatarevsky (ca. 1873–1945), with his 1899 melodrama *Der yeshive bokher* [The Yeshiva Boy], was the first Yiddish playwright to follow Jacob Gordin in Judaizing Shakespeare. Zolatarevsky was intimately acquainted with *The Jewish King Lear*, having played Dovid Moysheles in a touring company in 1895. He had tried playwriting by then, and a few years later, sold Boris Thomashefsky his new adaptation of *Hamlet*, which premiered simultaneously in New York and Philadelphia in February of 1899. The play was an unexpected success, running steadily for the rest of the season.

Ironically, for all Zolatarevsky's subsequent notoriety as the author of *The Jewish Hamlet*, the initial newspaper advertisements indicate neither his authorship nor the play's Shakespearean lineage:

Windsor Theatre
45–47 Bowery
Friday, Saturday and Sunday evenings,
The 3rd, 4th and 5th of February
For the first time
— The —
JEWISH MARTYR
or *The Yeshiva Boy*
Performed by Thomashefsky
Music by Friedsel[34]

Thomashefsky was certainly a big enough star to eclipse many a young playwright, but here, even the composer — albeit a prominent one in the American Yiddish theatre at the time — gets billing where the playwright's name is omitted.

Further down in the advertising columns, appears a play more obviously connected to Shakespeare: *Der yidisher Hamlet*, premiering at the Arch Street Theatre in Philadelphia on the third and fourth of February. In fact, *Der yidisher martirer* and *Der yidisher Hamlet* are one and the same, but it was Thomashefsky who put Zolatarevsky's play on the theatrical map. The Philadelphia production starred Max Rosenthal, the leading Yiddish actor in that city at the time, as Avigdor; Thomashefsky played Avigdor in New York, where it became a signature role for him. There Zolatarevsky himself played the role of Yankl Khazn, a role he wrote specifically for the New York production.[35]

Thomashefsky seems to have romanticized somewhat his initial involvement with *The Yeshiva Boy*. At the bottom of the title page of a script prepared specifically for a benefit for Zolatarevsky on 13 April 1935, appears a note entitled, "History of *Yeshive bokher*": "Produced for the first time in Philadelphia by Max Rosenthal — flopped — had to perform another play the second night — Thomashefsky bought the unsuccessful work and the *Yeshive bokher* lives, and will live as long as I live."[36] The tone of this miniature "history" of the play suggests that Thomashefsky recited it onstage at the beginning of the benefit performance. It also presents Thomashefsky as a sort of theatrical faith healer who brings the play back from the dramaturgic graveyard. The initial newspaper advertisements, however, reveal the "history" to be only partly accurate. The play does seem to have flopped in Philadelphia, since its title quickly disappears from the Arch Street Theatre ads, but Rosenthal and Thomashefsky premiered the play simultaneously.

Der yeshive bokher takes place in an eastern European Hasidic community whose *rebbe*, or spiritual leader, passed away six weeks before the action of the play begins. It is now the wedding day of Dvoyre, the late rebbe's widow, and Todres, his step-brother. Todres has also been named the new *rebbe*, though we quickly see how unqualified he is, since he falls asleep during important meetings and bungles his every attempt at learned commentary. Even his adjutant sneers at him openly, constantly addressing him by such names as "*gazlen*" (robber) and "*balegole*" (coachman).

When Avigdor returns home after two years studying abroad, he learns of dramatic changes. In typical Yiddish theatrical fashion, Zolatarevsky structures the action to heighten the emotionality of the events. Where Hamlet learns of both his father's death and his mother's remarriage before the audience first sees him, Zolatarevsky places both of these discoveries onstage, thus showing his hero's immediate reaction to them.

Zolatarevsky builds upon the emotional impact of Avigdor's discovery by closing Act I with the recitation of the *kaddish*, the Jewish prayer for the dead, which serves here both to honor the deceased and to reproach those who are celebrating too soon. Avigdor has Dvoyre remove her wedding veil and extinguishes all the lights except for one candle, with which he says *kaddish* to the accompaniment of music by Louis Friedsel. Composer Joseph Rumshinsky, himself one of the most prolific and respected Yiddish theatre composers, had high praise for Friedsel's music: "If Louis Friedsel had written nothing besides the prelude to the *kaddish* from *Der yeshive bokher*, he would have earned the reputation he had at the time. Those eight bars played on the viola and clarinet always gave me — and still do to this day — the feeling of death, but without fear: something of eternal rest."[37] Rumshinsky was not alone in his praise, for Friedsell's *kaddish* took on a life of its own in at least half a dozen recordings, including one by Thomashefsky and two by David Kessler.[38] Within the context of the play, Avigdor throws open the curtains covering the ark where the Torah is held after he completes the *kaddish*, and sees his father — not anthropomorphized as a ghost, but purely in Avigdor's imagination.

Act II begins on Purim, but the holiday's festive nature contrasts ironically with the dire events to come. At first, the tone is pleasant enough, for Avigdor and his beloved, Esther, are about to sign their marriage vows. But the mood changes when Avigdor is given a letter from the late *rebbe*: "I had a step-brother, younger than I by twenty years. Todres is his name. For the last ten years I noticed that my wife was not indifferent to him. I kept silent, kept it to myself, until one day I saw them together in a way that made me go mute on the spot from sickness and weakness! I am dying before my time. Take vengeance on that man — have pity on the woman, she is a mother." The letter serves all of the expository function of the Ghost scenes in

Hamlet without any of the sense of the supernatural — a shift of perspective captured in Anglo-Jewish writer Israel Zangwill's comic sketch, "The Yiddish 'Hamlet,'" in which a Lower East Side poet adapts *Hamlet* for a Yiddish theatre in New York and asks, "Now, how can a ghost affect a modern audience which no longer believes in ghosts?"[39] By replacing the Ghost with other devices, Zolatarevsky adapts Shakespeare's use of the supernatural to a more rationalistic world.

Other documents further complicate the plot. The innkeeper announces that he informed the police that Avigdor is a socialist, and has papers to substantiate the claim. But the innkeeper absent-mindedly leaves the papers behind, and Avigdor's friend, who has overheard the intrigue, grabs them and stashes them in his shirt. Clumsy moments like this show Zolatarevsky's inexperience at writing melodramas; he has the ingredients, but sometimes has trouble combining them artfully.

The situation grows more and more violent. A supporter of Avigdor is beaten by Todres's followers for speaking out against their rebbe. Todres calls for the stoning of Avigdor, whom he deems a heretic. Dvoyre tries to intercede on her son's behalf, and when Todres stops her, she escapes him by jumping out the window. A bloodied Avigdor is brought in by a crowd, and is soon followed by his mortally injured mother, who manages to give Avigdor his father's ring before she dies.

Act IV takes place exactly one year later, with Avigdor having recently escaped from the mental institution where he was committed just after his mother died. His friends suspect that he may return to visit his mother's grave on the anniversary of her death. Esther, whose health has suffered greatly from all the anxiety, enters disoriented from a visit to Dvoyre's grave. When someone reports that Avigdor has been spotted nearby, Esther dies from the shock.

The final scene finds Avigdor at his parents' graves when Esther's body is carried onstage. Avigdor leads the *kaddish* for her while standing in the grave. He comes out, says that they can only be united in death now, and falls dead. The chorus sings, "Blessed is the true Judge." In the manner of the most popular melodrama of all time, George Aiken's adaptation of *Uncle Tom's Cabin*, the action is resolved in the world to come. Aiken closed the play with a tableau showing the good characters united in heaven. Zolatarevsky suggests a similar working of divine justice by ending with a Jewish formula acknowledging the finality and justice of God's judgment in all things.

At first glance, *Der yeshive bokher*'s tremendous popularity may seem surprising. Little of its language could be called poetic, the intrigue is obviously contrived, and characters have a terrible habit of keeling over and dying, upon the slightest provocation, at dramatically convenient moments. But taken on its own terms rather than on its merit (or lack thereof) as a reworking of *Hamlet*, *Der yeshive bokher* had much to recommend it to contemporary audiences. Zolatarevsky strove for grand sentimental effects rather than metaphysical musings, most markedly by closing three of the four acts with the hero mourning the death of a loved one. The play also offers both comic relief and social commentary, often simultaneously, thus giving the audience the opportunity both to laugh at and condemn characters whose values clashed with their own, especially where religious practice was concerned. Hasidim and other Orthodox Jews decried Yiddish theatre. For one thing, it caused Jews to break the Sabbath — the very evening, in fact, when *Der yeshive bokher* premiered. In the play, hypocritical orthodoxy is responsible for tyranny, adultery, and even death, if not exactly murder. By equating Hasidism with moral corruption, *Der yeshive bokher* affirms the nontraditional Judaism of its audience, where theatre is acceptable, but tyranny is not.

Princess Hamlet

A couple of years after Thomashefsky helped popularize *The Yeshiva Boy*, Bertha Kalish (often spelled Kalich or Kalisch) took *Hamlet* in a very different direction. 1901 saw the premiere of two Shakespeare productions that went a long way toward putting the Yiddish theatre on the broader American cultural map. One was Jacob Adler's interpretation of Shylock in a production of *The Merchant of Venice* that was visited with great interest by theatre impresarios and critics from uptown. Adler impressed them so much that two years later, he returned to the role, in Yiddish, surrounded by an English-speaking cast. Bertha Kalish's performance of Hamlet would serve as a different sort of springboard to Broadway. It too drew the attention of the uptown critics, and helped gain her the wider audience she needed to make a breakthrough on English-language stages. The Shubert brothers, the dominant American producers of their day, would offer her a long-term contract in 1905, allowing her to succeed outside of the Yiddish theatre on a far greater scale than any other American Yiddish actor of her generation.

Bertha Kalish's career provides a striking example of the sort of multilingual, cross-cultural journey common among many Yiddish actors of her generation. Born in 1872 in the Austro-Hungarian city of Lemberg (now Lwów, Ukraine), Bertha Kalish attended music school as a girl, and later studied at the Lemberg Conservatory. At the age of thirteen, she was hired to sing in the chorus of *La Traviata* in a Polish theatre. After performing in the chorus of several other productions, she accepted the offer of a fellow actor, Max Gimpel, to join his new Yiddish theatre in Lemberg. When the company's leading lady (who would later play Ophelia to Kalish's Hamlet) left for America, Kalish became the troupe's prima donna, starring in such plays as Avrom Goldfaden's operetta *Shulamis*. Gimpel's Theatre would become one of the world's most prominent Yiddish theatrical venues, but it did not take Kalish long to be recognized by an even more powerful figure. When Avrom Goldfaden saw her perform at Gimpel's Theatre, he so admired the beauty of both her person and her voice that he hired her to join his company in Romania.

Much of her subsequent career followed a similar pattern: a series of increasingly lucrative and prominent offers that led her from Bucharest to the Bowery, from the Bowery to Broadway. After performing in various cities in Hungary, Romania, and Galicia from the late 1880s until 1896, she was persuaded by the management of the Thalia Theatre in New York to join the company for the salary of thirty-five dollars per week. She quickly became as popular with New York audiences as she had been in Europe, and her salary jumped to 150 dollars per week for her second season in New York.[40]

By the early 1900s, Bertha Kalish was more than just another Yiddish star; she made such a tremendous impact in several of the roles she created that no other actress dared touch them. Most prominent in her repertoire were leading roles in three of Jacob Gordin's most popular plays: Etenyu in *God, Man, and Devil* (1901), Sophia Fingerhut in *Sappho* (1901), and Ettie in *The Kreutzer Sonata* (1902). Gordin wrote the latter two plays specifically for Kalish. When she crossed over to the English-language stage, where she would meet with greater success than any other Yiddish actor of her generation, these dramas dropped out of the Yiddish performance repertoire.[41] Kalish also appeared in more conventional Yiddish performances of Shakespeare before playing Hamlet, having played Desdemona and Juliet on the Bowery in the late 1890s.

While the twentieth century "has tended again to see female Hamlets as experimental,"[42] they were fairly commonplace in the decades leading up to Bertha Kalish's debut in the role. Sarah Siddons was probably the first woman to play Hamlet, around 1775, though never in a London theatre;[43] those who followed her included fellow Englishwoman Alice Marriott in the 1860s, and American star Charlotte Cushman beginning in the 1850s.

As the tradition of female Hamlets grew, it also grew less remarkable. Most of the critics who attended Kalish's *Hamlet* did not dwell on the issue of an actress playing a man, though it did bother A. H. Fromenson: "No woman, not even Bernhardt, much less Kalisch, can enter into all the various conflicting, contradicting, soul-rocking emotions that racked the tortured spirit of the unfortunate Prince of Denmark. It is essentially a man's part. . . . It is, therefore, not to be wondered at that Miss Kalisch could not attain the heights she sought to reach."[44] Other critics touched on the gender issue only in passing if at all, one finding Kalish's Hamlet "handsome and manly,"[45] another seeing her as "a pleasing, though plainly a feminine, Hamlet."[46] On the whole, the critics seem to have found the issue of cross-dressing hardly more noteworthy than the phenomenon of an American playing a Dane.

Of all her female predecessors in the role, contemporary French sensation Sarah Bernhardt clearly served as Kalish's inspiration. Two of Bernhardt's roles had already entered the Yiddish repertoire. Kalish had previously starred in Zeifert's translation of Victorien Sardou's *Fédora* (1882); billed in the Yiddish press as "the best work in Sarah Bernhardt's repertoire," the play premiered on 11 November 1898.[47] Just two months later at the same theatre, Keni Liptzin starred in Gordin's translation of Octave Mirbeau's *Les mauvais bergers* (1897), which opened on 6 January 1899. While the lavish spectacle of Sardou's play and the socialist orientation of Mirbeau's had numerous counterparts in the Yiddish repertoire, neither French playwright was otherwise prominent on Yiddish stages. Shakespeare was quite another story, of course, and once Bernhardt took on the role of Hamlet in Paris in 1899, it seems natural for Kalish to have taken advantage of this intersection of a classical icon with a contemporary one. Indeed, she fairly leapt at the role after Bernhardt first brought her Hamlet to New York, where it opened at the Garden Theatre on 25 December 1900. Just over a month later, Kalish followed with a Yiddish version (fig. 8)

Kalish capitalized on the publicity generated by both Sarah Bernhardt's and Boris Thomashefsky's recent performances of the role in order to attract as broad an audience as possible. Thomashefsky had gained notoriety for his appearances in both translated and Judaized versions of the play. Bernhardt's Hamlet evoked equally divergent opinions from audiences and critics in both Europe and America. As her biographer Cornelia Otis Skinner writes, "Opinions regarding Bernhardt's own performance were varied and heated. Many found it superb. Others couldn't bear it."[48] Some were clearly put off by her sex and her age. Critics agreed that she did not even try to conceal her femininity; Max Beerbohm quipped that her Hamlet was *"très grand dame."*[49] She was also much older than the role as written, though at fifty-four she was far from the oldest to have played the young prince.

Perhaps more important than such physical attributes was Bernhardt's insistence on embellishing her performance with a great deal of stage business. She knocked Rosencrantz's and Guildenstern's heads together; kicked Polonius in the shins and caught a fly on his nose; used Ophelia's hair as a screen through which she viewed *The Mousetrap*; kneeled before the ghost; and died standing up.[50] Outrageous as these choices may sound, Robert Speaight reminds us that "since Mounet[-Sully] saw the performance ten times and Maurice Baring described it as 'the ultimate triumph of intelligence,' her impertinent challenge cannot be written off as a bad joke."[51] Yet the praise was often drowned out by a chorus of disapproval, such as William Winter harshly pronouncing the performance "well calculated to commend itself to persons interested in the study of freaks."[52] The conflicting reactions to both Thomashefsky's and Bernhardt's interpretations opened a middle road for Kalish.

THALIA THEATRE.

טהאליא טהעאטער, 46־48 בוערי.

עקסטרא !

צום ערשטען מאהל דיזען יאהרשען
טהעאטער עקספסירים

מאדאם
בערטהא קאליש
אלס האמלעט

עהרען בענעפיט פארשטעלל.;
פיר

עקסטרא !

צום ערשטען מאהל דיזען יאהרשען
טהעאטער עקספסירים

מאדאם
בערטהא קאליש
אלס האמלעט

עהרען בענעפיט פאר־שטעללונג
פ'ר

מאדאם בערטהא קאליש

מיטוואך אבענדם 30 יאנואר

צור איספיהרונג קאסמט
זעקספיעירס בעריהמטע דראמא

האמלעט

מאדאם בערטהא קאליש אלס האמלעט

אין נואוירונג און פערפאסמואערסליכע ראללען וערלבע איז ביז יעצט בלויז און סקע,נ׳נ: געשפיעלט נעוואירען, שפיעלט צום ערשטען מאהל קאליש
מים דער מיטוויירקונג דער נאנצער מאדאם טהאליא טהעאטער קאמפאני.

ווערטהעם פובליקום : — האמלעם איז ביז יעצט געשפיעלט נעוואירען מאן דיא גרעסטען קינסטלער דער וועלט און נור סענונר.   דיא איינציגע פריוא
וועלכע האם זיך אונטערנאמסען צו שפיעלען דיא ראללע מאן האמלעם וואר נור סאראה בערנהארד.   מאדאם קאליש וועלכע האם איממער
נאמסאהן איהר בעסטסטען אין אירגענד וועלכע ראלל די דורכצופיהרען מים נרעסטר פּארטיקבינים. נעסם אויף זיך יעצט דיא נעוסאנע אויפנאאבע צור
איהר עהרען בענעפים צו שפיעלען דיא ראללע מאן האמלעט.   דיים 6 מאנאטען דאס זיא שטודירט איהר ראלל האמלעט מים איינגעם מאן איינגעם
נרעסטען פראפעסטארן אין ריעזען מאך אונטעט דעם נאמען ל. מ. נאללען שמא, דער וועלכער פּאראהנאר האם אונטערריכטעם דיא נרעסטען
קינסטלער, וואו : פאוטעה, מאאר אדאמס, עגני רעסטעל אונד נאך אנדערע, אונד דיא פּערפּורטכם אלזא אנצאאוינערן דאם דער אבנער האם
30מען יאנואר: וואל פּערקבליכבן פיר אין ארדענטקעין בייא יעדען צושויער;   מיר ביא נאצע טהאליא טהעאטער קאמפאני פאן אונזער ־ זייטע
וערדען צור עהרע אונוער קאללעגין קינסטלערין וועלבע האם פערלאסם אונד פערשפעאם נעהרע אונד כבור טים איהר ערשיינען טים אונו צואאסטטען
איוא עיין ביהנע וועלכע פ׳ כאסוד זעלבסם האם איהר נעשענקבס אלזע סעלות וויא איהר נעשענקבם. מיר וועלבע דיא נעטסמע
ריישיקער וויא בראבפאנענל אונד אברעצע האבען מים דעם נאמען קינסטלערין.   וערדען מיר אאלעם מעגליכעם אם פיטסעטתעל־
פּאן איהר דערקער איהרע זעטטע ראל דורכצופיהרען מים פראקם אונד נלאנץ.   קוסמ אין יעטאם, אונד מהיילם צו עהרע דיר עהרע נעביירוז.   אכפטונגסמ׳;,

ריא טהאליא טהעאטער קאמפאני.

דיים אויסמעריקואם אויף דעם דיעל וועלכע האמלעם האם מים לעאירטעס.

קינדער אונטער 5 יאהר וערדען נים אריינגעלאזען.

טיקעטם זינר שוין צו בעקומען אין באקס אפים פון טהאליא טהעאטער.

י. ליפשטאדט, יונגע סטים פרינטער, 1401 נרענד סטרים, ני יארק

8. *Bertha Kalish as Hamlet. From the Dorot Jewish Division, the New York Public Library, Astor, Lenox, and Tilden Foundations.*

Reviewers were quick to note parallels and contrasts to the Hamlets of both Bernhardt and Thomashefsky. Kalish acquitted herself well, though the *Commercial Advertiser* critic observed,

> It would perhaps have been as well if Mrs. Kalisch had never seen Bernhardt. Her conception of the Dane is wholly different from the Frenchwoman's, and so her direct copying of much of Bernhardt's melodramatic business with Polonius and at the play is out of place. Still, it is a worthy effort and a success, and well deserves repetition from time to time, especially as it is so much better than the other Bowery Hamlets and than many more famous ones.[53]

Alan Dale noted that Kalish modeled her costume after Bernhardt except for the blond wig (an innovation that Charles Fechter had introduced), which she exchanged for a long dark one. Dale praised Kalish's interpretation in general, finding that it occasionally "suggested Sarah at her best. It rarely recalled Sarah's Hamlet at her worst."[54]

Kalish also fared well in comparisons to Thomashefsky, with the critic from the *Commercial Advertiser* concluding:

> The general adequacy of the performance showed that *Hamlet* is something of a tradition on the Bowery. Thomasheusky [*sic*], at the People's, and Kessler, at the Thalia, have both tried their hands in versions of the melancholy Dane. The production of the former, who is known on the Bowery as the Yiddish Hamlet, is much inferior to the present production at the Thalia. Throughout, the actors give a performance dignified, serious and, as a whole, quite faithful to our English conception of what the play ought to be.[55]

Yet accustomed as many of them were to the phenomenon of *Hamlet* in Yiddish, the critics often wrote at length on Yiddish culture's appropriation of the play.

Alan Dale seemed particularly tickled by the experience of hearing an English classic performed by Yiddish actors. His review included a reproduction of a page of the program, followed by the caption, "Curious spelling of the names of the famous characters in Shakespeare's play. In Yiddish Ophelia is 'Affolio,' and other names are similarly treated without fear or favor." Later in his review, Dale reminded his readers of the Jewishness of the actors: "The names of

the players themselves read like a directory of the East Side. Moskow-
itz was Claudius, and Mrs. Nadolsky was Gertrude. The Ghost fell to
the lot of Mr. Goldstein, and Ophelia was interpreted by Mrs. Tanz-
man. There was a Marcus, and a Feinstein, and a Friedman and a
Tornberg." [56] Dale does not elaborate on this "directory," but the condescension drips from his remarks, as if he had proclaimed, How
quaint for these denizens of the Jewish ghetto to take on one of
the greatest English masterpieces! Perhaps he would have been more
comfortable if the actors had changed their names to less conspicu-
ously ethnic ones, just as he chose an Anglo-Saxon *nom de plume* rather
than his legal name, Alfred J. Cohen. [57]

The script of the translation used by Kalish, prepared by B. Vilenski, carries on a number of traditions in Yiddish translations of *Hamlet*, such as cutting characters and speeches in order to speed the pace
of the play and censoring sexually suggestive double entendres. Vilenski's text also underscores certain ideas with broad gestures, at times
blossoming into elaborate spectacle. Thus Hamlet's encounter with
the Ghost bears strong similarities to Thomashefsky's staging of it.
Upon first seeing the ghost of his father, Hamlet falls back into Horatio's arms and loses his hat, just as Thomashefsky had done. The
Ghost's command to "Swear!" is then accompanied by flashes of
thunder and lightning, a scene that Dale watched "with many thrills
and keen enjoyment." [58]

Act I ends with Hamlet declaring, with upraised sword (again like
Thomashefsky) his eagerness to avenge his father's murder: "Hear
me. Your avenger lives, and he will fight for you until his last breath.
So help me God" (23). As Mikhl Goldberg had done for Thomashefsky, Vilenski cut the lines from Shakespeare that show Hamlet's reluc-
tance: "The time is out of joint — O cursed spite, / That ever I was
born to set it right!" (I.v.188–9). The reviewers' comments suggest
that Bertha Kalish may have given the Yiddish lines a more subdued
reading than Thomashefsky did, but the text itself still presents a
Hamlet far more eager to avenge his father's death than is Shakespeare's Hamlet at the same point in the play.

A less ambivalent Hamlet makes for a less complicated tragedy.
Such an interpretation is consistent with other simplifications in the
text Kalish used; Dale summed up the changes as follows: "The most
significant things, psychologically, in the alterations of the text, are

those which point out what elements of Shakespeare would be unintelligible to the average Yiddish mind and education. . . . Metaphor they either abandon or simplify."[59] While Dale's condescending tone returns to haunt this passage as well, his observation is essentially accurate. Such adjustments follow in the tradition of many earlier Yiddish translations, which tended both to simplify the plays' narratives and to lessen the character flaws of such heroes as Hamlet, Romeo, and Coriolanus.

As Act II opens, Vilenski simplifies the action by eliminating several secondary characters, thus condensing exposition and getting Kalish back onstage as quickly as possible. Here she could begin demonstrating her ability to portray either real or feigned insanity. The critics read her interpretation as the latter, Dale viewing her Hamlet as "a very sane and lucid gentleman of a somewhat rollicking turn of mind,"[60] the *Dramatic Mirror* seeing it as "a romantic Hamlet — not an insane Hamlet, nor a philosophical Hamlet."[61] The adjective "rollicking" matches Vilenski's stage directions for Hamlet throughout the scene. After Hamlet delivers his first line to Polonius, he spins around, an action he repeats a few lines later. As if this were not disconcerting enough, he also stares at Polonius when the latter asks, "Do you know me, Prince?" and fans through the pages of his book three times as he announces that he is reading "Words. Words. Words."

Vilenski excised the double entendres in this and subsequent scenes; nowhere did Kalish's Hamlet speak of "country matters." Act II closes with Hamlet's soliloquy, amplified with the exclamation, "At the play! At the play!" (40) — again, a more exuberant outburst than Shakespeare's straightforward, "The play's the thing / Wherein I'll catch the conscience of the King" (II.ii.604–5). After the last line, Hamlet freezes in a pose between the curtains, a common device in the nineteenth century for ending acts and plays.

Typical as it was to create a *tableau vivant* as the sole focus at any given moment, it was a far different choice to present such an image while some other, more central, activity was taking place. Kalish's production did just that during the most famous speech in dramatic literature. Ophelia kneels in prayer just before Hamlet enters for the "To be or not to be" soliloquy and remains in that position throughout his musings over whether he should his quietus make. Whatever one thinks of the merits or shortcomings of such a production choice, keeping Ophelia onstage at that moment was an artistically generous move for a star to make at a time when most Yiddish actors of Kalish's stature did all they could to minimize the other actors' presence as a way of enhancing their own.

Kalish played a Hamlet increasingly agitated following the "get thee to a nunnery" exchange, letting out a "terrible scream" (48) before remarking, "Let the doors be shut upon him," and twice starting to exit in mid-sentence before returning. A. H. Fromenson regarded the scene as the zenith of Kalish's performance: "Only once did Miss Kalisch reach the greatest height. She had one truly great scene, and for this alone the production was worthwhile. Hamlet's scene with Ophelia, where the prince orders his sweetheart to 'go to a cloister and become a nun,' was sublime, and not even the divine Sarah could have rendered it better." [62] The next stage direction giving a clue to Hamlet's state of mind comes at the conclusion of the *Mousetrap* scene; after Claudius has the play stopped, Hamlet approaches him and "stares straight at him" (58). Considering the critics' agreement that Kalish played Hamlet as anything but insane, the movement suggests a Hamlet confidently sizing up his uncle and unafraid to show Claudius that Hamlet knows all about the true circumstances of the elder Hamlet's death.

Staring at Claudius can serve as a prelude to a more extensive chastisement of Gertrude. The *Commercial Advertiser* reported approvingly, "In the closet scene she is particularly good when she upbraids Gertrude, but makes a very bad end by drawing her sword on her, and then repenting and crying 'Mother, mother!'" [63] While the staging and wording directly recalls Thomashefsky, Kalish apparently removed this stage business for a later production. [64] Since Bertha Kalish was often praised for depicting a subtler Hamlet than Thomashefsky's, the resemblances between the two performers' translations at such moments may indicate the concessions Kalish was willing to make to audiences weaned on Shakespearean performances that were presented more broadly than she would have liked. Once she established a Hamlet with her personal stamp, she seems to have gained the confidence to alter the text to suit her approach more appropriately.

Act IV of Kalish's production ends with a startling image, reminiscent of the fascination of Victorian painters like John Everett Millais with pictorial representations of the drowned Ophelia. When Gertrude describes Ophelia's drowning to Laertes, he remarks, "Too much of water hast thou, poor Ophelia, / And therefore I forbid my tears" (IV.vii.185–6). The Vilenski production has Ophelia's body brought onstage by this point, thus turning Laertes' apostrophe into a direct address to his sister's corpse. This addition, typical as it was of the American Yiddish theatre of its time, also manages to out-Shakespeare Shakespeare. Showing the drowned Ophelia puts on stage the embodiment of Gertrude's vivid description of the drowned girl (which in Shakespeare precedes Ophelia's body being brought out for burial) while heightening both the sentimentality and the visual spectacle of the moment. It also echoes any number of moments in Shakespeare when a character addresses a deceased or seemingly deceased loved one — Lady Anne to Edward VI, Lear to Cordelia, and Romeo to Juliet, to name but a few.

Not surprisingly after the presentation of Ophelia's drowned corpse, the production makes an impressive spectacle of her funeral. Four pallbearers carry her body on a bier bedecked with flowers; they are accompanied by two clergymen, four pages, courtiers, ladies in waiting, and Claudius, Gertrude, and Laertes. Vilenski keeps the rest of the action in the graveyard (again as Goldberg had done for Thomashefsky), to the chagrin of one critic. While praising the text's overall faithfulness to the original, the *Dramatic Mirror* felt that this choice made "the final tragedy come abruptly. This destroys the power of the closing incidents of the story and sadly weakens the character of Hamlet."[65] The ending was made to appear even more sudden by omitting Fortinbras entirely and giving the last lines to the dying Hamlet, who tells Horatio, "Now you are freed of your oath. Tell everything that you have seen on this terrible night" (114). As he dies, the audience hears a flourish of trumpets, and the sounds of people weeping offstage.

The critics submitted generally favorable verdicts. Dale concluded: "I have seen very many worse performances, with highly advertised actors in the cast. . . . There were no airs. There were no frills. . . . There were no poses, no struggles for elusive effect. [Kalish] got down to the solid bed rock of the idea and hammered at it."[66] Her

large audience, according to the *Dramatic Mirror*, was even more enthusiastic: "The old playhouse . . . was fairly packed from orchestra
rail to topmost tier. The spectators belonged to every class and type
of the Hebrew race. That she triumphed, in the opinion of her admirers, was proved by the thunderous applause that brought her again
and again before the curtain at the conclusion of each act."[67]

Kalish clearly carried the production, her supporting cast receiv-
ing mixed reviews from the critics. Berta Tantsman was said to lack
charm, or to be "not in her best element," as Ophelia.[68] Sabine Weinblatt, who replaced her, was "hugely fat and lusty," according to the
ever sarcastic Alan Dale: "She was richly attired in Nottingham lace
curtains, cut low in the neck, and her hair was tied back in Grand
street style. She was a very beautiful person, but not at all wistful."
Dale deemed Samuel Tornberg's Polonius "a very humorous individual, just as in the Sarah version. He wore a sort of velvet gaberdine,
rich and kosher, and seemed to enjoy his life extremely."[69] Tornberg
and Maurice Moscovitch (Claudius) were said to perform well "within
limits, but each is given only one note."[70] Fromenson, though, had
high praise for Moscovitch, even though the rest of the supporting
cast demonstrated that "taste and rehearsal are practically unknown
on the Jewish stage." According to Fromenson, "The young actor
plays with a polish and reserve that indicates a very intelligent mind,
and if he does not allow himself to be dragged down by the degrading
influences at work on the Yiddish stage, there is a brilliant future in
store for him. He played with a quiet dignity that made his thankless
role stand out brilliantly."[71] Moscovitch would fulfill the promise of
his "brilliant future," perhaps nowhere more strikingly than with his
interpretation of Shylock.[72]

Bertha Kalish's *Hamlet* was no mere drawing-room experiment. It
was popular theatre — popular enough not only to remain in her repertoire as long as she remained in the Yiddish theatre, but also to
appeal to the "uptown" critics, thus helping her gain the notoriety that
would sweep her along to a successful career on the English-speaking
stage.[73] No longer linguistically marginalized in the Jewish theatrical
ghetto, Bertha Kalish could now join such contemporaries as Helena
Modjeska and Alla Nazimova, whose European accents distinguished
them as exotic without preventing them from being appreciated and
applauded by the English-speaking public.

A "*Tragi-Tragic*" *Hamlet*

While most American Yiddish versions of Shakespeare — Judaized or not — originated in New York, audiences in the "provinces" enjoyed the occasional opportunity to see a homegrown Shakespeare production. Such was the case in the fall of 1917, when Joseph Kessler (no apparent relation to David) led a serious-minded troupe at Chicago's Haymarket Theatre. Little record of his performances as Romeo and Shylock that season survives. His Hamlet (fig. 9), on the other hand, is better documented, in an extant manuscript of his acting version, as well as in reviews from Chicago, and also from London, where he performed the role again several years later at the Pavilion Theatre.

By the time Joseph Kessler first played Hamlet, a generation had passed since Thomashefsky and Kalish took on the role. A generation of Yiddish audiences had had the chance to become more comfortable attending English-language theatres, and perhaps even studying Shakespeare in the original in school. Similarly, the professional Yiddish theatre had matured; indeed, it was about twice as old at the end of World War I as it was when Thomashefsky and Adler were assaulting each other with Shakespeare posters in 1893. The text Joseph Kessler used for his *Hamlet*, accordingly, tends to tone down some of the theatrics used by translators like Goldberg and Vilenski, though it still gives actors a number of opportunities to display their emotions in the grand manner.

As in previous Yiddish versions, Kessler's production begins in Elsinore, where men and ladies of the court stand in two rows as the orchestra plays and the King and Queen enter. The action quickly moves to an abridged exchange between Laertes and Ophelia (again with Polonius' verbosity considerably curtailed) and on to the Ghost scenes, which Kessler's translator combines into one, following what has become a Yiddish tradition. Rather than falling backward upon first seeing the Ghost, Hamlet's response here is more muted; he simply takes a step back when first learning of the Ghost from Horatio. Then, when addressing his father's spirit, Hamlet kneels, holding his sword by the hilt and bearing it as a cross. The scene also involves dramatic effects, with a rumble of thunder and a flash of lightning each time the Ghost commands, "Swear!"[74]

9. Joseph Kessler as Hamlet.
From the Archives of the YIVO Institute for Jewish Research.

Kessler's text tends to be far more attentive to Shakespeare's use of language than most earlier Yiddish acting versions of Shakespeare. In particular, it strives to preserve Shakespeare's use of rhyme in Hamlet's note to Ophelia, the entire play-within-a-play, and Ophelia's song. On the other hand, Kessler's version takes tremendous liberties by adding scenes to compensate for certain cuts or to clarify the overall action or individual characters' motivation.

When Claudius spells out to the audience his plan for having Ham-

let removed from his path, he does so far less obliquely than in Shakespeare's wording:

> Ah, you unfortunate prince, you are going to England never to
> return — the letter I am sending with you to the King of England
> is your death sentence. He will have you beheaded without asking
> why. You must die, for you know more than a madman could. Yes,
> yes, such is the fate of every criminal once he causes but one death:
> he must then cover his first bloody act with a second death. I can-
> not do otherwise. Go, unfortunate one, you will never see Den-
> mark's soil or your mother again.

This translator seems to have been thinking of another Shakespearean usurper at the same time, for Claudius' soliloquy bears shades
of Macbeth's "It will have blood, they say; blood will have blood"
(III.v.121). The translator also replaces Hamlet's explanation to Horatio of the King's abortive plot against him with an interpolated scene
between Horatio and Gertrude that redeems some of her motherli-
ness. After Horatio describes how Claudius tried to kill Hamlet —
something we never see her directly discover in the original (indeed,
Horatio himself does not learn about it until much later) — she commands him, "Go to him, Horatio, tell him that his mother is very
worried about him and asks him to delay his return slightly. Warn him
to be careful. Tell him that, Horatio, and bring him my dagger."

If Kessler performed opposite a softer Gertrude than Shakespeare's text seems to indicate, he also had a tougher Laertes to combat. Shakespeare's Laertes is certainly the consummate soldier, and
more than willing to repay Hamlet for the deaths of Polonius and
Ophelia. In Shakespeare, though, Claudius continually eggs him on,
afraid that the young man's thirst for vengeance (like Hamlet's, ironically) might weaken with time. But Kessler's acting version makes
Laertes' vengeful sorrow positively villainous; he sounds like a figure
out of a Jacobean revenge tragedy in the speech that closes Act IV:

> O mayn got. Dertrunken! Tsufil vaser hostu mayn oreme shves-
> ter — darum halt ikh tsurik mayne trern, — o Hamlet ven du zolst
> afile voynen baym altar, — vel ikh dikh fun dortn arunterraysn un
> mit mayne fis de[r]tretn! Lebt vol mayn kenig! Nor di rakhe ken

mayn tserisn harts vider heyln, — den vey vil vey, un shmertsn for-
dern shmertsn! Lebt vol! Rakhe! Rakhe! far mayn foter un shvester.

[Oh my God! Drowned! Too much of water hast thou, my poor
sister, and therefore I hold back my tears. Oh Hamlet! Even were
you to stand by the altar, I would tear you away from it and trample
you under foot! Be well, my king! Only revenge can heal my broken
heart. For one pain demands company, and sorrows demand more
sorrows! Be well! Revenge! Revenge for my father and sister.]

For all its relative sensitivity to Shakespearean language, the text implicitly acknowledges an audience weaned on melodrama, and thus
fine-tunes the shades of gray enveloping Shakespeare's characters
into sharper blacks and whites. Nowhere does this come through as
clearly as in the duel. During one of the breaks (just after Gertrude
drinks from the poisoned goblet), Hamlet kneels by his mother, who
wipes the sweat from his brow. As she does so, Laertes tells Claudius,
"Your Majesty, now I will wound him!" The complicated tangle of
alliances, rivalries, and intrigues now boils down to something simpler: the good Hamlet and his wayward but repentant mother being
destroyed by an evil king and his eager, unsportsmanlike henchman.

A critic watching Kessler play Hamlet in London in 1922 thought
the actor gave a particularly Jewish slant to the role: "Mr. Joseph
Kessler gave us the tragi-tragic Hamlet, the 'Job' who cries from his
troubles, wants consolation, and cannot find it. Better stated: Herr
Kessler gave us a Jewish Hamlet, who suffers more deeply than the
non-Jewish Hamlet, pays more dearly for his sorrows, and rages at the
world in his pain."[75] It is unusual for a Yiddish critic to remark on an
actor giving a Jewish flavor to a non-Jewish role, though the Jewishness of Yiddish Shylocks will form a motif in reviews of Yiddish
versions of *The Merchant of Venice*.

The London critic felt that Kessler never went out of character.
This was not the case in 1917, according to a reviewer who saw Kessler's Hamlet that year in Chicago. Kessler's company at the Haymarket Theatre, the reviewer felt, had not sufficiently studied their roles,
but they could hardly be blamed for that: "the gods themselves would
not have performed any better if they had to study, in three days'
time, *Kreutzer Sonata*; *Khantshe*; *God, Man, and Devil*; *The Cripple*; and
Hamlet."[76]

By the same critic's assessment, the audience at the Haymarket seemed unfazed by any lack of polish on the part of the actors. And like earlier generations of Yiddish theatre critics, this reviewer gave the audience credit for its enthusiastic response to the production, pointing to "the tremendous applause, which also shows that the intelligent audience knows when to applaud. . . . The theatre was packed with intelligent theatregoers, among them many Christians. We hope that Herr Kessler will realize that [staging] better things pays, and that he will present more plays by world-famous writers."[77] The London reviewer echoes his American colleague's observations of the audience as well as his hope for further artistic offerings in the future: "The audience burst out into thunderous applause, and let us hope that from now on, there will be a permanent Yiddish theatre, which is so necessary for the people."[78]

In retrospect, Moyshe Zeifert was at least half correct in his assessment of "the Plague of the Classics." There was nothing that could stop the Yiddish actors from performing Shakespeare as long as the Yiddish theatre was a vital cultural force, and they would often fall short of the greatest Shakespearean interpretations of their counterparts performing in other languages. But in a remarkably short time, Zeifert's colleagues progressed from performing in rough translations like his to more carefully crafted versions. These translations, like most other Yiddish versions of Shakespeare, sought to provide clear, theatrically compelling texts for use in performance, not literary texts that would convey all the metaphorical and poetic nuances found in the original English.

The journey *Hamlet* traveled from its first appearance in Yiddish to Zolatarevsky's adaptation and Bertha Kalish's star vehicles reflects a number of significant aspects of the overall course of the American Yiddish theatre. *Hamlet* began in New York and ultimately moved to the *provints* of other American cities. It started as a means of providing new theatre material and of asserting the company's credentials as performing artists — indeed, in a head-on battle of dueling Shakespeares with the theatre company across the street — and continued to serve as a source of advertising hokum. Meanwhile, it offered a legitimate opportunity for actors to demonstrate that they were legitimate, and that the relatively limited audience for Yiddish theatre was not a reflection on the limits of their talents. The career of one of the more high-minded performers of Shakespeare in Yiddish, Joseph Kessler, also illustrated that the designation "American Yiddish theatre" sometimes had porous boundaries, for there was a regular flow of personnel, productions, and scripts between North America and other venues — particularly Europe, but also South America and Israel.

Hamlet served as a two-way bridge linking American Yiddish culture to American and European culture at large. It helped bring the Yiddish theatre to the attention of non-Yiddish-speaking critics and audiences, for it was familiar enough not to require translation, and thus served as a useful test for evaluating the talents of Yiddish actors. On the other side of the cultural divide, its availability to Yiddish audiences in whatever form made familiar for them one of the most treasured jewels in the crown of Western culture. Within a decade, the American Yiddish theatre went from taking its first tenuous steps in Shakespearean costume to making *Hamlet* its own.

chapter 3

An *Othello* Potpourri

On 27 May 1892, an intriguing advertisement appeared in the
New York Yiddish press. Although the production of *Othello* promoted in the ad would not be performed in Yiddish, it would be
mounted in a Yiddish theatre. The advertisement raises issues that
will resurface throughout the history of Shakespearean production on
the American Yiddish stage in such a striking manner that it merits
being reproduced here almost in its entirety:

Thalia Theatre
46–48 Bowery
Monday evening, the 6th of June, 1892
JUST ONE PERFORMANCE

By the tragedian recognized by all the greatest and
most world-famous European newspapers

MR. MORRIS MORRISON [fig. 10]
Born in Galatz, Romania, as
OTHELLO

The Moor of Venice, by Shakespeare. With an exceptional first-
class German company of artists. The great artist Herr Morris
Morrison has played this role of Othello in the following major
cities in Europe and America: London, Berlin, Petersburg, Moscow, in the Meininger Hoftheater, in Dresden, St. Louis, Philadelphia, Cincinnati, etc. etc.

On Monday, the 6th of June, in the Thalia Theatre, Morris Morrison, the greatest artist of our time, will appear in the role of
"Othello," supported by a first-class, exceptional company of German actors. Herr Morrison was born in Romania, has made the
greatest name for himself in the greatest cities in Europe and
America, and stands on the same level with Salvini, Rossi, etc.
The following are translations from various English and German

10. Advertisement for Morris Morrison's Hamlet *and* Othello *at the Windsor Theatre. From the Dorot Jewish Division, the New York Public Library, Astor, Lenox, and Tilden Foundations.*

newspapers. The German newspaper from Philadelphia. Germania Theatre . . . "The guest performance by the Duke of Meiningen court actor Herr Morris Morrison has been extended for one week. Friends of the theatre will thank the director Heinemann, for he has kept the great artist on for one more week. . . . Rarely on the German stage of Philadelphia has stood an artist of such brilliance and ability, equal to Herr Morrison's power in voice and facial expression. With his handsome, manly appearance, he wins the interest of audiences of the highest caliber."

Translation from an English newspaper: "Of all the Shakespearean roles that Herr Morris Morrison plays so masterfully, he stands higher in the role of 'Othello' than anyone else who plays the role. Herr Morrison is blessed by nature with all the means to be a great tragedian. He has a beautiful, manly appearance. His voice is strong and sweet, and his acting exhibits an admirable talent. In Europe he has long been compared to Salvini, Rossi, Booth, and McCullough."

Another English newspaper: "The great European tragedian Herr Morris Morrison is a talented artist from the famous Meininger court actors. He has a beautiful appearance and a deep, musical voice, so it is a pleasure both to see and hear him. Everywhere Herr Morrison has appeared, he has enjoyed the greatest triumph." One of the greatest European newspapers writes the following about Herr Morrison's Othello: "With the role of Othello, Herr Morrison has reached the highest level of Shakespearean tragedians. His Othello is unsurpassed; his speech in the court when he wins the heart of Desdemona, his acting in the jealousy scene, are incomparable. He performs with all his soul. Wondrous is the scene when he forces Iago to speak and he attempts to kill his beloved Desdemona," etc. . . .[1]

While neither Morrison's name, the play in which he will appear, nor the language in which it will be performed necessarily indicate his ethnic background, readers might have assumed that he was Jewish by virtue of his being born in Galatz, Romania, a city whose Jewish community experienced a rich but turbulent history. The mention of Morrison's birthplace assures the reader that he is what Yiddish-speaking Jews call a *landsman* — literally a countryman, but more broadly, a fellow eastern European Jew. On the other hand, the names of several other cities, both European and American, should assure prospective audience members that if Morrison can make it everywhere else, he can make it in New York. The dual identity of the Yiddish actor — as an artist unencumbered by ethnicity or nationality on the one hand, and as a Jew with a Jewish following on the other — would continue to color the way audiences perceive Yiddish actors throughout the history of the American Yiddish theatre.

The roll call of European and American actors serves essentially the same purpose here as Morrison's illustrious itinerary, indicating that reliable authorities (that is, non-Yiddish newspapers) have recognized that Morrison has earned the honor of having his name mentioned in the same breath as those of his illustrious colleagues. Furthermore, Morrison comes with weighty credentials: as a former member of the renowned Duke of Saxe-Meiningen company, whose name the ad repeatedly invokes, almost like a mantra. But while such references would make perfect sense for audiences familiar with Western theatre, a Yiddish theatregoer in 1892 would be unlikely to recognize any of these names. Assuming that the newspaper reviews cited here are translated more or less faithfully, the references might have made sense to most of their original readers. When transferred to a Yiddish newspaper, on the other hand, this information seems to be dropped into a cultural vacuum. The "Emperor's New Clothes" effect, however, should have sufficed to impress the Yiddish reader, who would probably have sensed that one should be impressed by such names as Salvini and Booth even if they meant nothing in and of themselves.

The advertisement does not shy away from superlatives, but pretends to balance its own subjectivity by relying on "facts" and authorities: newspaper reviews, the actor's background, and his place in the theatrical pantheon. As the Yiddish theatre in the United States develops, the interaction between Yiddish and non-Yiddish theatre escalates, and Yiddish actors and audiences become increasingly — even intensely — aware that other theatrical venues exist. Critics and actors spend a great deal of energy trying to figure out the position of Yiddish theatre within the context of world theatre, and audiences take great pride in pointing out influences of the Yiddish theatre on the English-speaking American stage and screen.

Just as interesting as what the advertisement emphasizes is one significant detail that it hardly mentions. The play's authorship, while cited at the beginning of the text, clearly takes a back seat to the biography of the star performer. References to scenes from the play — again, perhaps instances of information in a vacuum — serve as specific testimonials to the quality of Morrison's acting. In fact, these references may work better in a vacuum than to those familiar with the play, who may find some of the descriptions a bit odd. Othello has already won Desdemona's heart by the time he pleads his case to the Venetian senators; she simply affirms his description of their courtship. And to say that he "attempts" to kill her is an understatement, but then to say anything more about this to an audience unfamiliar with a play could seem like giving away the ending of an Agatha Christie mystery.

Though once an illustrious performer, Morrison had fallen on hard times, and a few months earlier would have been an unlikely candidate to play any Shakespeare character besides perhaps Caliban or the Porter in *Macbeth*. Boris Thomashefsky and his wife Bessie, in memoirs written two decades apart, both describe how Morrison showed up at the Standard Theater in Chicago when Thomashefsky's company was playing there, apparently in the middle to late 1880s. Their accounts diverge in a number of respects, but both agree on the following: Morrison first came to them in tattered clothes and a long beard, and told them his name was Davidson. He eventually landed odd jobs around the theatre, and at one point or another revealed that he was actually Morris Morrison, former star of the German stage.[2]

Beyond that general outline of the story, the couple's recollections of Morrison's arrival differ in several noteworthy respects. Both memoirists describe the mystery that surrounded this strange, very tall, and somehow noble figure, but Bessie's description takes on a religious tone. She dwells on the cast's curiosity about the stranger while he is doing odd jobs around the theatre. Some suggest he may be a king in exile, others a bankrupt tycoon, and still others, a *lamed-vovnik* — according to Jewish folklore, one of the thirty-six saintly people who exist in every generation.[3] The latter theory gains credibility when the cast members notice the disdain with which he seems to look upon their rehearsals; they see a touch of contempt for Yiddish theatre as the sign of an artistically healthy soul.

All doubt as to his saintliness disappears when he intervenes in a fight between a skinny Jew and a strong Gentile, whom Morrison thrashes mercilessly. Afterwards, he reveals his true identity: "He became extraordinarily friendly and spoke with us willingly, justifying himself by saying that he did not mean to beat the poor Gentile so much, but he could not look on while the weak Jew was being beaten, because he himself is a Jew, he told us. And his real name is Moyshe Cohn, but, he smiled amiably, 'On the German stage, my name is Morris Morrison.'"[4] The anecdote resonates with the aura of tales from many religions in which holy men reveal themselves. Given the ambivalence of Yiddish actors toward their own repertoire and practice, the subtext of Bessie Thomashefsky's description rings with a messianic note. This larger-than-life, mysterious figure reveals himself as a man endowed with knowledge and experience from another world: the realm of Gentile theatre.

But Morrison would not be the one to "open a new way" for Yiddish actors. Though some observers, such as Bernard Gorin, saw Morrison as the first to bring "the influence of the better drama" to Yiddish stages,[5] Morrison continued to perform in German rather than in Yiddish. Indeed, in a tribute to Morrison following the actor's death in 1917, Abraham Cahan would remind readers that the actor had performed exclusively in German, adding, "had Morrison learned to perform in plain Yiddish, he would certainly have lost seventy-five percent of his popularity with us."[6] Cahan's assessment rings true, consistent with the Yiddish theatre's inferiority complex at the time. Even the most ardent supporters of Yiddish theatre saw Morrison as a privileged being, one whose Jewishness did not confine him to performing for Jews. Boris Thomashefsky recalled that the first time he went to see Morrison perform, at the German-language Irving Place Theatre in New York, "I was very jealous of that Jew Morrison, who plays in the German theatre before such a public, who come in carriages, dressed up as for a holiday, in frocks and evening dresses."[7] It was this recognition of the German theatre's greater cultural prestige that had led Thomashefsky to call at the Irving Place Theatre when he needed coaching to play Hamlet.

Morrison's final performance, again as Othello, ended a career that straddled different realms of the Diaspora, as an actor performing in German outside of Germany, and occasionally in Yiddish theatres, but never in the Yiddish language. The paradoxical prestige he held as a non-Yiddish-speaking "Yiddish" actor held out the promise of similar kudos to his Yiddish-speaking colleagues. They could not re-invent themselves as stars of the German stage, but they could help give the Yiddish theatre a Shakespeare transfusion.

Morrison's *Othello* in June of 1892 may have helped launch an era. The following October, Jacob Gordin's adaptation of *King Lear* — the first full-length Yiddish play to advertise itself as a Shakespearean adaptation at the time of its premiere — was produced in New York. *Othello* itself would remain a regular offering in the American Yiddish repertoire in subsequent decades, although not in as wide a variety of forms as the Yiddish variations on *King Lear* and *Hamlet*.

A Fully Yiddish Othello

However floridly his supporters praised him, Morrison oc-cupied a peculiar place in the Yiddish theatre — not only by not speaking Yiddish, but by performing a repertoire that had not really taken hold in Yiddish yet. A generation later, Rudolph Schildkraut, already a star on Austrian and German stages before his Yiddish de-but, would resemble a sort of second coming of Morris Morrison on a grander scale.[8] In the meantime, *Othello* would make other appear-ances in Yiddish, starting in the mid-1890s. While neither the script nor reviews of Boris Thomashefsky's 1894 debut in the play seem to have survived, a version by Mikhl Goldberg from approximately the same period remains intact, and offers a glimpse into what Yiddish audiences would have experienced when finally watching *Othello* in Yiddish.[9]

In terms of the text alone, Yiddish audiences would have seen one of Shakespeare's most tightly focused tragedies streamlined even fur-ther, so that the spotlight would shine even stronger on the actors playing Othello and Iago. Goldberg frequently tones down, or elimi-nates altogether, the play's earthy sexual and racial imagery, and shows little interest in finding Yiddish parallels to Shakespeare's use of po-etry. What he provides instead is the essence of a thrilling tale of intrigue.

The American Yiddish theatre, squeamish as it tended to be about sex in this period, would hardly have been comfortable with Shakespeare's opening scene. Shakespeare packs it with brutal metaphors, such as Iago's taunting Brabantio by hinting crudely at the potential offspring of Othello and Desdemona: "You'll have your daughter covered with a Barbary horse; you'll have your nephews neigh to you" (I.i.114–5). No such language appears in Goldberg's text. And when Roderigo chimes in, claiming that Desdemona has gone "To the gross clasps of a lascivious Moor" (I.i.126), Goldberg softens the line by simply saying that she "went with the Moor."[10] Comparable cuts and emendations are made throughout the translation, perhaps most markedly in the near absence of the courtesan Bianca. She appears briefly in Goldberg's version, but more as a mover of props and deliverer of messages than anything else, and certainly not as a prostitute connected to Michael Cassio. Goldberg's changes tacitly acknowledge that while no theatregoer could miss the fact that the plot of *Othello* revolved around a case of sexual jealousy, there was no reason to get into details about, as Iago puts it (but not in Goldberg's version), "the blood and baseness of our natures" (I.iii.328).

Othello is, of course, as famous for its treatment of race as it is for being a parable of jealousy, but Othello's blackness is barely hinted at in Goldberg's version. The translator cuts, for example, most of Brabantio's first speech to Othello, accusing the Moor of binding Desdemona in "chains of magic" without which she never would have "Run from her guardage to the sooty bosom / Of such a thing as thou" (I.ii.70–1). One can only speculate on the reasons for a Yiddish theatre company to be as timid about racial matters as about sexual ones. Indeed, this may seem surprising given the fascination that Yiddish writers would have with the subject a generation later, when such poets as A. Leyeles (1889–1956), H. Leyvik (1888–1962), Berysh Vaynshteyn (1905–1967), and the Communist-oriented Proletpen writers of the 1920s and 1930s would continually revisit the subject. These writers were firmly entrenched in the political culture of the United States. In the 1890s, however, perhaps the audience of Jews who had so recently immigrated — many fleeing persecution in their countries of origin — had weak stomachs for watching a hero mocked for his racial identity. Given the many anecdotes about turn-of-the-century Yiddish audiences' difficulties distinguishing between art and life, a translator like Goldberg may not have trusted them to separate the playwright's point of view from those of individual characters on such a delicate issue.

By eliminating the coarser sexual and racial references, cutting classical allusions that would mean nothing to most of his audience, and translating for clarity rather than poetry, Goldberg provides an expurgated potboiler. His version of *Othello* does not attempt a nuanced treatment of human psychology, but rather a thriller of jealousy, ambition, and murder that might just as easily have been written by a contemporary manufacturer of melodramas of the sort so popular in the contemporary European and American theatre.

Iago, My Yidishe Mama

When Boris Thomashefsky decided to stage Leon Kobrin's *Der blinder muzikant, oder, der yidisher Otelo* (*The Blind Musician, or, the Jewish Othello*) in 1903, he may have been seeking to replicate his success with Zolatarevsky's *The Yeshiva Boy* a few years earlier. Kobrin, born in the Byelorussian city of Vitebsk on 15 March 1872, received a traditional Jewish education, but also fell under the spell of Russian literature. By the age of fifteen, he had sent several stories in Russian to the Russian Jewish journal *Voskhod*, though they were not published. Soon after emigrating to the United States in 1892, Kobrin began publishing Yiddish stories, which won him admirers among New York's Yiddish intellectuals. In 1898, he published his first novel: *Yankl Boyle*, with an introduction by Jacob Gordin.[11]

At about the same time, Kobrin also started taking his first steps toward becoming a playwright. He would later recall being among the audience of Lower East Side intellectuals who gathered during the winter of 1898–1899 to hear Gordin give a lecture series in Russian on the plays of Shakespeare, Molière, and Ibsen. When a Russian immigrant in the audience asked why this primarily Jewish audience was learning about great Gentile writers instead of trying to develop new Jewish ones, several participants were inspired to establish the Fraye yidishe folksbine [Free Yiddish People's Stage], whose purpose was to raise the artistic level of the Yiddish theatre. Charter members included Gordin, Kobrin, and Joel Entin, a Columbia literature student who would eventually become an important Yiddish theatre critic.[12]

Despite its charter, the Fraye yidishe folksbine soon began preparing a production of Ibsen's *Enemy of the People*, in a translation by Gordin. Meanwhile, Kobrin read his first play, *Mina*, to Entin, who was sufficiently impressed to try to get it produced. Gordin, on the other hand, found "some dramaturgic flaws," and according to Entin, attacked the play "without pity." The ensuing debate between Kobrin's supporters — the majority in the room — and Gordin's faction, led the latter group to withdraw from the organization that evening, thereby bringing about its instant demise.[13]

Ironically, Gordin later wrote to Kobrin at Jacob Adler's behest and offered to help shape *Mina* into a stageworthy play. According to Entin, Gordin wrote terse scenarios for the play in Russian, upon which Kobrin elaborated in Yiddish. Gordin either took or was given most of the credit on the posters announcing the play, which opened at the Windsor Theatre on 13 January 1899. Nevertheless, the Yiddish theatre community in New York knew that Kobrin supplied more than just the "idea" for which the ads credited him, and *Mina* launched his career as a dramatist.[14] By the time he wrote *The Blind Musician* for Thomashefsky in 1903, Kobrin had written for each of the "big three" American Yiddish actor/managers — Adler, Kessler, and Thomashefsky — and could boast both critical and box-office success with such works as *Nature, Man, and Beast* (1900) and *Paradise Lost* (1902).

The Blind Musician premiered at the People's Theatre in New York on 6 November 1903. Just as Gordin had been inspired not only by *King Lear*, but by Turgenev's retelling of the story in prose, Kobrin combined sources from Shakespeare and from contemporary Russian fiction, though in Kobrin's case the Russian source was not a new version of the Elizabethan drama. Kobrin took the main title of his play, as well as some of its central themes, from Vladimir Korolenko's novel *The Blind Musician* (1886), which was familiar to many Yiddish readers by the time Kobrin's play opened. The novel had been serialized in a Boston Yiddish weekly, *Der emes*, in 1895, and was reprinted in the *Forverts* in the spring of 1903. Perhaps this reprinting gave Kobrin the idea to make an overt reference in his title to two works that would be well known to Yiddish audiences by the time his play premiered.[15] Polish-Yiddish critic Noah Prilutski would later scoff at Kobrin's habit of borrowing famous titles: "Milton created *Paradise Lost*; Korolenko wrote *The Blind Musician*. Kobrin stitches together two *shund* plays for the American Yiddish stage in his 'shop,' and he has the audacity to name one after the famous English poem, the second after the beautiful Russian étude." [16]

In fact, *The Blind Musician* resembles neither of its ostensible sources so much as it does Gordin's *The Jewish King Lear* and *Mirele Efros*. Korolenko's protagonist, Pyotr, blind from birth, is raised in the country by his mother and uncle, finds his calling in performing the peasant music of his region, and ultimately marries his childhood sweetheart. Kobrin's title character, Yozef Finkelshteyn, a classical composer living in New York City, has been gradually losing his eyesight, and constantly bemoans his affliction from the moment it sets in. His likeness to Pyotr lies only in the externals — that he is blind and is a musician. Similarly, he resembles Othello only in that he erroneously accuses his wife of infidelity, strangles her, and repents his mistake.

Shakespeare's plays had been retold to fit contemporary Jewish life before, but Kobrin was apparently the first Yiddish playwright to adapt a Shakespeare play to an American setting. His characters speak Americanized Yiddish, peppered with such expressions as "never mind," "sure," and "Don't be so fresh." The critic Shmuel Niger, in discussing Kobrin's respect for the Yiddish language (by no means the norm among Yiddish playwrights at the turn of the century), explained that Kobrin used Americanisms because "he wanted, as a naturalist, to be 'true to life,' not because he was untrue to his linguistic instrument." [17] Locales as well as language help establish the play's American environment; Carnegie Hall, the site of Yozef's anticipated debut as composer, hovers promisingly over most of the play.

The play opens in the home of Feygele Finkelshteyn, a wealthy widow, whose mother-in-law, Etl, reflects back on her life as she looks forward to her grandson Yozef's wedding. While the opening monologue provides the sort of bald exposition typical of Yiddish dramas at the time, Kobrin shows his ability to convey vital information artfully, as when Etl muses sadly over her travels "from Minsk to New York, from my husband's grave to my son's grave." [18]

By 1903, opening a Yiddish play with Jewish customs had itself become customary. Here, the occasion is a wedding; Bessie, Yozef's sister, and Sam, her fiancé, bring in lights for the wedding canopy. Bessie shows her grandmother her arm, red from the pinches of Michael Pomp, the foreman in her mother's shop. The womanizing Michael is also a "bluffer" — American Yiddish for a congenital braggart — and a bully. When he picks a fight with Sam, Bessie urges her fiancé to fight back, reminding him, "You told me you can fight like Fitz" — an allusion to the British boxer Bob Fitzsimmons, who won world titles in three different weight classes between 1891 and 1903.[19] Michael kicks Sam, prompting him to give a lesson in American manners: "Say, don't fight like a greenhorn. . . . An American fights with his hands, not with his feet."

Relationships among the characters echo both Gordin and Shakespeare. Etl left most of her fortune to her son, whose gratitude his wife did not share. Feygele's marriage to Michael a bit later in the play harks back to those of Gertrude/Claudius and Dvoyre/Todres in being an unwise match that ultimately causes harm to the son. Mikhl Goldberg toned down the sexuality of *Hamlet* in his translation, but Kobrin puts an image in Yozef's mouth that, with a slight emendation, could easily be uttered by Hamlet: "Mother, your bed is polluted with shame and with the blood of your children." The central theme of blindness also recalls both *Lear* and *The Jewish King Lear*. Unlike Korolenko's protagonist, but like both Gloucester and Dovid Moysheles, Yozef begins the play with his sight intact. His mother wants to marry him off while he still can see — not out of concern for him, but to get him off her hands — and has deceitfully told him that the doctor said his eyes will heal on their own.

Act I ends with the combination of marriage and mourning used so effectively in both *Mirele Efros* and *The Yeshiva Boy*. Guests enter and dance, and then listen to the memorial prayer "El mole rakhmim" (God, full of mercy), for which Yozef has composed a new melody. Kobrin heightens the sentimentality further, for as the prayer comes to an end, Yozef realizes that his blindness is now total: "Rosa, grandmother, where are you all? I don't see you any more, it is dark around me . . . darkest night, I am blind." He falls, and so does the curtain.

It is a highly contrived moment, of course. Prilutski found the scene to be thoroughly unconvincing when Thomashefsky brought the play to Warsaw in 1913: "In the very midst of the festive ceremony, on that very spot beneath the four poles [of the bridal canopy], Kobrin's hero suddenly goes blind. Why not deaf? That would be a greater catastrophe for à musician! But that is what the playwright wants, and so we must be satisfied as well. At least the curtain fell at that moment, so one could go for a smoke in the foyer."[20] Valid as Prilutski's complaints may have been, such moments made American Yiddish audiences "lick their fingers," as the Yiddish expression goes. Furthermore, the theme of blindness may have struck a deep chord with Kobrin's original audience of recent immigrants, whose entry into the promised land at the turn of the century hinged largely on the health of their eyes:

> At this time, trachoma, a severe and contagious form of con-junctivitis that can cause blindness, was widespread among the European emigrating classes, and — though it was curable — the United States authorities regarded its presence in an arriving im-migrant as grounds for immediate deportation. There was, conse-quently, a separate station for eye inspection, and the quick though necessarily uncomfortable maneuver performed there by the ex-aminer . . . was to become a virtual medieval horror in immigrant folklore, all the more so because the possibility of rejection at this point was frighteningly real.[21]

This ordeal, recent history for much of Kobrin's audience, could lead them to empathize with Yozef's plight all the more strongly.[22] Prilutski, on the other side of the Atlantic, may not have appreciated the potential evocativeness of such moments. He also belonged to a distinctly "high-art" circle of critics and writers, who tended to scoff at American Yiddish melodramas. Back in America, on the other hand, the critic for the *Fraye arbeter shtime* found Yozef's situation compelling, and argued that while Kobrin "followed closely in Shake-speare's footsteps" in the exploration of jealousy, he found a more effective way of exploring this emotion:

> The jealousy that Kobrin depicts in his drama comes across in a stronger, more passionate form, since it is the jealousy of a blind man.
> Love, goes an adage, is blind. The nature of jealousy, however, is that it makes you see things that never existed. . . . Such jealousy,

be it ever so passionate, always has a comic element. . . . With a blind man, the comic element falls away, and we have before us the terrible feeling of jealousy in all its horror.[23]

Indeed, by having eliminated the elaborate villainy of an Iago, Kobrin needs a device like blindness to make the protagonist's jealousy plausible.

Act II begins three months later, on a pretty autumn morning in a back parlor at Feygele's. Cigarettes and cards lie strewn about the messy room, with empty bottles and glasses on the table. Michael and Feygele have gotten married, but he is as unruly as ever. He tells Rosa that her beauty is wasted on a blind man; after she rebuffs him, he flirts with the maid. Meanwhile, Yozef's self-pity foreshadows the undoing of his own marriage; in one of his weaker moments, he pedantically tells Rosa:

> They say that the great Russian writer Fyodor Dostoyevsky felt the greatest pleasure when he had a toothache. You seem to seek the same sort of pleasure, but such pleasure is sick, unnatural. I want you to have natural pleasure, but I can't give it to you. Rosele, your love for me is nothing more than a toothache. How it tortures me, how it torments me! How much longer can you suffer and savor this toothache?

The so-called toothache threatens to increase in intensity at the slightest provocation, which comes, of course, in the form of Michael Pomp. While Yozef gives the family a preview of the love song he has composed for his Carnegie Hall debut (fig. 11), Michael stealthily approaches Rosa and kisses her. Yozef, his other senses heightened to compensate for his loss of vision, senses something amiss, but Rosa tries to spare her husband any unnecessary discomfiture by keeping silent. Her plan backfires, though, when the jealous Feygele exposes her husband. Rosa, confident that her innocence speaks for itself, refuses to defend herself. Yozef unconvincingly insists on his wife's innocence, then falls to the ground in torment, the physical darkness that precipitated his earlier fall now intensified by an emotional morass as well.

Act III takes place three days later. Unlike Desdemona, Rosa sees her husband's jealousy in its early stages, and having no patience for his unjust accusations, she has moved back to her father's house.

11. Leon Kobrin's The Blind Musician, *Act I.*
From the Archives of the YIVO Institute for Jewish Research.

Yozef pours his restlessness into the piano, although it is only six o'clock in the morning. When Michael returns drunk from a successful night of gambling, Yozef flies at him and knocks him down.[24] Etl runs in and finds her grandson on the ground, and he complains to her that everyone knows that Rosa really belongs to Michael.

Yozef gets a second chance with Rosa, but she returns to him only to find him more suspicious than ever, and decides that they can no longer be together. Nevertheless, she agrees to stay until after the concert, and he proclaims as if she were not there, "She stays . . . yes . . . her bloody throat." He grabs her by the throat, she screams, and he pulls her to him, bringing Act III to its puzzling conclusion.

To make matters curiouser and curiouser, we still find Rosa with Yozef as the curtain goes up on Act IV. She sleeps through the ominous thunder and lightning, but he cannot, and when she awakens, he asks her to sing his love song to try to calm him. But it has just the opposite effect, and he cries: "False! False! That was created out of self-deception! I should not have created a love song, but a song about a deceived, blind artist!" He tears up the music, strangles his wife, then immediately regrets the act. His cries rouse the rest of the household, and when his mother asks, "Yozef, what have you done?" he responds bitterly, "You have eyes; you can see. Mama, be a mother at least and strangle me." A policeman arrives to arrest Yozef, who tears himself away to fall upon Rosa's corpse as the final curtain falls.

The Blind Musician met with mixed critical reception. The *Fraye ar-beter shtime*'s two-part review hailed the play as Kobrin's best to date, though "he has yet to write his masterpiece."[25] The chief faults, complained the critic, were an entirely superfluous fourth act and the presence of too many unnecessary characters; he suspected that Kobrin had included some of them only to provide work for the entire People's Theatre company, a troupe whose composition made it necessary for some of the actresses to play male parts.

The *Fraye arbeter shtime* critic defended many of Kobrin's artistic choices, including the drastic one of removing from his adaptation a Iago-like villain who orchestrates his foe's downfall in an almost inexorable manner. Kobrin's erstwhile friend Joel Entin[26] was less impressed by the juxtaposition of jealousy and blindness: "From the plot synopsis alone, the reader can tell how the two things trip up the playwright and he doesn't know how to unravel them."[27] In particular, wrote Entin, the absence of a true villain led Kobrin to contrive "caprices" for the otherwise exemplary Yozef in order to move the plot along:

> But even capriciousness is not enough to turn Yozef into a Jewish Othello. Shakespeare's Othello believed bad things of his Desdemona because of Iago, the smartest, and as Othello believes, the noblest person in the drama. But Yozef, the "Jewish Othello," hears how the most honorable, smartest, and noblest people in the play speak rapturously of Rosa, and only the most bestial, dishonorable, and lowly besmirch her with their unclean mouths.[28]

Entin suggests that Iago's effectiveness stems not just from his evil, but from his almost unanimously accepted semblance of virtue. Michael and Feygele, on the other hand, are unsympathetic from the moment they first appear. Since Yozef knows this as fully as the audience does, his acceptance of their slandering of Rosa does strain belief.

Kobrin gives up a great deal by excluding a villain on the scale of Iago, but the sacrifice makes some sense within the context of his aesthetics. First of all, Kobrin's dramaturgic style, following in the footsteps of such European contemporaries as Ibsen and Hauptmann, did not easily lend itself to a character like Iago, much of whose evil charm emerged in his many soliloquies, unacceptable devices in realism's world of fourth-wall illusion. Perhaps more important, Iago was too far gone in his villainy to appeal to a playwright like Kobrin, who sought to paint *lebnsbilder* (pictures of life) in his dramas. Less drastic villainy, like bullying, philandering, and ingratitude, was more to Kobrin's taste, though the *Fraye arbeter shtime* critic anticipated that some viewers would feel that Kobrin had already overstepped the bounds of decency: "Many wonder why it was necessary for the author to portray a Jewish mother as terrible as the one in *The Blind Musician*." [29]

Harshest among Kobrin's critics was Prilutski, who seems to have been disappointed by the boundless patience of the Warsaw audience: "not one putrid egg, not one rotten apple went flying through the auditorium that evening." [30] Back in New York at the time of the play's premiere, Joel Entin tempered his many critiques with a few words of qualified praise: "There are in the play a few strong moments, a number of psychological insights, a few living characters, and healthy humor in some places." Nevertheless, he was forced to conclude that "In short, the romanticism of Shakespeare's play does a dance with the coarse burlesque jokes of a vaudeville show." [31]

Shakespeare as "Art Theatre"

Shakespeare's plays managed to coexist with those of Gordin, Goldfaden, Lateiner, and Hurwitz. While several Shakespearean translations and adaptations would remain popular in revival, the teens brought the beginning of the end for new American Yiddish interpretations of Shakespeare. The Yiddish theatrical avant-garde began in the early 1920s — or more precisely, in 1922, with the landmark revival of Goldfaden's *Di kishefmakherin* [*The Sorceress*] by the Moscow State Yiddish Theatre (generally known by its Russian acronym, Goset). That production, directed by Alexander Granovsky and with a script adapted by Yekhezkel Dobrushin, helped establish Goldfaden as a home-grown "classic." [32] Throughout the 1920s, major troupes in the Soviet Union, Poland, and the United States led the way toward rediscovering the Yiddish repertoire by using the techniques of the contemporary theatre. With new ways of presenting familiar texts and a new wave of talent in the form of such writers as H. Leyvik, Osip Dimov, and Perets Hirshbayn, the Yiddish theatre was becoming less dependent on adapting the non-Yiddish repertoire and more focused on developing its own products. Yiddish theatre companies rarely competed with each other to produce Shakespeare's plays any more; one of the last holdouts in the United States was Maurice Schwartz's Yiddish Art Theatre.

The Yiddish Art Theatre presented three Shakespearean premieres during its three decades of activity, but the theatre's production of *Othello* in 1929 was its only treatment of Shakespeare qua Shakespeare, or in other words, of non-Judaized Shakespeare.[33] At first glance, the Yiddish Art Theatre might seem an ideal agent for bringing Shakespeare to Yiddish audiences. Maurice Schwartz (c. 1888–1960), its director, had studied the classics and performed with most of the major Yiddish interpreters of Shakespeare. Furthermore, he sought to raise the artistic level of the Yiddish theatre repertoire. The latter aim, in fact, partly explains the scarcity of Shakespeare plays among the more than 130 different productions the company mounted. One of the Yiddish Art Theatre's most important achievements was its contribution to an indigenous Yiddish drama; in addition to reviving classics by Gordin, Kobrin, Sholem Aleykhem, and others, it helped launch the careers of a new generation of playwrights, such as Leyvik and Hirshbayn. The overall health of the American Yiddish drama was strongest when it relied on Shakespeare least.

Yet even when the reserve of talented Yiddish playwrights was richest, the Yiddish theatre did not entirely turn its back on the Gentile playwright who had provided it with so much source material. The mainstays of the Yiddish Shakespearean repertoire, such as *Hamlet*, Gordin's *Lear* variations, and Zolatarevsky's *The Yeshiva Boy*, enjoyed continued revivals, and on 31 January 1929, at a benefit performance for Maurice Schwartz, the Yiddish Art Theatre presented a new translation of *Othello*, starring Schwartz as Iago, Ben-Zvi (Paul) Baratoff as Othello, and Celia Adler as Desdemona (figs. 12, 13).

The translator, Mark Schweid (1891–1969), had already made a name for himself as an actor and poet, and signs of his skill emerge at numerous points in the text. Schweid's translation, more than

12. Maurice Schwartz as Iago at the Yiddish Art Theatre, 1929.
From the Archives of the YIVO Institute for Jewish Research.

any extant text that had been produced in the United States before it, carefully follows Shakespeare's rhyme scheme. Schweid not only shifts from prose to verse whenever Shakespeare does, but even tries to find a Yiddish approximation for Shakespeare's rhymes. Take, for example, the Duke's comments following the reconciliation of Othello and his new father in-law, Brabantio:

13. Ben-Zvi Baratoff as Othello with Celia Adler as Desdemona at the Yiddish Art Theatre, 1929. From the Archives of the YIVO Institute for Jewish Research.

What cannot be preserv'd when Fortune takes,
Patience her injury a mockery makes.
The robb'd that smiles steals something from the thief;
He robs himself that spends a bootless grief. (I.iii.206–9)

Schweid renders the Yiddish as follows:

Vos s'lozt zikh nit farhitn, loz dem falshn glik
Un far zayn krenkung gib im mit geduld tsurik.
Baroybst dem royber, ven a shmeykhldig baroybter bist,
Der ganvet bloyz bay zikh, ver s'paynigt zikh umzist.[34]

Schweid conveys the meaning of the passage as he creates a rhyme scheme parallel to the pattern of the original, but in doing so, he makes the verse difficult for the actors to speak. Where Shakespeare delivers the rhyme in elegant iambic pentameter, Schweid's rhymes come in Alexandrine form, with the third line above stretching to a fourteen-syllable gallop that might easily turn the Duke a royal purple. Such passages led critic Nokhem Bukhvald to conclude, "The translation loses almost all of the magic of Shakespeare's poetry. . . . What [Schweid] has given us in Yiddish is very nice, but it is not Shakespeare."[35]

Bukhvald's critique of the text itself placed him in the minority, for the other Yiddish critics tended to praise Schweid's work, albeit without specifying why. Both viewpoints have some merit; Bukhvald correctly recognized that Schweid failed to make Shakespeare's poetry soar, but perhaps what Schweid's champions admired were both his careful attention to, and clear understanding of, the original. At least the fragment of the text that survives — about two-thirds of the play — follows the original in both the meaning of the lines and the arrangement of the scenes more than was customary in the American Yiddish theatre.

At the same time, the production called attention to its own experimental endeavors. The play's director, Soviet-trained Boris Glagolin, offered a sharply stylized production whose "modernistic" set impressed *New York Sun* critic Stephen Rathbun:

There are tall columns, some painted orange, others painted black, and in one scene there is a banquet table placed at such an extreme slant that if it were aboard a ship no soup would be served until the storm had abated. These settings . . . were like a blending of the Russian style with a touch of the Norman Bel-Geddes magic. And certainly the scene with the banquet table on an incline was bizarre enough to suggest that cinema masterpiece, "The Cabinet of Dr. Caligari."[36]

Not everyone admired the production's modernistic trappings. While Bukhvald also recognized that the director "has adorned the play with outward spectacle," he added sourly: "But it is not an interesting spectacle." [37]

One element of the spectacle did manage to attract most of the critics' interest, if not their approval. In place of the orchestra pit, Glagolin had a tank of water built that could serve as a Venetian canal in Act I and the Cyprus harbor afterward. The proximity of the story's setting to bodies of water did not convince the critics that such an elaborate design served the play, and Glagolin's direction did little to help integrate the water into the action. The only direct uses he made of the water were to bring Iago and Roderigo onstage in a gondola at the beginning, and for a little girl to play with a ball, which rolled into the water later in the evening. The critics found these to be flimsy pretexts for building the water tank, on which they heaped their sarcasm. Cahan continually referred to it as a bathtub and Rathbun suggested, "All that was needed was some fish to make it the most popular feature of the production." [38] Bukhvald reminded his readers that the set of the 1924 Yiddish Art Theatre production of Perets Hirshbayn's *Ghosts Know What*, also included "several thousand gallons of real water. And just as we did not understand at the time why there needed to be real water in a play, we do not understand now either — unless it is to make fools marvel." [39]

Glagolin undoubtedly had nobler motives in mind: using the water not just for the sake of spectacle in and of itself, but also as a means of underscoring the play's Mediterranean flavor, in both its setting and its source. This would have been consistent with other production choices. Glagolin drew on the commedia dell'arte to make Othello's servant into a harlequin and Bianca into a columbine, and turned to more recent Italian arts for the production's music, from Verdi's *Otello*. [40] The *New York Times* critic was more receptive to these choices than his colleagues were, finding that "the orthodox impression of the play is lost in something else — something which is none the less impressive because of its strangeness. If it is Shakespeare, it is Shakespeare with a new tempo, a color which is Oriental and not Elizabethan." [41] The play's Italian setting may not have been the only impetus for using commedia elements; Glagolin's former countryman,

Vsevolod Meyerhold, began experimenting with such techniques in the early 1900s, and inspired other directors to do the same.

Glagolin also brought the role of Iago more in line with Shakespeare's source for *Othello*, a novella by Italian Renaissance writer Giambattista Giraldi Cinthio. As the *New York Times* reviewer observed, "The Iago of Glagolin and of Giraldi Cinthio is a despised and rejected suitor of Desdemona, whose sick passion for the Moor's white lady is in the acting of Maurice Schwartz persistently in evidence."[42] One bit of "evidence" in that direction was Schwartz's Iago picking up the shawl Desdemona dropped and clasping it to his breast.[43] Such moments added up to what the *New York Times* critic saw as "a new Iago": "As Mr. Schwartz plays the part and in the costume he wears there is a deal more Mephistopheles in the character than there is of Iago."[44] *Forverts* editor Abraham Cahan also found a different Iago than he had expected, but felt that the production suggested motivations other than diabolism for Iago's treachery: "Glagolin has turned Iago into a sort of psychopath, a sick man with not-too-healthy nerves . . . a dark demon in human form, a patient from a sanitarium. That is how Maurice Schwartz plays Iago, and if you forget about Shakespeare's Iago, he plays him very well."[45] Cahan concluded that Schwartz's interpretation led the critic almost to pity Iago. One certainly would have to "forget about Shakespeare's Iago" to appreciate such a response to the character who so coldly schemes to bring about so much destruction.

Schwartz led the rest of the cast in a broad, declamatory style of acting; in Cahan's words, "Just as they declaim with their voices, they also do so with their feet and hands."[46] Cahan took care to point out that such stylized acting could be worthwhile, and reminded his readers that the greatest Yiddish actors of the previous generation, such as David Kessler and Sara Adler, also tended to throw all their limbs into their performances. Nokhem Bukhvald was less receptive to such energetic gestures, concluding that Schwartz's Iago "sometimes descended to the level of an operatic villain."[47] Yet Bukhvald conceded that one quality in Schwartz's acting kept his performance from being a total failure: "He made a strong impression at certain moments from suspenseful silences, from dramatic stillnesses."[48] Cahan felt that Schwartz "shouts too much,"[49] and B. Y. Goldshteyn concurred: "If that man does not lose his voice by the end of the play's five-week run, it will be a miracle." [50] No miracle was necessary, though — just disinterested audiences. "Perhaps a Sunday afternoon audience is not of a very discriminating character," observed one reviewer, "but it was unfortunate that in two of the most dramatic moments something more than an audible snicker was heard in several parts of the theater." [51] Given such reactions, it should have come as little surprise that the production folded after just two weeks.

The Yiddish Art Theatre's *Othello* was far from the first American Yiddish version of Shakespeare to disappoint both audiences and reviewers. Nevertheless, Glagolin's production moved several Yiddish critics to ask, as Abraham Cahan bluntly put it, "Should we perform Shakespeare in Yiddish at all?" [52] At first glance, the question seems anachronistic, given the tradition by that point of some forty years of Yiddish Shakespeare in the United States. The same question had surfaced in print before, but the critical successes of such stars as Bertha Kalish and Jacob Adler seemed to put it to rest. The reappearance of this issue in 1929 suggests that critics saw Glagolin's *Othello* as separate from that tradition in ways that demanded the matter to be raised anew.

Variations on Cahan's question by other Yiddish critics who reviewed Glagolin's *Othello* indicate that those critics now demanded something more of Shakespeare in Yiddish than mere faithfulness to the text, or even a "mere" outstanding star performance. One aspect of the production's approach to the original that annoyed some of the Yiddish critics was its self-consciously experimental approach. Cahan sarcastically remarked,

> When Americans or Englishmen, Germans or Frenchmen go to see a Shakespeare play, they want to see Shakespeare's play itself. Our Yiddish theatre audience, however, has evolved much further than the Americans, English, Germans, and French — or so Mr. Glagolin and Maurice Schwartz have decided. For Jews, one cannot present Shakespearean Shakespeare. His Othello has to be cut up and presented anew. [53]

Echoing Cahan, Alexander Mukdoyni complained that "Germans, Englishmen, and Frenchmen find it suitable to give traditional Shakespeare productions, but we Jews want to give modernistic Shakespeare productions."[54] This generalization was hardly warranted by the example of just one production, nor were Shakespeare productions in other cultures so consistently "traditional," but to a critic of Mukdoyni's turn of mind, the American Yiddish theatre had not yet produced enough "Shakespearean Shakespeare" to support such unabashedly experimental efforts.

While Goldshteyn of the *Fraye arbeter shtime* also disliked the production's modernistic approach, he noticed the promise of a richer, more interesting work beneath the surface. He compared *Othello* to the same company's recent revival of *God, Man, and Devil*, Jacob Gordin's version of the Faust legend. Schwartz had played the Mephistophelian Uriel Mazik, who dons traditional Jewish clothing to lead astray the pious protagonist; Celia Adler played Freydenyu, a niece of the Faust figure:

> Maurice Schwartz very successfully transformed Iago into Uriel Mazik. . . . When he neither Urieled nor Maziked, he failed. Celia Adler be-Freydenyued Desdemona so beautifully, and whenever she recalled that she was playing not Freydenyu, but a Shakespearean heroine, she failed. M. B. Shmuelovitsh played a Hasidic rabbi, a community leader, not a Venetian Doge. . . . If they had not translated *Othello*, but simply Judaized it, we would have had a fine production.[55]

Goldshteyn had history on his side; American Yiddish audiences embraced Shakespeare most warmly when his plays were reconfigured to suit a Jewish idiom. Perhaps Schwartz and Glagolin missed a golden opportunity to present an *Othello* with a Jewish flavor, if not an extensively Judaized version of the play.

The production's shortcomings have conspired to overshadow its place as a cultural landmark, albeit it a flawed one. The art theatre movement had taken hold in the major centers of Yiddish theatre — particularly New York, Warsaw, and Moscow — a decade before, yet Shakespeare had been essentially absent from their repertoire. Throughout his career at the helm of the Yiddish Art Theatre, Schwartz would prove a master of balancing the demands of the box office and his artistic ambitions, and one way of doing so was to keep

an eye on what his counterparts in Europe were doing and then emu-
lating them, directly or indirectly. Yet when it came to staging Shakespeare, it was Schwartz who was in the vanguard; it would not be until
the mid-1930s that the most significant productions of Shakespeare's
plays in Yiddish would be mounted in Europe: *King Lear* at the Moscow State Yiddish Theatre in 1935, starring Solomon Mikhoels as
Lear and Benjamin Zuskin as the Fool; and Aaron Tseytlin's version
of *The Tempest* at the Folks un Yugnt-Teater in Warsaw in 1939, with
Avrom Morevski as Prospero.

Othello moves so inexorably toward the hero's downfall, with so
little distraction from the main line of action, that it seems not to have
needed Judaizing in the way that some other Shakespeare plays might
have in order to fare well in Yiddish. Then again, the same might also
be said of *Macbeth*, which "Moyshe" received far more coolly. D. M.
Hermalin's translation of the Scottish play ran at the Thalia Theatre
on the 3rd and 4th of May 1895 — then vanished as if in a puff of
smoke from the witches' cauldron. Yet crystal-clear though the story
line of *Macbeth* may be, an audience of new immigrants struggling to
get to the next rung above the bottom of the socioeconomic ladder
might have had trouble relating to a cautionary tale on the evils of
ambition.

Othello, on the other hand, offered domestic tragedy, and what
theatregoer had not felt pangs of jealousy? This community may have
had particularly strong reasons to empathize with Othello's plight: a
husband who had immigrated to America before his wife might begin
to doubt whether she had remained true to him; the wife left behind
might well wonder whether some American beauty had turned her
husband's head. Perhaps the Yiddish audience, whose children and
grandchildren would champion liberal causes so passionately, also
sympathized with the plight of a protagonist shunned and reviled because of his race.

But *Othello* never became much of a "problem play" in Yiddish —
at least not in an overt sense. Perhaps that is because it was inherently
the right play for the right audience — a play that spells out its characters' emotions in bold capital letters. One would have to struggle
against the text to downplay Othello's emotions. Just a moment into
the action, for example, Iago describes the general's elaborate rhe-
torical style:

> Three great ones of the city,
> In personal suit to make me his lieutenant,
> Off-capped to him . . .
> But he (as loving his own pride and purposes)
> Evades them with a bumbast circumstance
> Horribly stuff'd with epithites of war . . . (I.i.8 –14)

Other characters frequently allude to Othello's passionate nature, setting him up for an emotionally spectacular fall. As Iago goads him further and further into the throes of jealousy, Othello "falls into a trance," which Cassio comes upon:

Cassio: What's the matter?
Iago: My lord is fall'n into an epilepsy.
This is his second fit; he had one yesterday.
Cassio: Rub him about the temples.
Iago: [No, forbear,]
The lethargy must have his quiet course;
If not, he foams at mouth, and by and by
Breaks out to savage madness. (IV.i.49 –55)

A Morris Morrison or a Boris Thomashefsky would have been only too happy to illustrate such a graphic description.

To say that the American Yiddish audience had little patience for understatement is . . . well, an understatement. In that sense, *Othello* may have been the most purely entertaining Shakespeare play from the Yiddish vantage point. Yiddish adaptors of other Shakespeare plays found ways to convey powerful messages to their audiences in cleverly rewritten parables mounted on a Shakespearean foundation, but that never happened with *Othello* — perhaps because there was no need to. *Othello* already had the right ingredients without trying to give it a Jewish flavor. If a Yiddish Shakespearean wanted to send a message, he could call King Lear. Or Romeo and Juliet . . .

chapter 4

'Parents Have Hearts of Stone'
Romeo and Juliet

If Jewish parents found in *King Lear* the ultimate parable of
filial disloyalty, their children could turn to *Romeo and Juliet* to teach
the older generation a lesson about the consequences of parental tyranny. In the latter play, after all, it is the children who are sacrificed
on the altar of their parents' petty hatred; as the Prince chastises the
patriarchs at the close of the tragedy,

> Capulet! Montague!
> See what a scourge is laid upon your hate,
> That heaven finds means to kill your joys with love. (V.iii.291–3)

The eastern European Jewish immigrants to the United States came
to a society that held different assumptions than theirs about both romantic love and arranged marriages, two subjects pivotal to Romeo's
and Juliet's predicament. By extension, such differences reflected a
broad range of others that would often drive a wedge between the
generations of immigrant families: religious traditions, clothing, language, leisure, and so on. By making his versions of *Lear* end happily,
Gordin had told the older generations that it was all right to follow
their children while goading the children to respect their parents'
point of view. The translators and adaptors of *Romeo and Juliet*, on the
other hand, frequently teach by negative example, as they preserve
(and often amplify) Shakespeare's tragic ending.

The Great Lover

Out of the whole gamut of Shakespeare's tragic heroes, Romeo was clearly best suited to Boris Thomashefsky's temperament.
Few descriptions of Thomashefsky's acting indicate that he could
be entirely convincing playing Hamlet's introspectiveness, Lear's rage

and grandeur, Othello's jealousy and majesty, or Shylock's menace and humiliation. But romantic love was Thomashefsky's stock-in-trade, both onstage and off. Given the long list of love affairs that dominates his autobiography, the actor may have had to think hard to imagine Romeo's fatal constancy to one woman, but playing the romantic leading man was what Thomashefsky did best.

Thomashefsky's company at the Thalia introduced the play to Yiddish audiences on 14 September 1894, resuming the war of words it had launched when it pitted its *Hamlet* against the Windsor's *Othello*:

> Victory! Triumph! Art! Poetry! The Thalia Theatre has taken upon itself the difficult and holy task of familiarizing the Yiddish public with the divine work of Shakespeare, and will therefore produce *Romeo and Juliet*. Only the Thalia Theatre trusts the Yiddish theatregoer, and when we presented *Hamlet*, our competition made fun of us. How can "Moyshe" go to Shakespeare? How can the little Jew understand such a divine, serious work? The astonishing effect of *Hamlet* showed that the Yiddish public loves, esteems, and understands great, instructive, serious works, and we are going on to present *Romeo and Juliet* as well. . . . Shakespeare's *Romeo and Juliet* should be a temple of writing and a school for learning and understanding.[1]

It was actually Windsor Theatre, presumably the "competition" alluded to here, that beat the Thalia to the punch in producing Shakespeare, and the Thalia's advertisement suggests that Thomashefsky is still smarting from the insults heaped upon him when the Windsor's *Othello* went head-to-head with the Thalia's *Hamlet*. Here the Thalia co-opts the Windsor's rhetoric, giving itself sole responsibility for "the difficult and holy task of familiarizing the Yiddish public with the divine work of Shakespeare." This may have sounded peculiar coming from the company that specialized in operettas, but the Thalia was not about to let its most commercially successful products keep it from venturing into more critically respected territory. A subsequent press release reinforced this message, asking rhetorically, "Where else can you find so classic a *Hamlet* and so poetic a Romeo as Thomashefsky?"[2]

Thomashefsky performed his poetic Romeo regularly once he added it to his offerings in 1894. Surviving playscripts, in fact, indicate that not only did he appear in the role often, but that he used several related but distinct versions of the play over the years. It is not clear which of them was first produced at the Thalia. All of the texts share a number of striking characteristics, suggesting that either the first of them or a common source had a direct influence on the rest. They all make cuts, changes, and additions designed to maintain the focus on the title characters, heighten the sentimentality of their love for each other, and maximize the pathos of the final death scene. Within these parameters, however, each translation has its own personality, its own unique approach to certain scenes and passages. Examining these translations collectively provides us with a composite portrait of how *Romeo and Juliet* was presented to American Yiddish audiences.[3]

All of the extant translations cut the Prologue as well as the opening dialogue, consisting of banter between two of the Capulets' servants. The Yiddish versions begin with raw action rather than words: the sword fight between servants of the Montagues and Capulets. This is logical enough; Shakespeare's opening dialogue is filled with wordplay that would be all but impossible to translate, and in terms of sheer exposition, the dueling that comes a moment later tells us what we need to know.

Against this background of the ongoing feud, Shakespeare introduces Romeo, who it may be worth reminding ourselves is pining away at this point not for Juliet, but for a young lady named Rosaline. His friends argue that he dotes on her only because he has not seen enough other women: "Compare her face with some that I shall show, / And I shall make thee think thy swan a crow" (I.ii.86–7). The fact that Romeo can fall so quickly for Juliet after his initial lovesickness over Rosaline suggests that he may be at least as much a paragon of fickleness as of romance. Friar Lawrence, for one, is scandalized by the rapid change in Romeo's affections:

> Holy Saint Francis, what a change is here!
> Is Rosaline, that thou didst love so dear,
> So soon forsaken? Young men's love then lies
> Not truly in their hearts, but in their eyes.
> Jesu Maria, what a deal of brine
> Hath wash'd thy sallow cheeks for Rosaline!
> How much salt water thrown away in waste,
> To season love, that of it doth not taste! (II.iii.65–72)

The Friar's lament does not appear in the Yiddish versions, which bend over backwards to avoid making Romeo seem capricious. One script (1302C) has him yearning for an unnamed woman early in the play, while all of the others explicitly name Juliet as the source of his sorrow right from the beginning: "O Juliet, Juliet," he sighs in one version (1302D). Another goes a few steps further. After sending his friends ahead of him to the Capulet ball, Romeo delivers the following soliloquy:

Zol komen vos es vil, nokh eyn mol vil ikh mayn Yulye zen. Durkh mayn maske verde ikh ir mayn laydenshaft tsaygn. Ober mayn no-men must zi nikht visn. Tsvar vird der has tsvishn unzere eltern fon tog tsu tog farmert, ober tsvishn mir un Yulye izt es grade umgekert. (1302A)

[Come what may, I want to see my Juliet one more time. I will show her my sorrows through my mask, but she must not know my name. The hatred between our parents grows from day to day, but it is quite the contrary between Juliet and me.]

In providing this glimpse into Romeo's thoughts, translator Mendl Teplitski also borrows an Elizabethan dramatic technique by ending the scene with a rhymed couplet: "*farmert / umkegert.*"

The Yiddish versions also erase Romeo's accidental involvement in his friend Mercutio's death. Shakespeare's Romeo, attempting to break up a sword fight between Tybalt and Mercutio, actually makes things worse. After he is mortally wounded, Mercutio asks Romeo, "Why the devil came you between us? I was hurt under your arm" (III.i.102–3). Not so in the Yiddish theatre, where Romeo is kept at some remove from the duel, and Mercutio's line is cut.

The translators often change certain key details about Juliet as well. All of them, for example, make her somewhat older than Shakespeare does. Shakespeare's Nurse figures out that her charge is fourteen, but for reasons of either verisimilitude, propriety, or both, the Yiddish Juliet is made a few years older: seventeen in some cases, eighteen in others. One version also removes any hint of lessened devotion to Romeo, however fleeting. In Shakespeare, immediately after she spends the night with Romeo, Juliet assures her mother how much she hates him for having killed Tybalt. Later in the same scene, she seems to feign agreement — which she disavows in a brief soliloquy a moment later — with the Nurse's plan that she marry Paris. Mikhl Goldberg does not let Juliet go even this far. Not only does she refrain from bad-mouthing Romeo for her mother's benefit, but she paraphrases part of the Shakespearean soliloquy in a passionate speech addressed directly to the Nurse: "Get away from me! You and my heart are strangers from now on. I am going to Friar Lawrence. If he cannot help me, I still have enough power to die" (1302, page 31).

All of these changes suited an aesthetic that shied away from ambivalence in dramatic heroes and villains — or to put it another way, preferred melodramatic characters to tragic ones. And just as translators often clean up Romeo's and Juliet's dialogue to ensure that their love comes across as pure and unwavering, actors and directors often further eliminated ambiguity through carefully conceived stage pictures. All of the tableaux described in the different versions derive from an acting style that tended to rely more on gesture than on tone and diction; as Jacob Mestel observed of the Yiddish actor, "The less emphasis he lay on the spoken word, the richer his gesture and mimicry had to be."[4] Shakespeare concludes Act I with the Capulets' ball, where Romeo and Juliet meet, dance, and fall in love (though not necessarily in that order). As Romeo leaves the party with the other guests, Juliet learns that he is a Montague and thus her family's enemy. Someone then calls for Juliet from offstage, and she exits with her Nurse. Goldberg has Romeo call Juliet from offstage, which elicits a more elaborate reaction from Juliet than Shakespeare calls for: "Juliet falls in a chair [a bit of business repeated in Teplitski's text], Nurse (enters) with light" (1302B). Rather than having the Nurse lead Juliet off, Goldberg has her literally illuminate Juliet's feelings. The anonymous version follows Shakespeare more closely in the lovers' first meeting, but adds a tableau at the end of the scene. After Juliet sighs, "Ah, Romeo, Romeo," she stands pensively, then grows fearful as Romeo starts to leave. He bids her goodnight, the dance whirls around them, and the two of them pose in the midst of it. The curtain falls slowly (1302D).

The Hermalin/Vilenski version offers the most detailed choreography for the Capulet ball, threading an item of stage business through the scene to underscore the dialogue with corresponding nonverbal communication. At the start of the ball, Juliet dances with Paris, much to the Nurse's satisfaction. When Juliet catches sight of

Romeo, "both gaze at each other in amazement." She drops the flowers she is holding, and Romeo hands them to her. She mimes thanks, and looks at Romeo before disappearing with Paris into the crowd. Towards the end of the scene, the translators give Juliet a soliloquy spelling out her feelings:

> Dos fayer iz entflamt! Es roysht in mayn tifer brust, vos izt dos? Ken mir yemand zagen vos badaytet eyn shneles ungehoyer herts klapen und dennokh zalkhe zise gefiln? Dokh shtil mayn herts. Mayne muter ervartet mikh yetst. (1302C)

> [The fire is lit! It stirs deep in my breast. What is it? Can someone tell me what it means to have a fast, powerful heartbeat followed by such sweet feelings? But be still, my heart. My mother is waiting for me now.]

As she is about to leave, Romeo reappears. A surprised Juliet heads towards the door, turns around, "gives him a loving look and throws him the flowers. He picks them up and kisses them" (1302C).

The use of vivid gestures and tableaux continues the next time the lovers meet, during the balcony scene. One version has the orchestra quietly playing a waltz during the lovers' tryst (1302D). Another specifies that the curtain take "a couple of minutes" to fall at the end of the scene (1302A). And Goldberg makes use of Juliet's handkerchief in a manner echoing Hermalin and Vilenski's use of the flowers. She drops her handkerchief to Romeo on her parting line, "A thousand times good night." Romeo, left alone, responds with a partial translation of Shakespeare's "Sleep dwell upon thine eyes, peace in thy breast! / Would I were sleep and peace, so sweet to rest" (II.ii.186–7). Goldberg, however, changes the meaning toward the end:

> Zol der shlof vonen af dayne oygn un der fridn in dayn brust, ikh volt mir yetst gevinshn tsu zayn shlof un fridn, um tsu zayn nebn ir.

> [Sleep dwell upon thine eyes, peace in thy breast! Would I were sleep and peace, so I could be near her.]

Romeo then kisses the handkerchief, kneels, and sighs, "My Juliet! My Juliet!" (1302B).

Fond as Yiddish plays tend to be of ceremony, some of the translators take the opportunity to elaborate on Friar Laurence's ministrations to the couple in his chambers. Shakespeare does not show them getting married; rather, the Friar announces, "Come, come with me, and we will make short work, / For by your leaves, you shall not stay alone / Till Holy Church incorporate two in one" (II.vi.35–7). Teplitski tones down the Christian reference, changing the last lines to, "You will not stay alone until God makes two from one" (1302A). That version and Goldberg's then show a wedding tableau, with Friar Laurence kneeling, Bible in hand, with eyes heavenward (1302A, B). As they did in the ball scene, Hermalin and Vilenski elaborate more than any other translator, here giving Friar Laurence a whole new speech:

> My heart beats for joy seeing that your love is stronger than a person can express. Yes, my children, your eyes say more in one second than your tongues could in a century. Come here, we will make it brief. I will give you my blessing and ask the Almighty to protect you forever and always. (*They go to the altar. Laurence stands in the pulpit. Romeo and Juliet kneel below him, holding hands.*) Almighty Father in Heaven, bless and protect these two innocent children, bless their union and keep them from evil and need! (1302C)

Shakespeare's Friar is too skeptical of Romeo's intentions for such exclamations, but by cutting any mention of the Friar's doubts, the Yiddish versions have no qualms about reinforcing his enthusiasm.

The assorted alterations of Shakespeare's imagery, language, and characterization made by the Yiddish translators culminate in a final scene designed to make the most of the pathos inherent in the lovers' predicament. Most of the versions radically rewrite the ending by eliminating everyone but the two lovers from the final scene, thus cutting Romeo's killing of Paris,[5] the Friar's explanation of the tragedy, and the "glooming peace" reached by the two families. Explanations and implications are left outside the action, which keeps the lovers' tragedy in the foreground.

Shakespeare's Romeo dies without realizing that Juliet lives, but in every Yiddish version, the Apothecary's poison works slowly enough for the lovers to say good-bye, thus making the tomb scene resemble *Aida* as much as it does *Romeo and Juliet*. Just after Romeo drinks the poison, Juliet awakens, understandably disoriented. Cleverly, the translations have her think she is still being forced to marry Paris as she awakens: "Why are you forcing me like that? My strength may be flagging but my will is firm. I will not marry Paris. Romeo is my husband." Similar wording appears in all of the versions, thus showing the influence of the first translation upon all of the others. In each of them, Romeo then tells Juliet that he has taken poison, and bids her farewell. She pleads with him not to die, then stabs herself. In one version — probably the first to be produced — Romeo manages to reflect on the forces behind the tragedy before he dies:

Eltern hobn shteynerne hertsn. Keyne treren kenen zey shmeltsn. Di natur betct unzoynst. Kinder musn ungliklekh zayn. (1302D)

[Parents have hearts of stone. No tears can melt them. Nature pleads in vain. Children are destined to be unhappy.]

What the Yiddish versions sacrifice by cutting the last 140 lines of Shakespeare's text is the notion that the deaths of Romeo, Juliet, and their peers can be made meaningful by teaching the Montagues and Capulets to bury their enmity. While we may view Shakespeare's resolution of the action as the necessary restoration of order, a different sort of theatrical sensibility — indeed, the same one that led Mikhl Goldberg to cut Fortinbras out of the final moments of *Hamlet* — may see it as anticlimactic. If this play is all about Romeo and Juliet, who cares what happens to the other characters after the lovers die? The Yiddish translations leave the audience with the emotional knockout punch, not the smelling salts to bring them to their senses.

Thomashefsky's Anti-Romeos

Romeo and Juliet was by far Thomashefsky's greatest Shakespearean success, if we disregard adaptations such as *The Yeshiva Boy*. He often appeared as Romeo after his debut in the role in the mid-1890s, and seems to have been trying to replicate this coup in a flurry of other Shakespeare translations that he staged during the same period. None of them lasted long in the repertoire, however — a fact that might not have been a great surprise to close observers of the actor. Perhaps to an even greater extent than his contemporaries,

Thomashefsky loved playing the hero. Indeed, according to his wife Bessie, he would even go so far as turning a villain into a hero in mid-performance, as she says he did in Lateiner's *Ezra, oder der eybiker yid* (Ezra, or the eternal Jew), which premiered in 1891. Lateiner had written the play for the star couple, but according to Bessie Thomashefsky, the rest of the company was so tired of Boris getting all the applause that they went on strike until the leading role was assigned to another cast member. When Max Karp was given Boris's role and Boris cast as the villain, the Jew-hating Pan Schweininski, Bessie did not take the change lying down: "I asked my husband to play Pan Schweininski, but to put on his best clothing so he would look attractive and the public would love to look at him. My husband followed my advice and dressed up like an ancient prince, with tights and beautiful boots. He was lovely to behold."[6]

Nevertheless, it was the other actors who were getting all the credit, since Thomashefsky "did not have any 'bombastic monologues' for which the audience would applaud."[7] Yet Thomashefsky managed to turn the tables on them:

> Then came a scene in which Pan Schweininski was supposed to condemn the Jews before the king, and the Jews would jeer at him like they did Haman [the villain of the book of Esther], but Thomashefsky reversed the speech, delivering an impassioned monologue praising the "poor Jews." The audience thundered, giving him an endless ovation. . . . In my husband's hands, the evil Schweininski became a philo-Semite, a true saint. The role demanded otherwise, you say? Well, what does an actor not do for applause?[8]

Could such an actor ever pour heart and soul into playing Richard III, one of the most diabolical villains in Elizabethan drama? His reputation as a ladies' man would have served him well in Richard's devilish courtship of Lady Anne, but one wonders how convincingly he could have carried off other aspects of Richard's villainy.

Advertisements for Thomashefsky's *Richard III*, which premiered at the Thalia on 1 November 1894, fell back on the familiar strategy of dropping what must have been largely unfamiliar names of actors and critics from other cultures in order to assert the play's greatness:

> The greatest masterpiece Richard the Third by the greatest master William Shakespeare. Attention! On the greatest Yiddish stage, the

Thalia Theatre, by the greatest Yiddish actor, Boris Thomashefsky. Hear what the world's critics say. . . .

"'Richard the Third' is a play beloved by audiences around the world, and the greatest actors — Barnay, Possart, Sonnenthal, Booth, and all the other great actors in the world — have shown their artistry in this masterpiece. . . ."

Schlegel the dramaturg says in his Shakespeare criticism:

"Although Shakespeare inserted a world of history into 'Richard the Third,' it is so clearly written that every person, even those who are not experts . . . must easily understand the play. . . . Small and large, educated and uneducated, all nations, Germans, Russians, Frenchmen, Englishmen, kings and servants, capitalists and workers — all, all take off their hats to 'Richard the Third' — all run to see him on the stage — all wonder at him all love him and all honor him."

Should the Yiddish stage fall below other stages? No! ! !

Our Yiddish Shakespeare tragedian Mr. B. Thomashefsky, who has not rested until he has seen the Yiddish stage equal the other stages of the world . . . has now taken another step in his ascent towards the highest level of art, up to "Richard the Third." He hopes not to rest until he reaches his goal of making the Yiddish public equal to all the other nations of the world and the Yiddish stage into a world stage.[9]

Puffery alone could not sustain the production, which was performed for only three nights. In spite of its potential attractions, *Richard III* may not have had a chance with audiences used to a Thomashefsky so ingrained in heroic roles that even his villains turned over a new leaf by the end.

Thomashefsky would have no more success playing Cassius in *Julius Caesar*,[10] or the title role in *Macbeth*,[11] both for very short runs in 1895. A few years later, he would play Coriolanus, a role Sigmund Feinman had attempted in a short-lived production in 1901. Perhaps playing Coriolanus was a way of eating one's cake and still having it, combining the gravitas of a villain with the moral authority of a hero. Where Shakespeare's protagonist is a career soldier who excoriates his men when they show less bravery than he, the Yiddish version by Mikhl Goldberg paints a more gentle picture of the Roman warrior. The most telling sign of this comes in Act III, where Coriolanus, whom the Roman senate wishes to name as a consul for his brave military service, bluntly expresses his contempt for the common people and the cowardly tribunes. Shakespeare gives Coriolanus a series of three speeches, each harsher than the one before, scoffing at those who have agreed to dole out free corn to the Roman people. Coriolanus insists that they have not earned the corn, since they recently abandoned him in his successful defense of the city against the Volscians:

> They know the corn
> Was not our recompense, resting well assur'd
> They ne'er did service for't; being pressed to th'war,
> Even when the navel of the state was touch'd,
> They would not thread the gates. This kind of service
> Did not deserve corn gratis. (III.i.120–5)

The cumulative effect of the speeches is to give Coriolanus' enemies the verbal ammunition to turn the people against him and have him banished from Rome. Goldberg's version, on the other hand, cuts all three passages. Coriolanus thus comes across as less extreme, and the Romans have less reason to banish him. Yiddish audiences, on the other hand, would quickly banish *Coriolanus* from the stage. There seems to have been little to make them warm to either the play's protagonist or to its central themes, and for all the play's battles, Goldberg's translation often substitutes speech for action. That the speeches tend to revolve around such issues as duty and honor — concepts that would not have been likely to resonate with Thomashefsky's audience — undoubtedly helped hasten the exit of *Coriolanus* from the Yiddish repertoire.

Romeo and Shulamis

Romeo and Juliet, on the other hand, was practically a guaranteed money-maker with Thomashefsky's audiences, according to the actor himself, and one of only a handful of world favorites to fare so well in Yiddish theatres. "*Romeo and Juliet* was a great success. Girls would bring their boys to learn from Thomashefsky and Sophia Karp how one should love."[12] Showing the same sort of reverence for

Shakespeare as he had displayed when preparing to play Hamlet for the first time, Thomashefsky exhorted his Juliet to do the same: "Even a talented actress must study the role of Juliet for a long time. As if it were a small matter: Shakespeare's dialogue, his love-language! I explained to [Sophia Karp] that she must truly prepare herself to play Juliet. After all, this was not a role from [Lateiner's] *Ben Yankev* or [Goldfaden's] *Kuni Lemls*."[13] Sophia Karp, however, was not a quick study.

Karp, in Thomashefsky's account, was as poor at learning lines as she was beautiful of face and voice, and she possessed those qualities in abundance. The prompter, a fixture in Yiddish theatres at the time, would help remedy this difficulty to a certain extent from his box under the stage, but she would get lost the moment he had to stop to cough or sneeze. Rather than wait for him, she would begin speaking dialogue from other plays, and as Thomashefsky reverentially editorializes, "Of course, one cannot make up one's own dialogue in *Romeo and Juliet*."[14]

As extra precautions against his leading lady's sieve-like memory, Thomashefsky installed not one but two prompters when he staged *Romeo and Juliet* at the Windsor Theatre in New York. "I myself," he adds with all the pride of a schoolboy who has gotten a perfect score on his spelling test, "did not need the prompter, having learned my role by heart."[15] He also had Juliet's balcony built at a spot strategically located between the two prompters. This arrangement worked well at the Windsor, but when Thomashefsky brought the production to Philadelphia, family business kept him from overseeing the construction of the balcony and hiring an extra prompter. The result was a fiasco.

What reached Thomashefsky's ears on the stage of the Arch Street Theatre that evening were not Shakespeare's lines translated into Yiddish, but rather the distressed cry, "Boris, I can't hear the prompter!" Thomashefsky tried cueing her himself, but she could not hear him clearly either, and began reciting dialogue "from [Lateiner's] *Alexander*, from *Ben Yankev*, from [Goldfaden's] *Shulamis*."[16] So angry did Thomashefsky become at his co-star's lack of professionalism, he claims, that he jumped off the ladder and into the wings, changed, packed his bags, and caught the next train to New York. The theatre manager, Thomashefsky's brother-in-law Morris Finkel, was forced to bring down the curtain and announce to those in the audience who were willing to stay that Mr. Thomashefsky had suddenly fallen ill, and the company would start over again with a performance of *Shulamis*.

If Thomashefsky's behavior sounds inconsistent — insisting on getting the dialogue right but bailing out of the play in mid-performance — it fits the actor's image, to those who knew him best, as a curious mixture of craftsman and showboat. Playwright Leon Kobrin observed two sides to his friend and colleague:

> I would call one "Thomashefsky-the-good" and the other "Thomashefsky-the-bad." . . . That is also how he is on the stage. One with that stiff, starched, top-hat tone, without life and soul, the Thomashefsky of cheap *shund* plays and even cheaper operettas; and the other — with that lively, truly artistic tone, full of soul and fire, which he always revealed in the better plays.[17]

Thomashefsky portrays himself as changing his modus operandi when performing Shakespeare, so committed to the playwright's work that he was willing to restructure both stage and crew in order to make the production a success. This Thomashefsky would rather have abandoned the whole endeavor than see it compromised.

Thomashefsky's anecdote not only describes an extraordinary scene; it also bears a curious resemblance to William Kaiser's 1897 sketch, "The Mistake on the Stage," in which the prompter Yeshaye, suffering from a cold, tries to coach a pair of actors performing "a new play à la *Romeo and Juliet*." They have had insufficient time to learn their lines, and due to the combination of Yeshaye's congestion and the position of the prompter's box, neither of the performers can hear him properly. As a result, the words they think they hear turn the meaning of the written dialogue on its head, and change the tone of the scene from loving to loathing. Yeshaye gets increasingly annoyed, until he can contain himself no longer. Leaping onto the stage "in a wild fury," he knocks the actors to the ground, and "the curtain, out of sorrow, falls too."[18]

Whether or not Thomashefsky consciously transposed this sketch to his own autobiography, his account gives him a moral authority parallel to that of the prompter in Kaiser's piece. The prompter's name is no accident. Like his namesake, the prophet Isaiah, Yeshaye lashes out at those who stray from the sacred text, although the prompter uses force where the prophet made his point in angry poetry. Thomashefsky chooses a different form of protest: the eloquence of abstention.

To the extent that we can trust the actor's version of these events some four decades after the fact, this episode also suggests what happens when the Yiddish theatre cannot pull off a performance of Shakespeare. Quite plausibly, it reverts to its own "classics," for a Sophia Karp would either not have had such problems memorizing Shulamis' lines (many of which were set to music in any case), or would not be held to such high standards of accuracy in a Goldfaden opera as in a Shakespearean tragedy.

"Between Shaykevitsh and Shakespeare"

Another pillar of the Yiddish dramatic canon would provide his own alternative to Shakespeare's star-crossed lovers. Gordin's *Di litvishe brider Luriye* (The Lithuanian brothers Luria), which premiered at the Thalia Theatre on 25 August 1894 with Boris Thomashefsky in the starring role, explores what happens when the two lovers live to have a say in their own destiny. Although the *Brothers Luria* was not even advertised as a Jewish *Romeo and Juliet* initially, critics were quick to see the parallels. This time, however — unlike the managers who promoted *The Jewish King Lear* — no one seems to have asserted Gordin's superiority.

Tuvye and Gedalye Luria, the drama's titular brothers, had a falling out over their inheritance years before the play's action begins. Their paternal grandfather survived their father, and willed all of his sizeable inheritance to Gedalye because the boy was learned in Jewish subjects while his brother was not. Tuvye has bristled at the slight ever since, but where he simply begrudges his brother the fortune, Gedalye hates him with a passion. So when Tuvye plans to expand his mill, which would obstruct the view from his brother's house, Gedalye appeals to the town rabbi to intervene.

Gordin molds his rabbi in the kindly spirit of Shakespeare's Friar Lawrence.[19] Reb Shraga is generous to a fault — indeed, his wife constantly berates him for giving away gifts and donations he considers "superfluous," but which she insists are necessities (like flour and money for food). As generous in spirit as he is with material matters, Reb Shraga calls the two brothers together to try to mediate their dispute. But when Gedalye learns that his daughter Rivke has been speaking to Tuvye's son Yankl, he becomes increasingly impervious to reason.

We do not see Yankl and Rivke fall in love — that is a fait accompli by the time we meet them — but our first glimpse of them is enough to show that they are kindred spirits. Both children offer money to the rabbi's charities in their first lines of dialogue. Moments later, in the midst of their fathers' bickering, both demonstrate a lack of comprehension of, and lack of patience with, their fathers' decades-old dispute. Typical Gordin lovers, they show their suitability for each other not through romantic chemistry, but through compatibility of character.

We have seen how *The Jewish King Lear* almost failed to see the light of day because Gordin's actors protested its departures from the conventions they expected to find in a Yiddish drama. Again in *Brothers Luria*, Gordin peppers what he clearly intends to be a drama of ideas with enough physical action to hold the attention of actors and audiences who might lose patience with just talk. The quarrel in the rabbi's house at the end of Act I deteriorates first into puerile name-calling, then a curtain-closing fistfight. Such emotionalism could allow for intensive scenery-chewing, as in a sold-out performance in which Bessie Thomashefsky took part, some years after the play's premiere. By this time, the *Brothers Luria* had become a warhorse in the repertoire, and the production in question was what the Yiddish theatre deemed a "combination performance"; that is, featuring major stars in all the leading roles. Boris Thomashefsky played Gedalye Luria; David Kessler, Tuvye Luria; Jacob Adler, Reb Shraga; while Bessie herself played the rabbi's wife, Sore-Dvoyre. In her memoirs, Bessie Thomashefsky recalls her fellow stars' behavior toward the end of Act I:

Thomashefsky has a scene in which he throws a plate to the ground and breaks it, so he throws two plates at once. Kessler does not take this lying down and also picks up some dishes; he is a star too, after all. When Adler sees that these two stars will walk away with their success, he does not stay quiet either, and he — the good, elderly rabbi — starts to "star" too: to break dishes, that is.

Before the end of the act, our three stars broke all the dishes on the stage and were about to lay into the furniture . . . but the good curtain suddenly came down and the furniture got away with its life — until the subsequent acts.[20]

The violence — whether the fisticuffs indicated in Gordin's script or interpolated plate-throwing — grows far worse in Act II, which revolves around Gedalye's efforts to betroth Rivke to the son of a rich and powerful man who Gedalye hopes will help him ruin Tuvye's business. Knowing how short his own temper can be, Gedalye recruits Reb Shraga to help him persuade Rivke to accept the match. Yet though Rivke obeys her father's order not to speak to Yankl any more, she readily expresses her love for her cousin, first to the rabbi and then to her father:

> *Rivke*: Daddy dear, order me to walk through fire and I'll obey you, but I can't obey you by loving someone my heart tells me not to love.

> *Gedalye*: Your heart! I'll tear out your dirty heart and stomp on it, I'll tear out your eyes that look at what they shouldn't, you impudent slut![21]

It does not take long for Gedalye's abuse of his daughter to move from the verbal to the physical. A moment later, he slaps her, then smashes her hand with a stick. When her mother, hearing her screams, calls for a doctor, Rivke stoically remarks, "Sha, what are you shouting for? What are you afraid of? It's no great tragedy. Better to lose a hand than one's soul and one's entire life, isn't that right, Daddy dear?" After a pause, he responds, "Oy, Rivkele, my only daughter," and embraces her as the curtain falls on Act II (26).

This moment condenses the entire father-daughter relationship of *The Jewish King Lear* into a few hair-raising lines. Dovid Moysheles's misunderstanding of his daughter Taybele, and the sequence of events that grew out of his disowning her, would stir generations of Yiddish audiences. But Dovid Moysheles never raised a finger against her, and even his mean-spirited older daughters never inflicted physical violence on him. In Gedalye Luria, Gordin's audience got to see an even prouder, more severe counterpart to Dovid Moysheles. (The parallel would have been even more striking had Adler originated the role that Gordin had written for him, but this was not to be. When the actors at Adler's theatre went on strike, claiming that he exploited them, Gordin took their side and brought the play to Thomashefsky, who premiered in the role at the Thalia Theatre.)[22]

Act III takes place on the street, where one glimpse of the brothers' homes shows how the tables have turned. Gedalye's far fancier house is now darkened, and Rivke lies within, desperately ill. Tuvye's simpler abode is lit up, and sounds of his singing workers emanate from it. Indeed, we learn that he has paid his workers to sing loudly and disturb his brother's family's rest — a moment that Yiddish writer Yitskhok Leybush Peretz condemned for "descending from tragedy into farce."[23] Throughout his review of a 1906 production in Warsaw by a visiting company led by Jacob Adler, Peretz taunts Gordin for positioning himself between what Peretz sees as the cheap sensations of Yiddish writer Nokhem-Meyer ("Shomer") Shaykevitsh and the lofty dramaturgy of William Shakespeare: "Whenever Shakespeare has nothing to offer, out comes Shaykevitsh and hocus-pocus!: no more tragedy!"[24]

Peretz has a point. At times, Gordin's play offers moments of true power, and is particularly Shakespearean in its depiction of the humbling of Gedalye, who loses all his pride in the wake of his outburst of violence. When Rivke's doctor learns that the brothers' feud and the consequent separation of the two lovers have brought about the nervous fever that now jeopardizes her life, he urges Gedalye to mend the situation quickly. Gedalye readily does so, knocking on his brother's door and pleading for cooperation in order to save his daughter. Tuvye admits him when he learns the reason for his brother's visit, and Gedalye collapses on the threshold on his way inside.

Act IV further elaborates on the humiliation of a once proud community leader. The brothers are again meeting at the rabbi's house, but this time they are drawing up a contract that will resolve their dispute and pave the way for their children's marriage. The terms, dictated by Tuvye, are draconian to say the least; one might almost call them Shylockian. Gedalye will pay Tuvye half of their grandfather's inheritance, with interest for twenty years, as well as all of Tuvye's legal costs involving the dispute: 4,475 roubles and 35 kopecks. He will also offer Tuvye a public apology in the synagogue on the morning of the Sabbath. The rabbi is astonished at how vengefully Tuvye is behaving in triumph, but Gedalye hardly reacts to these extraordinary demands, being focused entirely on his daughter's recovery.

Rivke, though, is every inch Gedalye's daughter, and though he signs the document, she tears it up. No matter that she almost died pining away for Yankl: "I would be the unhappiest woman in the world if I knew that my happiness was bought for such a terrible price — that you should want to make my father, the great Gedalye Luria, so small and lowly!" (45). The force of her convictions, and rivers of tears from both the rabbi and Gedalye, finally make Tuvye relent. The cantor and his apprentices who came to sing at the wedding are called in, and joyous singing and dancing bring down the final curtain.

Gordin was only a couple of years beyond the success of *The Jewish King Lear* when he wrote *The Lithuanian Brothers Luria*, and though he uses Shakespeare far more loosely here, he clearly has not shaken off the yoke of his own success. *The Lithuanian Brothers Luria* begins to resemble *Romeo and Juliet* once it introduces two lovers separated by a family feud, but it accumulates large doses of *King Lear* along the way, and Rivke ends up performing a balancing act. Peretz called the result a cross between Shaykevitsh and Shakespeare. In Rivke's case, it is a cross between Juliet's insistence on the man of her choosing and Cordelia's loyalty to her father. It will not be the last time that the spirit of Dovid and Taybele hovers over Yiddish adaptations of other Shakespeare plays.

O True Apothecary!

Romeo and Juliet would serve as the inspiration for several more Yiddish adaptations, ranging from a frivolous comedy to versions that make extensive use of Jewish imagery to reimagine the play for contemporary audiences. In the former category falls Joseph Groper's (c. 1866–1911) one-act operetta *Romeo un Zhulyete* [Juliet], probably first performed in New York around the turn of the century.[25] Groper's Juliet is the daughter of a count; her Romeo, a humble shepherd. It is Juliet who takes the initiative, aided and abetted by her nurse. When Juliet declares her love to Romeo, he worries about the potential consequences: "A false hope steals its way into my heart as you talk, and that hope can make an end of my life." Juliet shrugs off these fears, though — "God will help us," she assuages him — and they sing of their undying love for one another.

Groper offsets the banality of his leading lovers with a couple who act as their comic foil: an anti-Romeo-and-Juliet who bicker constantly and end their every scene with a contentious duet. When we return to the main plot, the Count walks in on his daughter and the shepherd embracing, locks Romeo up in the cellar, and declares that Juliet will immediately marry a nobleman he has picked out for her. "But," she protests, "I don't know him at all." "That doesn't matter," her father replies. "I do." The situation makes Juliet contemplate poisoning herself, but she hesitates and sets the bottle aside. A few moments later, her thirsty Nurse comes across the bottle and gulps down its contents. Her cries of agony make Juliet and the Count come running, but just when it seems that the lovers' agony will bring death to others, the Count breaks out into hearty laughter: "Ha ha ha, Varvara has poisoned herself with castor oil."

Once Juliet's father realizes that she was contemplating suicide, he dramatically softens his position:

> *Count*: Daughter, I see that your love is too strong. You are my only child and I do not want to lose you. I give you my permission to marry him. (*Calls out*) Hurry, bring the shepherd from the cellar.
>
> *Juliet*: I thank you, father. You have made me happy — the happiest girl in the world.

Romeo is brought up from the cellar, the couple receives the father's blessing, and the chorus cheers their future happiness.

One cannot accuse Groper's operetta — *Romeo and Juliet* Lite — of any great ambition to reinvent Shakespeare. Quite the contrary; it extracts the inherent pathos out of the dilemma of two lovers kept apart by forces beyond themselves, mirrors their situation with a comic subplot, and breezily rearranges the miscues at the end to make sure no one gets more than a bad stomach ache. But by calling his little diversion *Romeo un Zhulyete*, did Groper set out to attract an audience in search of higher-minded entertainment? Perhaps, though as a one-act piece, Groper's operetta would have appeared on a bill with either other short pieces or one longer one, and thus may not even have been named in advertisements for the evenings on which it would have been performed.

Nobody *Expects the Spanish Inquisition!*

Frequent visitors to the Yiddish theatre could have expected to witness dramatizations of the Spanish Inquisition with some degree of regularity. The first generation of American Yiddish theatre audiences saw a fairly regular treatment of the theme, featuring such titles as Pinkhes Thomashefsky's *The Lonely Cedar Valley, or, The Jews Under the Inquisition* (1883), Shaykevitsh's *The Spanish Inquisition* (1886), Hurwitz's *Don Joseph Abravanel*, Weissman's *Don Isaac Abravanel, or, Judith the Second* (1887), Sharkansky's *Kol Nidre, or, the Secret Jews in Madrid* (1896), and Jacob Adler's *The King of Spain and the Jews* (1899).[26] The Inquisition motif itself fit perfectly into the broader category of dramas of Jewish persecution. Inquisition dramas offered depictions of a historical parallel to ordeals that much of the audience had experienced firsthand, while the distance of some four hundred years undoubtedly made theatrical representations of the Inquisition — grim though the subject was — less disturbing to watch than contemporary events that hit closer to home, such as pogroms in Russia or a blood-libel trial in Hungary.

Sam Shneyer's melodrama *Yehudis*, staged at the Perry Street Theatre in Cleveland around the turn of the century, capitalizes on the Spanish Inquisition recipe, to which it adds a pinch of Figaro, a soupçon of Romeo, and other ingredients to thicken the stock and enhance the flavor. *Yehudis* relies even less on *Romeo and Juliet* than does Groper's operetta. In an apparent effort to appeal to as broad a spectrum of the audience's associations as possible, Shneyer uses the flimsiest of pretexts to set the play in fifteenth-century Spain, in the time of the Inquisition.

Indeed, Shakespeare's drama plays so tangential a role in Shneyer's play that we need not delve too deeply into the plot of *Yehudis*. In brief, though, the story takes place in Inquisition-era Spain, whose king has ordered his Jewish finance minister, Don Joseph Abravanel (a fictionalized counterpart to Portuguese statesman and biblical scholar Isaac Abravanel), to raise a peace dividend to avoid war with Morocco. Meanwhile, the anti-Semitic Spanish field marshal, Romeo, plots to ruin Don Joseph while courting his daughter, Yehudis. After various reversals of fortune based on lost and found documents, duels, and discoveries, Yehudis saves her father's life and restores him to his former prestigious position, while Romeo is arrested and his evil plots undone.

So wherefore Romeo in all of this? He seems more like Richard III than like the Romeo we know, but Shneyer gives the character's romantic endeavors — a sort of unsuccessful counterpart to the wooing of Lady Anne — a Monta-Capulesque twist. Romeo has written Yehudis a letter, which his friend Figaro (here a postman rather than a barber, though given the play's Spanish setting, still potentially from Seville) opens and reads aloud: "I am the unhappiest man in the world . . . my heart burns like a fire . . . an iron wall stands between us, and you can knock it down with one word . . . I love you . . . my dear Yehudis."[27] What Figaro omits, but we learn later, is Romeo's threat: that if Yehudis does not marry him, he will destroy her father. She stands firm, however: "I would rather be the daughter of a beggar than marry the man who would make my father a beggar." Later, she gives another reason for refusing: she cannot marry a Gentile. Nevertheless, when he offers to convert — a response she may not have anticipated — she still refuses.

To the extent that *Romeo and Juliet* enters Shneyer's plot at all, the family feud has become a matter of Jews pitted against their oppressors. Shneyer, however, dismisses this story line as soon as he introduces it. Instead of offering two lovers who attempt to transcend their differences, he creates one torn between lust and politics and the other wanting nothing whatsoever to do with the romance. Rather than looking to Shakespeare to find a Jewish idiom for a classic source, Shneyer simply drops Romeo's name as part of an accumulation of elements that would be familiar to the audience: Romeo, Figaro, Abravanel, Spanish Inquisition. He then pastes those associations onto a story better known to that audience than any of these components, for in its broad outlines, *Yehudis* is essentially a retelling of the book of Esther with some alterations in names and plot details.

A Tragedy of the Jewish Culture Wars

Shneyer's *Yehudis* and Groper's *Romeo un Zhulyete* did not so much adapt Shakespeare as ride his coattails. A far more extensive attempt to reinvent Shakespeare in Jewish terms, in the tradition of *The Jewish King Lear* and *The Yeshiva Boy*, came in 1903, with Nokhem Rakov's *The Oath on the Torah, or, the Jewish Romeo and Juliet.* Lithuanian-born Rakov (1866–1927) headed west in 1887 for political reasons and settled in London. He gained entrée to the theatre via the prompter's box, which he occupied in London Yiddish theatres managed by Max Rosenthal, Rudolph Marks, and Jacob Adler. But as Rakov's English improved, he took to adapting plays from English to Yiddish in the superficial manner of the time, figuring out "how to turn a priest into a rabbi."[28] In his first plays, he parlayed current events into dramatic form, in such works as *The Greenhorn in London*; *The Strike in London*; and *Captain Dreyfus, or, Emile Zola.*

Around 1902,[29] Rakov left London for New York, where he found that such writers as Hurwitz, Zeifert, and Zolatarevsky had already capitalized on the most interesting events of the day for their plays. Rakov's first play in America, *In Wild Russia* (1902), brought little money into the box office, and he soon turned to Shakespeare for source material.

The Oath on the Torah opened at the People's Theatre in New York on 10 April 1903, the same day that another Rakov play, *The Idler*, opened at the Thalia.[30] The action begins on Simkhes Toyre (or Simchat Torah), one of the most festive holidays in the Jewish calendar. But on this day when Jews traditionally carry the Torah scrolls in a joyous dance around the synagogue, the action begins with two groups of Jews throwing rocks at each other. Gordin had shown these factions — *misnagdim* versus Hasidim — at loggerheads in *The Jewish King Lear*, but kept the antagonism strictly verbal. *The Yeshiva Boy* depicted bloodshed, but placed the violence offstage. In *The Oath on the Torah*, the rocks actually take to the air. Just as the Yiddish translations of *Romeo and Juliet* had done, Rakov supplants the war of words that follows Shakespeare's Prologue and moves right to the physical confrontation, although as in Shakespeare's version, nobody suffers any injury yet.

Shortly after the opening skirmish, the audience meets Raphael, the only child of the Hasidic rebbe. Raphael confesses to his friends Itsikl and Binyomin that he is in love, and Itsikl teases him in the manner of Mercutio. Rather than conjure up Mercutio's pagan imagery of Queen Mab, however, Itsikl draws upon biblical allusions:

> And just because you're in love, does that mean you have to sigh? Just go to your father and say, "Papa, I want to get married," and [he] will send Gedalye the sexton throughout the land to choose a bride, just as our forefather Abraham did by sending his slave Eliezer to find a wife for Isaac. And Reb Gedalye will find some Khavele, or a Rivkele, or another girl standing by a carriage and feeding a goat and you'll get married and . . .[31]

And like Romeo, Raphael cuts short his friend's speech.

But Binyomin and Itsikl continue to tease their friend about his lovesickness, and suggest an antidote. Raphael should come to Simchat Torah services, where he will see that his beloved is but one among many beautiful girls. Raphael resists their suggestion. Various Hasidim and *misnagdim* bring Act I to a close not by throwing stones, but by an activity far more conducive to the finale of an act of an operetta: singing the praises of their leaders. This ending completes an act focused far more on the feud than on the love story; indeed, we have not yet met Sheyndele, the Juliet to Raphael's Romeo.

She first appears at the beginning of Act II, set in her family's house. As in Shakespeare, she discusses marriage with her grandmother (Rakov's equivalent of the Nurse) and her mother, and agrees to marry whomever her parents choose for her. But Sheyndele plants the seeds of rebellion when she expresses her wish to attend services at the Hasidic synagogue. Her father, the Orthodox rabbi, forbids her.

Where the tragic romance of Shakespeare's lovers indirectly shows the folly of the feud that keeps them apart, Rakov's lovers directly indict their parents for perpetuating such mindless hatred. Sheyndele calls the quarrel ridiculous; after all, she points out, the Hasidim are Jews too. Ignoring her father's prohibition, she attends the holiday services at the Hasidic synagogue. The reviewer for the *New York Evening Post* applauded Rakov's transposition of the ballroom scene: "Each holiday finds [the Orthodox Jew] in the synagogue in his best

attire, giving free vent to his love and all the noble feelings which
animate the breast of man. It is fitting, then, that in translating Shakespeare into Yiddish the author should replace the Capulet ballroom
by the synagogue."[32] Since dancing plays a prominent role in the Simchat Torah festivities, this holiday provides an especially apt parallel
to the Capulet ball. And just as Romeo and Juliet end up dancing
together, Raphael and Sheyndele steal a moment alone: "Then there
is the procession around the altar, which resolves into a choral dance
of men and women, the younger men breaking into an ecstatic pas
seul. . . . And so, when the tide of religious joy surges to one side,
[Raphael and Sheyndele] meet at a corner of the altar and kiss."[33]

The balcony, like the ball, belongs to the synagogue, where Juliet
ascends to the women's section and Romeo stands below at the altar. Rather than ask, "What's in a name?" Sheyndele wonders aloud,
"Raphael, my Raphael, why did God fill our fathers' hearts with hatred and their children's hearts with love?" She then descends from
the balcony to the altar, the focal point of the synagogue and site of
the lamp symbolically called the eternal light, "representing the inde-
structibility of Jewish faith and Jewish life."[34] The staging of the oath
underscores how this symbolism relates to the eternal love between
Raphael and Sheyndele, as Raphael holds "the Eternal Light in one
hand, the fingers of his love . . . in the other."[35]

While the lovers create this symbolic tableau, they make their vow
on the Torah as Raphael invokes sacred witnesses:

Zayn zol der omed un der ner tomed
Eydes af imer, mir sheydn zikh nimer.
Zayn zol di toyre un di menoyre
Eydes gor tsu unzer shvue.

[May the cantor's desk and the Eternal Light
Be witnesses forever, we'll never part.
Let the Torah and the menorah
Be witnesses to our oath.]

The oath recalls not only *Romeo and Juliet*, but another prototype as
well: Avrom Goldfaden's operetta *Shulamis*, one of the most popular
plays in the Yiddish repertoire. Early in that play, Shulamis, lost in the

desert near Jerusalem, falls into a well, from which she is rescued by Avisholem. They fall in love, and swear by the well and a wild cat that happens by:

O der brunem, o der!
Un di kats, o di, o!
Zoln zayn, vi ikh shver,
Eydes tsu unzer shvue.[36]

[O, the well and the cat!
Let them be, as I swear,
Witnesses to our oath.]

Given Rakov's experience as a prompter, he undoubtedly knew *Shulamis* by heart, and must have known what he was doing when he echoed this scene that had charmed a generation of Yiddish audiences on both sides of the Atlantic.

After Sheyndele spurns Froyem (Ephraim), the suitor her parents have chosen for her, and quarrels violently with her father, the action moves to the synagogue. Naturally, Shakespeare's Friar would be out of place here. Rakov therefore changes him to a Cantor, who leads a melodic ending to Act II as he makes the lovers' union official in song.

Act III opens with an exchange that could come right out of a Yiddish operetta. Rakov presents a lighter side of the feud: Itsik/Mercutio asks two *misnagdim* if they want to become Hasidim. They reply that they will when they see the *rebbe* perform a miracle. This leads to a musical parody of the countless Hasidic folktales describing the wonder-working powers of various *rebbes*. Critic John Corbin remarked of another comic interlude shortly after this one, "It is not pretty, all this, but the audience enjoy it, and it refreshes them for the . . . tragic scenes to come." Yet Corbin appreciated the scene's theatrical merit: "In matters of this kind it is easy to be all too superior. Who was it that wrote the passages of bawdry in the original 'Romeo and Juliet,' the devil-portering scenes in 'Macbeth'? In its naive and unabashed expression of the popular taste the Yiddish plays of the Bowery are on the precise plane of the plays that delighted the Bankside under Elizabeth."[37] As other critics for the English-language press have done, Corbin finds in the Yiddish audience's unselfconscious love of theatre a modern manifestation of Shakespeare's legendary groundlings, with all their working-class vitality intact.

As with the raucous Shakespearean scenes that Corbin invokes, the action in Rakov's play quickly turns more serious. Since he omits an equivalent to Tybalt, Rakov allows for no justification to have Raphael banished. Instead, sheer pragmatism makes Raphael decide to leave town. Raphael has no means of supporting Sheyndele, so the Cantor offers letters of introduction to friends in Vienna who will help the young man learn a trade. Raphael agrees, and the Cantor promises to help Sheyndele keep her parents at bay until Raphael can return and make the marriage public.

Rakov, as he has done elsewhere, finds a Jewish replacement for Juliet's "Gallop apace" soliloquy by having Sheyndele sing from the Song of Songs while waiting for her grandmother to return from the Cantor's with news of Raphael. It is a fitting equivalent, for while Jewish, it expresses eroticism in a manner analogous to the sexually charged imagery of Juliet's monologue.[38]

After her father rejects Sheyndele's plea to break off the arranged match, Sheyndele and Raphael say their farewells in the moonlight. Ephraim enters just in time to see them embrace, and causes an uproar when Sheyndele's family and other *misnagdim* arrive. When he learns of the tryst, Sheyndele's father threatens to strangle her, but Raphael intervenes: "You dare not lay a hand on my wife." The grandmother confirms that the couple have indeed married, and Sheyndele's father faints as the curtain falls.

Six months pass between Acts III and IV. Raphael has sent many letters from Vienna, but his father-in-law has destroyed them all, and Sheyndele's distress has grown exponentially. Her father has also sent a follower to Vienna to bribe Raphael to sign divorce papers. When he receives a report that the divorce is official, Sheyndele's father tells her that she may go to Vienna on the condition that if Raphael no longer wants her, she will return and marry Ephraim. But as she is preparing for the journey, the divorce papers arrive in the mail. Sheyndele comes out of her swoon long enough to say, "Father, Mother, congratulate me. I am free, free."

The scene changes to the Cantor's quarters, where he learns of the divorce and agrees with Itsik's conclusion that the papers must be fraudulent. Raphael's friends resolve to bring him home immediately in order to stop Sheyndele's wedding to Ephraim, scheduled for the next day. Despite the Cantor's insistence that the wedding be called off, the preparations continue.

The play concludes with an aborted wedding ceremony. The guests lead Sheyndele and Ephraim onstage and leave them alone. Traditional Jewish weddings do not leave the bride and groom alone at the beginning of the ceremony, but since Rakov's plot does not allow for the moment to come later, he creates a variation of the law of *yichud*: "The symbolic consummation of the wedding takes place in a private room after the ceremony. This is not a custom, but a firm requirement of the law that must be testified to by witnesses. It is the final act . . . that seals the marriage. When the couple emerges from *yichud*, they are man and wife."[39] During their brief moment alone, Sheyndele tells Ephraim that he can have her body, but not her heart. Rakov creates an anti-*yichud*, not only in its placement in the order of the wedding, but also in its function. Instead of uniting with her future husband, Sheyndele uses the time alone with her groom to establish her autonomy. As soon as he leaves, however, she takes a different tack altogether, deciding that she cannot live any longer and swallowing a glass of poison as she declares, "Raphael, I lived for you and die for you."

The guests return at this point, and the blessing over the couple begins. It is interrupted by the entrance of Raphael, his friends, and the Cantor. Raphael and Sheyndele embrace, and she dies in his arms. He mourns her, but not so hysterically as to be unable to derive a lesson from her death: "Look at her, see your sacrifice. . . . You thought you could buy off a person's heart. No, money cannot buy someone's heart. Look, look: dead, my Sheyndele, my wife."

Raphael's father arrives at the point where the play is supposed to reach the pinnacle of tragedy, but his entrance line would be all but impossible to deliver seriously today: "Raphael, you've come all this way and went straight to your enemy without visiting your father first?"[40] Raphael responds didactically, "You see, father, the fruit of your hatred." And as if to punctuate his point, Raphael shoots himself. Standing over the corpses, Sheyndele's grandmother recalls how the lovers took their vow and concludes, "And so they stay united. They kept their oath."

The oath most immediately represents the lovers' devotion to each other in the face of adversity, but their vow works on an allegorical level as well. The family feud that makes it impossible for Raphael and Sheyndele to live together in peace involves millions of combatants. In purely quantitative terms, then, the lovers' oath is greater than that of *Romeo and Juliet*; it represents a belief in the essential unity of the Jewish people, even in the face of factions that keep that unity from being realized.

Romeo of the Tenements

Rakov, like other Judaizers of Shakespeare, molded his source material in ways calculated to resonate with an American Jewish audience in the early 1900s. American Jewish life would undergo a number of radical transformations over the next half-century, and those changes are vividly reflected in a short sketch entitled *Romeo un Dzhuliet* [Romeo and Juliet], by Gershon Einbinder (better known by his pen name, Chaver-Paver), published in 1956. The glory days of the American Yiddish theatre had passed, and with them, the grand spectacles, the larger-than-life passions, the god-like status of the star actors (except a few, mostly comedians like Molly Picon and Menashe Skulnik, who continued to enjoy a cult following). Corresponding to such changes in theatrical conditions, Chaver-Paver gives us *Romeo and Juliet* in miniature, a charming evocation of life on the Lower East Side from an earlier era, with a wink in Shakespeare's direction.

As the piece begins, we see a tenement apartment in that district at the beginning of the twentieth century. Dave, a nineteen-year-old student, pores over his English homework while his mother Malke fights off sleep in order to do the tailoring piecework that allows her son to get an education. Adorning their humble surroundings are emblems of their family's journeys, metaphors for certain central trends in modern Jewish history: a photograph of Malke and her late husband as newlyweds; another of her father, a stately man with a long beard; and glass shelves holding Jewish ritual objects and good dishes.

In the background, Susie, the girl who lives across the way, occasionally passes by in her apartment. Like every other detail in the sketch, the characters' names tell us something: Malke, Yiddish for "queen," gives off an Old World resonance. No girl Susie's age would wear the name Malke, just as no immigrant Jewish mother would ever have as all-American a name as Susie (who also has a Yiddish name, Zisl, indicating her sweetness). In between the two women's names in terms of degree of ethnicity versus Americanization is Dave, bearing the stamp of the Jewish David, but announcing in its abbreviated form that it has come to America. The ambivalent connotations of Dave's name suit his circumstances, for he is caught between two poles in just about every sphere of his existence. He wants to go to work to support himself, but his mother pushes him to get a college education. He tries to concentrate on his work, but is distracted by Susie. And in that plight so typical of the immigrant, the battle for allegiances between the mother and any prospective mate is compounded by the different mores they represent. Malke, noticing that Susie's presence makes it difficult for Dave to work, expresses her disapproval of the girl long before meeting her:

> *Dave*: It's nothing, Mama. She's a casual acquaintance. We just say "Hello."
> *Malke*: Better it should be "good-bye." [41]

Malke lumps Susie together with "today's American girls," who know more about dancing and kissing than how to run a home.

But Susie is no pushover. Malke first realizes this when she recognizes the tune Susie is humming. Malke, not Dave, knows the lyrics that Susie has left unspoken:

> You shouldn't go out with other girls,
> You should only be with me.
> You shouldn't go to your mother's house —
> And should only come to me. (60)

Susie has implicitly announced her position as Malke's rival for Dave's loyalty; the bloodless feud has begun.

Susie initially represents, in Malke's eyes, not only the sort of Americanized girl that Dave should not marry, but a more immediate threat as well, for she clearly distracts him from his homework. In contrast to Susie's Yiddish song and to another that Malke sang at the beginning of the play, Dave is studying a classic English text, Ben Jonson's "Drink to Me Only with Thine Eyes." After reading the English poem aloud, Malke reveals that both the writer and the ideas he expresses are new to her:

> *Malke*: Ben, is that like Benny, is he Jewish?
> *Dave*: No, not Jewish!
> *Malke*: An interesting person, comparing love to drinking and to wine! He must have loved his drink, that Ben Jonson. (61)

Dave then proceeds to sing the popular song based on the poem — ostensibly "for [Malke], but we see that he sings for Susie" (61). Malke sees it too, of course, and before falling asleep on the sofa, declares that she will look for another apartment in the morning, in order to get Dave away from Susie.

As a dramatic setting, the tenement apartment serves two crucial purposes for Chaver-Paver. Historically, the tenement was a fact of life for millions of Jewish immigrants to the United States. They also had balconies — or at least fire escapes — and therefore, like the synagogue women's section in *The Oath on the Torah*, came equipped with a natural parallel to Shakespeare's balcony scene. The charm of Chaver-Paver's balcony scene lies not in beautiful flights of rhetoric or romantic images. Quite the contrary; he surrounds Dave and Susie with the most prosaic of details, but shows them rising above their humble circumstances. Even when the setting offers traditionally romantic associations, the writer undercuts them:

> *Susie (looks out the window at the sky)*: Such a beautiful night!
> *Dave (also looks out the window)*: A wonderful night!
> *Susie*: Look, see how many stars!
> *Dave*: They are worlds. (*At that moment is heard the coughing of an asthmatic from a floor above them*).
> *Susie*: That's Max the painter, from the fourth floor. Every night it's like that. He should be living by the sea. (61)

The neighbor's coughing, far from dampening their romantic impulses, provides inspiration. Her mention of the sea gives Dave the opening to invite her to the beach with him, and they make a date for the following Sunday.

Susie, like Malke, sees through Dave quite easily, and does not fail to remark that his boldness with her probably owes something to the fact that his mother is asleep. The critical moment comes when, in a burst of gallantry, Dave tries climbing over to her balcony and tears a seam on his best pair of pants. He is not so head-over-heels as to forget who bought them for him:

> *Susie*: What happened?
> *Dave*: I'm embarrassed to say.
> *Susie*: Did something rip?
> *Dave* (*embarrassed*): Yes, the . . . the . . . what is it called . . .
> *Susie*: Ha, ha! I understand . . . But what's the big deal? Change into other . . .
> *Dave*: But she . . . I mean (*points to his sleeping mother*) — warned me to take them off. New pants that I wear to college . . .
> *Susie*: Such fear of a mother! What is she, a goddess?
> *Dave*: It isn't fear . . . It's . . . It's . . . You understand, works so hard, buys me things . . . (62)

Dave has apparently reached his nadir, both romantically and filially. While squandering his inheritance, he has managed to bungle the balcony scene too.

Susie can rescue him on both fronts, however, for she can sew. And in a milieu dominated psychically as well as financially by Malke, sewing means far more than just repairing seams. For starters, it enhances Susie's beauty in Dave's eyes: "You have great inner strength, just like my mother. . . . When you sit and sew, you're so beautiful" (62). Susie dismisses this with a laugh, but Dave's observation shows that his and Malke's notion of the ideal woman are not so far apart after all. When Malke awakes a few moments later to find her son *sans culotte*, the moment of truth arrives. Malke officiously calls for Susie to return them, but when she inspects the merchandise, she cannot even see where Dave ripped them. "She has golden fingers, that Susie," she marvels (63). She then asks her son to sing Ben Jonson's poem again, but this time not for her: "Sing it for that Susie-Zisl. A girl who can fix a pair of pants with such skill, not like some American girl . . ." (63).

Malke, acting as all the Montague and Capulet parents rolled into one, has been won over by the apparent enemy, who turns out to be an ally. Here, what's in a name is deceptive, for Susie's American name belies her traditional skills and values. When these become apparent,

Malke hyphenates the girl's name and adds its Yiddish component. Dave has managed to follow his romantic inclinations without paying a price, for what looked like rebellion turns out to be perfectly acceptable. Malke gives her final stamp of approval by sanctioning a song that she earlier dismissed on at least two counts: its use of a metaphor that made no sense to her, and its being directed over her shoulder to Susie. (And perhaps a third, with Jonson, disappointingly, turning out not to be Jewish in spite of *his* promising first name.) Now that Susie is kosher, Malke accepts the metaphor, and allows her son to use it in the way he initially intended.

Calling his sketch "Romeo and Juliet" calls attention to how different the action of Chaver-Paver's tale is from Shakespeare's. Malke plays the traditional blocking figure to Dave and Susie's union for a time, not because her values are at fault, but because she does not initially realize that Susie-Zisl represents everything Malke could want in a daughter-in-law. The writer packs his playlet with all the conflicts that other translators and adaptors of the play exploited in various ways, but ultimately makes his story into a utopian prehistory of the lives of his readers. Their parents and grandparents (or they themselves, as children) were Dave's, Malke's, and Susie's neighbors. They took home piecework, labored over their English homework, argued about changing customs and values in the New World. Each Yiddish version of *Romeo and Juliet* had something to say about those struggles. Traditionally, by keeping Shakespeare's tragic outcome intact even while significantly altering the dénouement of their source, Yiddish playwrights sent the message that the children were right. In an America where the Jews had clearly become more comfortable than they were half a century earlier, Chaver-Paver's readers could take greater comfort in his *Romeo and Juliet*, where the apparent conflict turns out to have been no conflict at all. Both the parents and the children were right.

chapter 5

'A True Jewish Jew'
A Shylock Quartet

"Of all of Shakespeare's works, *The Merchant of Venice* holds
the greatest interest for Jews," wrote critic Bernard Gorin in 1911.[1]
Gorin's observation may seem axiomatic today, but theatre practice
in the 1890s, when Shakespeare's plays were first staged in Yiddish,
would not necessarily have led to such a conclusion. The only recorded Yiddish production of the play in New York during that decade ran for just one weekend in February 1894, and such a commercial failure would have been an unlikely export to other American
cities.[2] Other Shakespeare plays, particularly the four explored here
so far, were initially far more successful than *Merchant* at American
Yiddish box offices, although in 1899 it became the first Yiddish
translation of a Shakespeare play published in the United States, in a
version by poet Joseph Bovshover.[3] Perhaps eastern European Jewish
immigrants, who had begun coming to America in large numbers only
a decade before, were not yet ready for such a delicate exploration of
the Jew's position in a Gentile world. Or maybe the play just needed
the right actor.

In 1901, Jacob Adler starred in the first Yiddish production of *The
Merchant of Venice* to make a lasting impression on critics and audiences. Over the next half century, three giants of the American Yiddish stage would periodically bring Shylock to life. Adler, Rudolph
Schildkraut, and Maurice Schwartz would use the role to explore the
Jew's place in the Diaspora more directly than most Shakespearean
translations and adaptations allowed. Yet since Shylock makes for
such a problematic Jewish role model, the major interpreters of Shylock on American Yiddish stages would seek various ways to make
the character more palatable, from softening the character to radically
cutting or even rewriting the play.

A fourth Jewish actor, who made no attempt at gaining sympathy
for Shylock was Maurice Moscovitch. His unsparing approach to the

role was made even more problematic by virtue of the fact that he performed it not in his native Yiddish, but in English. And not only in English, but in London's West End and later, in 1930, on Broadway. Because of his roots in the Yiddish theatre and the renown he had achieved outside it, his Broadway run was covered widely by Yiddish critics, who wondered aloud about its implications: what would Gentile audiences think of an unflattering depiction, performed by a Jew, of the most problematic Jewish character in all of dramatic literature?

Adler, Schildkraut, and Schwartz each played some performances of Shylock in non-Yiddish venues as well, thus attracting considerable attention from outside the Jewish cultural ghetto. Actress Bertha Kalish reported that Jacob Adler's Broadway debut as Shylock in 1903 drew several producers, including Charles Frohman and Harrison Grey Fiske, to the Lower East Side to scout for talent.[4] All four actors' Shylocks were reviewed extensively in the English-language press. The prominence of the actors playing Shylock, the publicity their performances generated, and the problematic treatment of Jews in the play, stirred heated debates about both Shakespeare's depiction of Jews and of the place of the Jew in the modern world. The play's center of interest for Jewish audiences — its treatment of the Jew's status in the Diaspora — remained constant. In production, however, approaches to the play changed over time. The most dramatic of these changes came in the aftermath of World War II, when the decimation of European Jewry radically altered how Jews looked at themselves, their neighbors, and the manner in which art depicts Gentile-Jewish relations.

Jacob Adler: From the Bowery to Broadway

The first Yiddish actor to achieve a significant impact as Shylock was Jacob P. Adler (fig. 14). Performing in both translations and adaptations, Adler had played a prominent role in bringing Shakespeare's plays to Yiddish audiences before appearing in *The Merchant of Venice*. In his memoirs, however, the tradition in which he places Shylock has less to do with Shakespeare than with a certain Jewish character type central to Adler's repertoire:

14. Jacob Adler as Shylock. From the Archives of the YIVO Institute for Jewish Research.

He is a patriarch. He is a higher being. And his personality is the accumulated legacy, the gathering force of generations, and it comes through in his language, his deportment, his appearance, his face, and his gait. There is a certain grandeur in this Jew, the triumph born of long suffering, of intellect, of a character raised by two governesses: high traditions and an endless series of spiritual sufferings.[5]

Accordingly, Adler set out to present neither the grotesquely comic Shylock that preceded eighteenth-century actor Charles Macklin's conception of the role, nor the cruel, petty, unbending Shylock of numerous other interpreters. Adler's Shylock was most akin to that of late nineteenth-century English actor Henry Irving, who called Shylock "a bloody-minded monster, — but you mustn't play him so, if you wish to succeed; you must get some sympathy with him."[6] Indeed, in Irving's hands, "The play was interpreted from Shylock's point of view: he never saw himself as a villain, and audiences usually accepted his opinion."[7]

Adler himself, in a 1902 interview, claimed to have seen Irving's Shylock many years earlier, in London: "Irving is the greatest actor I have seen. . . . But, strongly as I was impressed with the Englishman's Shylock, I felt all the more conviction in my own conception of the Jew of Venice, whom I would portray as a type, not as a caricature."[8] Adler, as might be expected from a Jewish actor, sought to go beyond Irving in making Shylock sympathetic, and felt that the character "should be shown well-dressed and proud of mien, instead of the poor and cringing figure which custom has made familiar."[9] This reading came across to the reviewers, who generally agreed that "Mr. Adler's conception of Shylock's demand for justice and the pound of flesh is not the bloodthirsty one to which we have grown accustomed."[10] Adler's Shylock therefore followed in the Irving tradition, but "not even Sir Henry Irving," wrote one critic, "has made an appeal for the sympathy of the audience such as Mr. Adler put into his performance."[11]

While also following Irving's lead in presenting a strikingly picturesque figure, Adler's Shylock was "a man of the people and thoroughly Oriental, not an aristocrat of the Ghetto, like Sir Henry Irving's."[12] In other words, "Mr. Adler has revived the Jewish Shylock. He takes a place in the synagogue; not among the nobility, but among those who are typical."[13] Typical, but by no means ordinary: "It is distinctly oriental — in the cast of the face, the swarthy coloring, the long, rich robes, and the dignity of bearing."[14]

Adler's *Merchant* — under the title *Shylock* — opened at the People's Theatre in New York on 5 December 1901. In time-honored Yiddish fashion, Adler used a script that drastically cut the original text to heighten the leading character's prominence. This is not difficult to do when the character is central to begin with; snip some of Polonius's philosophizing or a few of the Fool's riddles, and your Hamlet or Lear looms even larger. Shylock, on the other hand, appears in only five scenes out of twenty in the first place, making the power of his presence all the more remarkable. To make him the central character in terms of stage time requires a reworking of the plot, a restructuring of the text.[15]

Adler's acting version, following common nineteenth-century practice before Irving, put Shylock on stage for over half the play and ended with the focus on the moneylender by cutting Act V altogether. Adler was not the first to increase Shylock's stage time; indeed, he directly borrowed Irving's pantomime at the end of Act II, as described by George C. D. Odell: "The elopement of Jessica during the carnival celebration was accompanied by the greatest possible animation of masked crowds arriving in gondolas, running across the bridge, etc. But, after it was all ended, the return of Shylock over the bridge, across the silent stage, and his knock at the door of the deserted home!"[16] The Adler adaptation went much further, all but eliminating the double love-story plot and thereby drastically changing the tone of the play. This shift was surely intentional, for as problematic as Shylock is to a Jewish audience, a Jewish daughter abandoning her father and converting to Christianity is the stuff of tragedy, not comedy. After all, this was the culture that produced Sholem Aleykhem's Tevye the Dairyman, who went into mourning when a far more devoted daughter married a Gentile. There is little in *The Merchant of Venice* that would strike a Jewish audience as comic, but then the reading of the play that sees tragic dignity in Shylock is what would draw an Adler, a Schildkraut, or a Schwartz to the role in the first place.

The start of Adler's performance gave little sign of the coming tragedy. In Act I, he chuckled over the bizarre contract with Antonio — the "merry bond," as Shylock himself puts it. One reviewer saw Adler's drawing up of the agreement as "rather a merry quip — one almost imagines that he intends showing the unique bond to his colleagues on the Rialto with a laugh,"[17] but the actor added a gesture to the end of the same scene that seemed to suggest the opposite conclusion. Instead of sending Shylock off before the others, as Shakespeare does, the Yiddish text leaves him alone on stage after they go, and the curtain falls as he "raises his handkerchief and points with his staff."[18] In the words of one observer, "Round and round his hands he twists his great purple handkerchief, as though he were twisting Antonio tighter and tighter still. His grave face has turned all vindictive cunning."[19]

Shylock's wrath came to a head when he discovered that his daughter had run off, though Adler kept the character's anger contained until later. He entered to the accompaniment of quiet music, composed for the production by Joseph Rumshinsky, and knocked twice on the door with his staff. When he realized that Jessica had gone, he tore his garment in a symbolic gesture of mourning, sighed, and sank to the ground "as though he were gathering little by little all that has happened. A deep, shuddering, convulsive sigh" — "oy, oy," according to the stage directions (19) — "shows his realization of it. It is the simplest of means, and once more they prove the most moving."[20] In the next scene, though, Shylock's restraint vanished: "From a very low and quiet key he lifts his acting to the highest and sharpest. In the scene with Tubal it is all a fury of rage and revenge. Or it chokes with grief. Or it shrieks with avarice. Shylock's dignity and self-mastery are gone. He shakes his staff at the jeering bystanders. He clutches at Tubal. He barely totters off the stage."[21] He would maintain this tone in the beginning of the trial. In the meantime, the rest of the company took care of the subplot.

One of the most striking features of Adler's acting text is its treatment of Portia, played by Adler's wife Sara. Shakespeare introduces Portia in the second scene, but Sara Adler was kept waiting in the wings until the middle of Act III, where the entire casket subplot is summarily executed (in both senses of the word). That is, she and her servant Nerissa evaluate the suitors, Morocco and Aragon are omitted entirely, and Bassanio enters and chooses the lead casket without much deliberation. Such cuts do their utmost to limit not only the supporting characters' stage time, but their charm as well. One can almost hear the text heave a sigh of relief; now it can get back to Shylock.

Most critics agreed that Adler's performance reached its zenith in the courtroom scene. He began it like a cornered animal (which, in a sense, he is), leaping at Antonio until he was forcibly restrained. Adler told an interviewer that Shylock's apparent eagerness to do violence was purely for show:

> That such a court will interpret the law in his favor, the ironical Jew is not for one instant fatuous enough to suppose. . . . The real revenge that Shylock contemplates is *not* to take the pound of flesh which is legally forfeit to him, but to show the world that his despised ducats have actually bought and paid for it. His whetting the knife on his sole is a hyperbolical menace: his sardonic smile, accompanying this action, is the only sharp edge that shall cut the self-humiliated Merchant.[22]

At least one critic picked up on this reading: "When he sharpened the knife to cut the pound of flesh from the bankrupt . . . Shylock slyly noted whether the proud merchant quailed."[23]

Adler's Shylock regained his composure after lunging at Antonio, and demonstrated his dignity most profoundly in the moment of his deepest humiliation:

> Gratiano had been making a number of passes at him, which he had beaten off after the manner of a bird, with weak clutching of the hands; then he brushes the impress of Gratiano's hand from his sleeve, arranges his hair and coat, his beard, and with calm contempt for the court and all those interested in the wrongful miscarriages of justice, passes out, leaving a stern sense of disapproval of the whole proceeding.[24]

The production ended there. Concluding the play with Shylock's moment of triumph-in-disgrace rather than with the lighthearted resolution of the lovers' plot leaves the audience with the taste of persecution in its mouth. The thematic balance that Act V provides doubtless would not have impressed Yiddish theatregoers as much as the direct connection between the mood of Adler's ending and the anti-Semitism that so many of the immigrants in his audience had fled, and that many still feared.

This emphasis ultimately sets Yiddish interpretations of the role apart from those of their Gentile colleagues, as the eminent Yiddish poet Morris Vintshevski was quick to point out:

[As] hard as Henry Irving's task was to depict a human Jew while remaining true to the words of the great Englishman's play, it is all the more remarkable when a Jew undertakes to perform Shakespeare's words before a Jewish audience. That takes courage, and that alone deserves the attention of every lover of true art. . . .

Mr. Adler's Shylock will forever stand even higher than Irving's, for however great the latter may be, he can never sufficiently understand the Venetian Jewish merchant's pride . . . Adler's heart speaks where Irving's art paints . . . and he does not need a nose that looks like a half-moon . . . in order to portray his Shylock, to put flesh and blood and a living soul into Shakespeare's words. In short, his Shylock is a true Jewish Jew.[25]

To a critic like Vintshevski, who values Adler's ethnic authenticity in the role over Irving's mimetic skill, Adler epitomizes what Shylock should be: an apotheosis of Jewish suffering during centuries of anti-Semitism.

"What a beautiful figure of the Venetian Jew of the Middle Ages!" raved a critic. "And not an artificial man, no artistic effects. Every word, every movement is life itself."[26] Gorin agreed that Adler largely disposed of actorly artifice: "Mr. Adler's acting excels in its simplicity, naturalness, without exaggeration or affectation."[27] Sara Adler was praised for her "beautiful diction,"[28] but the rest of the cast did not come off as well: "It is a shame that the talented Yiddish artist has to perform with oafs who do not know how to move on stage and speak in German the entire time."[29] And Gorin chided the production's use of "superfluous" music, pointing out that "the audience that comes to see 'Shylock' is not the audience for [Hurwitz's] 'Ben hador' or [Lateiner's] 'Blimele.'" This audience, Gorin claimed, appreciated Adler's acting, thus proving "that the theatregoers are not such 'Moyshes' as they are made out to be."[30]

However gratifying Moyshe's appreciation may have been, Adler soon began to express an interest in reaching a wider audience, for "Adler is not as happy as could be expected in the laurels he has won playing in good drama . . . and his warmest wish is to appear one day before an American audience in one of the Broadway theatres."[31] Adler's fans at the People's were American, of course, but not in the sense implied here. They were not, simply speaking, in the English-speaking majority, and joining the majority promised an actor greater rewards, in terms of both wealth and recognition, than the greatest success in a minority culture could offer. Adler surely knew of the many precedents for mixed-language productions of Shakespeare in America, and seems to have realized that if ever he would have a chance to follow in the footsteps of a Salvini or a Coquelin, Shylock offered him the perfect vehicle.

Adler was given a chance to fulfill his wish in the winter of 1903, but is said to have twice refused producer Arthur Hopkins's offer to perform Shylock on Broadway with an English-speaking cast. "He did not want to play for strangers, did not want to leave his own public," writes his granddaughter and biographer. According to Adler family legend, the actor was spurred on by an "embattled Zionist" friend who joked, "You owe it to the Gentiles," and urged him, "Let them see how a JEW plays Shylock!" These exhortations reportedly spurred Adler to open discussions with Hopkins, leading to a tour of major cities in the Northeast that spring.[32] Adler's supporting actors, reported the *Jewish Exponent*, "have been selected from the first rank of the dramatic profession," and their performances were adorned by the "scenery, costumes and accessories used by the late Augustin Daly" for his spectacular staging of *Merchant* at Daly's Theatre in New York in 1888–1889.[33] Adler and company opened at the Academy of Music in Philadelphia, where it was reported that Adler's business manager, J. Abramson, "has seen to it that the first performance will be attended by the greatest men in Philadelphia and the greatest theatre critics in the land."[34] After Philadelphia, the production traveled to Baltimore, Boston, and New York, where it ran for one week at the American Theatre. The same theatre would host Adler's Yiddish Shylock two years later, in May 1905, also with an English-speaking supporting cast.

As the time for Adler's debut on the English-language stage approached, one Jewish critic writing in English felt compelled to prepare his readership for the event. The *Jewish Exponent* catered to well-heeled Philadelphia Jews, generally more akin in manners and taste to the upper-class Gentiles they sought to emulate than to the largely working-class Yiddish-speaking Jews they tended to keep at arm's length.[35] The newspaper's theatre critic, Louis Lipsky, predicted that "the audience may be led to ridicule or dislike by the language and the manners of this new interpreter." In order "to minimize as much as possible the incongruous effect he is likely to produce," Lipsky reminded his readers that all actors have certain physical limitations, and praised Adler's "histrionic abilities which would have opened the theatres of continental Europe to him if he had played in classic drama and spoken a continental language." [36]

Lipsky did not express any apprehension of overtly anti-Semitic responses to the play — at least not in so many words. Such reactions were rare, but a curious piece — it cannot really be called a review — in the *Evening Mail* began by pretending to quote pranksters in the audience calling Adler's Shylock "Svengali" or "Shylock Holmes." Turning his attention to the program, the writer claimed to find two advertisements for pawnbrokers. "We assume that they are relatives of the title-role gentleman, and we are wary." [37] As if writing a script for knockabout ethnic comedians, the critic also claimed to quote snippets of the production's dialogue:

> *Shylock*: Oy, oy, oy! A zwei Tausend Dukaten diamond. Gone! An that ain't no press agent yarn, neither. Ach muss ich suchen all over the place. Main Dochter ist mit a Goy eloped! [38]

Even the most powerful and sympathetic rendering of Shylock was not about to lead all reviewers in the America of 1903 to see matters from the Jew's perspective.

Setting this caricature aside, the actual reviews show that Lipsky's concerns had been well founded. While generally praising Adler's performance, English-language reviewers sometimes found his acting too flamboyant. The critic for the *Globe* observed that Adler's "extravagant gestures" did not always appeal to the Broadway audience, who "tittered at some of these things — and not unjustly. They were vivid, they were powerful, but for our more sluggish temperaments they were overdone." [39] The *New York Times*, on the other hand, found Adler at times too naturalistic for his own good: "Adler failed, in so far as he did fail, because his artistic good sense impelled him to give, on the whole, a simple, unaffected, and naturalistic rendering of the part, to eschew the Hebrew prophet of modern sentimentality, and to stick to the Shylock of Shakespeare — and of the Ghetto. He thus fell, as it were, between two stools." [40] Most other reviewers lauded Adler's performance for being neither too simple nor overly extravagant. In fact, the *Globe* and *Times* reviewers may simply have picked up on a central quality of Adler's Shylock, which offered sharp contrasts ranging across a wide emotional spectrum, from the subdued at one end to the nearly hysterical at the other.

Opinions on the quality of Adler's supporting cast were even more sharply divided. "Exceptionally incompetent," hissed one critic.[41] "Thoroughly competent," concluded another, singling out Meta Maynard for bringing "truly distinguished traits of delicacy and feeling" to her portrayal of Portia.[42] Most of the reviews, both in 1903 and 1905, gave solid marks to both the cast and the production values. "The play moved so smoothly," wrote an observer of the earlier run, "as to make one forget that this was its first production by this company on any stage. Scenically, too, this notable production left little to be desired. . . . The maskers in the street scene proved a picturesque feature, and Portia's house at Belmont was staged with elaborate and artistic effect."[43] A reviewer attending the 1905 revival thought "the scenery and effects were rather sumptuous for a stock company,"[44] perhaps suggesting that the Daly sets had been brought out of storage once again.

The Yiddish dialogue of Adler's Shylock amid the English of the rest of the cast both challenged the actor's ability to make himself understood, and further underscored his character's Jewishness. Even as late as 1905, one naysayer found it "unfortunate" that Adler would speak his dialogue in Yiddish, since "his performance therefore will possess small attraction for those who are unacquainted with the dialect."[45] Undoubtedly there was some truth in that, but after all, Adler had been sufficiently successful in the same bilingual format two years earlier to allow for a reprise of the experiment. During that earlier run, one reviewer for the Yiddish press paid close attention to the English-speaking audience, finding to his pleasant surprise that "a deep seriousness on the faces of these Americans. They understood Adler just as well as they did the rest of the actors, and in places even better. They showed this with both the attentiveness with which they listened to him and the applause with which they greeted the end of every scene in which he appeared."[46]

Many of the reviews in both the Yiddish and English press applauded not only Adler, but also the Yiddish language itself, which they welcomed into the fold as if it were a talented young actor who had finally made it to the big time after arduously honing his craft in obscure garrets and saloons. The *Jewish Exponent* paid Yiddish the backhanded compliment of being "a language which many of those who had heard it in the past had deemed harsh and raucous, but which seemed, as uttered by this actor, replete with gentle cadences and harmonies. It did not obtrude itself grotesquely, as many had feared it would, into the immortal English of Shakespeare, but proved a telling vindication of a language which . . . contains many gems of literature, both poetry and prose."[47] The *New York Herald* concurred, writing of the production's bilingualism, "it is not the smallest tribute to [Adler's] art that this fact interfered but little with the general enjoyment of his important scenes."[48]

The Yiddish press fairly beamed at how well the language had acquitted itself. Critic Moyshe Katz sounded like a proud father: "It is simply a pleasure to hear how a Yiddish monologue sounds on the English stage when it comes from the mouth of a great actor."[49] Another reviewer crowed that Yiddish "showed on the stage of the Academy of Music that it can be classic, that it sounds good, and that it can convey even Shakespeare's imagery."[50] Such claims for the artistic possibilities of Yiddish echo those that linguist Alexander Harkavy had made when he translated the "To be or not to be" soliloquy in order to demonstrate that Yiddish was "a language not just for simple dramas but also for sophisticated ones."[51] The performance of the English poet's work in Yiddish on English stages eloquently supported Harkavy's assertion.

In one sense, Yiddish speakers' excitement over the newfound recognition of their mother tongue was simply the next step in the process that had inspired the adaptation of Shakespeare into Yiddish in the first place; after the Yiddish theatre found a native audience, it started looking for a broader one. The latter quest can be seen as part of a larger struggle: eastern European Jews' efforts to find acceptance in the eyes of Gentile America. One Yiddish journalist expressed how this desire manifested itself on the eve of Adler's Broadway debut: "Jews felt a sort of patriotic warmth. Every one of us hoped that Adler would succeed, that he would be applauded, that the critics would have a high opinion of him. Every one of us felt that it would not be nice if the star of the Yiddish theatre should fail."[52] They were not disappointed.

Rudolph Schildkraut: From Berlin to the Bowery

Being the first actor to perform in Yiddish on Broadway made Adler a de facto ambassador to the Gentile world. In 1911, the New York Yiddish theatre welcomed another such envoy: one who, in fact, had already been applauded on non-Yiddish European stages. Rudolph Schildkraut (1862–1930) had had boyhood contact of a sort with Yiddish theatre, for in his home town of Galatz, Romania, his parents ran a hotel that frequently played host to Yiddish actors. Schildkraut, however (like Morris Morrison, another native of Galatz), entered the profession via the German-language stage. In his mid-teens, Schildkraut joined a troupe of itinerant actors, and after a few years of touring, was hired to act in comedies and operettas at the Raimund Theater in Vienna. His growing fame left him unsatisfied, for Schildkraut wanted serious dramatic roles. His chance to realize this aspiration came when the eminent German tragedian Friedrich Mitterwurzer (1844–1897) offered to make Schildkraut his protégé. Schildkraut readily accepted, thus gaining not only a gifted teacher, but also a vigorous promoter. This support vanished with Mitterwurzer's untimely death, but shortly thereafter, Schildkraut was hired by the director of the new Deutsches Schauspielhaus in Hamburg, where his Lear marked the high point of his five-year tenure as leading man. Before long, his performance of another Shakespearean role would win him even greater notoriety.

In 1905, a young Max Reinhardt invited Schildkraut to star in his production of *The Merchant of Venice* at the Deutsches Theater in Berlin. The play was staged in what was to become signature Reinhardt style — elegant, detailed, and lavish: "There were handsome sets, costumes out of Carpaccio and Veronese, street cries, snatches of song, incidental music by Humperdinck; a revolving stage reinforced the impression of a magical self-contained world given over to pleasure."[53] Given Reinhardt's emphasis on spectacle and on the play's more sanguine side, Shylock was not his primary focus, but Schildkraut still managed to make an impact: "A full-blooded actor and a conscious Jew, he entered into the feelings of a hunted, tormented and therefore unbalanced being, through whom generations of Jews voiced their shrill protest against their persecutors of all times."[54] Schildkraut would soon bring this interpretation to the United States, where his Shylock would decidedly take center stage.

Schildkraut's New York debut in 1911 created such a sensation that it threatened to relegate even the great Jacob Adler to the sidelines for a time, at least according to a cartoon in the Yiddish journal *Der groyser kundes* (fig. 15). The drawing shows Adler, his bloated body filling his box at the theatre, looking on with a grimace at Schildkraut's performance of Shylock. The caption, pretending to reveal Adler's thoughts at the moment, lampoons his reputed venality and callousness through a parody of Shylock's most famous speech: "Am I not a human being, as he is? If the actors' union hands me its demands, do I not cry? And if I am sued for breach of contract, do I not laugh? And if I cut a fresh porterhouse steak, do I not draw blood? So why can he act better than I?"[55] Fictional though the situation depicted in the cartoon was, it reflected at least one reality: Yiddish audiences' respect for Schildkraut's success as a German Shakespearean. Given earlier examples of the deference of Yiddish actors towards German culture — Thomashefsky's hiring of a German director to train him for *Hamlet*, for example, or the general awe of Morris Morrison once word got out of his experience in German productions — the interior monologue the *Kundes* put in Adler's head may not have been far from the truth either.

The combination of Schildkraut's German stardom and his strong Jewish identity led the Yiddish press to run story after story about him. Many observers found it all the more remarkable that his success on non-Jewish stages had not prevented him from taking unabashed pleasure in such Yiddish entertainment as the commercially successful melodramas listed in the following tribute: "They say he is a Jew, and what a Jew! A Jewish Jew, a Jew who gets inspired by the 'Pintele yid,' 'Yidishe neshome,' 'Yidishe harts,' and all the Jewish bastards and heretics who have flourished on our stage in the last few years. This is not because he is such an expert on true art, but because he . . . relishes everything Jewish."[56] In spite of the occasional recognition of a Bertha Kalish or a Jacob Adler, Yiddish speakers had by no means shed their perception of the inferiority of their mother tongue. Schildkraut's entry into Yiddish culture would add a new dimension; if a Jew voluntarily rejoined the fold after demonstrating his bona fides in the Gentile world, then surely Yiddish had worthwhile ingredients to add to the world's cultural melting pot.

The reviewer for *Der yidishes tageblat* felt that Schildkraut brought his Jewishness to the role so effectively that there was "certainly not a

15. Jacob Adler watching Rudolph Schildkraut play Shylock.
From *Der groyser kundes, 19 May 1911.*

more Jewish Shylock than the one Mr. Schildkraut presented." Furthermore, "He did not rage, he did not storm, did not make all of the broad gestures and declamations that one usually hears in classical drama, but played an old-fashioned Jewish merchant."[57] But not everyone was impressed with either Schildkraut's expression of his Jewish identity or his ability to play a Jew. Joel Entin suggested that

Schildkraut's success in Germany came at a price: "When someone has since childhood kept his distance from the Yiddish masses . . . it is difficult to rejoin them." Entin felt that this distance hindered Schildkraut's ability to create authentic Jewish characters, including Shylock: "Schildkraut turns the Spanish-Oriental Shylock of the time of the Venetian doges into a worthless Jew from the old market" and "entirely obliterates the little that is picturesque" about the medieval moneylender.[58] For Entin, as for many other reviewers, the Jewishness (or lack thereof) of Schildkraut's Shylock was crucial to the success or failure of the performance. After all, if the actor failed to present an authentic Jew, then the Christian characters' behavior toward him would no longer be authentic manifestations of anti-Semitism, and the focal point of the play for most Jewish viewers — as a commentary on relations between Jews and Gentiles — would therefore dissolve. Entin was also disappointed that Schildkraut, the "naturalistic artist," failed to find the beauty in the character: "His Shylock is naturalistically brutal, in one or two places somewhat melodramatic, and absolutely unsuited to the romantically elevated, poetic . . . Shakespearean drama."[59]

In 1911 at least, most of the critics who saw Schildkraut agreed. A few months before Entin entered his verdict, another critic contrasted the Shylocks of Schildkraut and his German colleague Ernst Possart, who played the role within two weeks of each other at the Irving Place Theatre, then a home of German-language performances: "Schildkraut makes his Jew a man socially inferior to Possart's. His is the money grabber, the low, vindictive Jew while Possart's is the gentleman, vindictive perhaps, but capable of restraining his hatred. Schildkraut gets comedy out of the part at every opportunity, while Possart is too serious to consider caricature. Schildkraut is more vigorous, ferocious and sometimes rants."[60] Two months later, a Yiddish critic reviewing Schildkraut's performance around the corner at the New Yiddish Theatre concurred, finding his Shylock "not the least bit idealized. He plays a Jew for whom money-making has become a consuming passion."[61]

Playwright and critic Leon Kobrin insisted that Schildkraut had failed to present a truly Jewish Shylock because he had so successfully uncovered the soul of Shakespeare's Shylock. Although "the great Schildkraut sought to embody in his Shylock the Jew who has been oppressed and persecuted for a thousand years," that was not the

Shylock Shakespeare created, according to Kobrin. Schildkraut was simply being true to Shakespeare's creation: "The more artistically the artist plays Shylock, the more dark and unsympathetic he seems . . . since the truly great artist reflects in his performance the spirit and the mood of the poet and of the poet's work. . . . Schildkraut presented the Shylock that Shakespeare created — if not the body, then certainly the soul. The mirror is not at fault for showing an ugly face." [62] Kobrin's dim view of Shakespeare's Jew was not far from that of critic Jacob Milkh, who declared in a 1911 article — inspired, he said, by seeing Schildkraut's Shylock — that the character as Shakespeare conceived him "has not a drop of Jewishness in him." [63]

Milkh's essay reveals a minute but telling detail of Schildkraut's stage business almost in passing. In his first scene, Shylock gives a Biblical precedent for charging interest and remarks by way of preamble, "This Jacob from our holy Abram was / (As his wise mother wrought in his behalf) / The third possessor; ay, he was the third" (I.iii.72–74). Milkh observed that during these lines, Schildkraut counted to three on his fingers, as if counting off the Hebrew patriarchs to himself. Milkh interprets the gesture as showing Shylock's minimal Jewish knowledge and, like Kobrin, does not fault Schildkraut for the choice. After all, it is consistent with Shylock's general ignorance of Jewish matters, such as his swearing by the Sabbath in the courtroom scene: "Shylock's declaration that he has sworn by the Sabbath to get revenge sounds like 'a Gentile speaking Yiddish.' One sees that a Gentile has invented a thing that is very precious to Jews. Well, the Sabbath is indeed a great and holy thing for Jews, but we do not swear by the Sabbath." [64] To Milkh, Shylock's Jewishness fails to run deeper than certain quasi-Jewish details on the character's surface, but one can interpret Schildkraut's counting off of the patriarchs in other ways. It can be seen as an example of his tendency to bring out the comedy in the role by letting Shylock enjoy an unusual moment of power over his oppressors and draw it out as long as possible. It could also suggest the opposite of Milkh's interpretation; perhaps Shylock is lording his biblical knowledge over Antonio and Bassanio. That is, he counts for their supposed benefit, not for his own. He knows perfectly well which patriarch Jacob is, but assumes that they do not. This last reading of the gesture is of a piece with another Schildkraut invention that intensified Shylock's Jewishness. A critic attending a 1920 performance said of Schildkraut's Shylock that "only such a Jew as he could mumble 'Shema yisroel' when he is commanded to convert."[65] By invoking the Shema — "Hear O Israel, the Lord is our God, the Lord is One" — Schildkraut put forth an intensely Jewish Shylock, a Jew who appeals to God as his Jewishness is being stripped away.

Theatregoers in 1911 may not have had the chance to hear this striking addition to the courtroom scene, for at the time Schildkraut presented a Shylock whom some critics found too flamboyant. Leon Kobrin felt that while Schildkraut achieved greatness at certain moments, "I do not at all like his falling to the ground when he loses" in the courtroom.[66] Kobrin was not alone. The critic from the *Mirror*, who had seen Schildkraut at the Irving Place Theatre, noticed many audience members "whose nervous laughter has to be checked by hisses. Not that they mean to be discourteous, but they are at a loss to know whether he means his Jew to be a burlesque."[67] Schildkraut considerably toned down his histrionics when he returned to the role in 1920 at the Jewish Art Theatre. David Belasco declared Schildkraut "the most natural Shylock I have ever seen, and I have seen all of the best Shylocks for a generation. I saw him some years ago and he was inclined to be theatrical, but his characterization is more mellowed now."[68]

Part of the critical success of Schildkraut's Shylock derived from his ability to pack a world of meaning into a small gesture, such as uttering the Shema, or, as critic Bernard Gorin described, "a small movement of the hand that Schildkraut makes when he curses his daughter. Before the curse can tear itself from his throat, he puts his hand over his mouth."[69] Even during the 1920 run, though, Schildkraut did not always resist broader expressions of Shylock's torment. Like Adler, Schildkraut placed his personal stamp on the pantomime after Jessica's elopement, a scene also described by Gorin:

> All that he says is "Jessica," and that is natural. He runs around the house and looks for his daughter; we hear this by the rapid steps on the boards and by the quickness with which the doors slam. He is not on the stage at all during this, but the audience can picture it as if it were played before their eyes. And when he comes out and

calls "Jessica," we hear such heartbreak in his voice and such desperation in his tone. . . . If Schildkraut were satisfied with that call and did not collapse on the bench in front of the house, the impression might have been much stronger.[70]

By 1920, Yiddish audiences had seen Shakespearean characters swoon time and again: Hamlet upon first seeing the ghost, Juliet after first meeting Romeo, Romeo upon learning of his banishment. On the whole, however, Schildkraut tempered his 1920 Shylock enough to impress both Yiddish- and English-speaking critics.

His supporting cast received mixed reviews. As Bassanio, Gustav Schacht gave "a virile performance of a wishy-washy hero."[71] Henrietta Schnitzer was lauded for playing Jessica "with much restraint,"[72] but the same critic condemned the rest of the actors as "astonishingly bad. It is evident that Yiddish actors, with rare exceptions, do not know how to play Shakespeare. They play, it is true, with much life and action, but they shout and act the buffoon and are always in the foreground and never in the background."[73] Another critic put a kinder spin on it, calling the cast "competent if somewhat boisterous."[74]

The spotty performances of the supporting cast surely cannot have helped the take at the box office, but Adler had managed to transcend indifferent acting from many of his fellow actors and achieve commercial as well as critical success. Schildkraut's *Merchant*, on the other hand, did not do well financially. B. Gorin has offered one explanation: "The Yiddish audience has no great love of *The Merchant of Venice*. . . . In a Yiddish theatre, one goes to see Shylock as a curiosity, or one comes to see the actor who plays Shylock, and such an audience is not a large one."[75] This was not the case with Adler, however, who kept Shylock in his repertoire for the rest of his career after first stepping into the role in 1901. But Adler went beyond even the famously sympathetic portrayal of Henry Irving, thus giving his audiences a Shylock they could live with. Although Schildkraut was an actor of high caliber, his Shylock may simply have been too raw, too unsparing, to be palatable to Yiddish audiences at the time. Meanwhile, a colleague was creating a Shylock that would make Schildkraut's seem as lovable as Puck.

Shylock, Strange but Familiar

While Schildkraut was returning to the role of Shylock in 1920, a fellow Yiddish actor across the Atlantic was dazzling English audiences with his chilling portrayal of the medieval moneylender. Maurice Moscovitch (1871–1940) had begun his acting career in a company led by Jacob Adler, toured the Yiddish-speaking world as an actor-manager, and settled in London in 1909, where he became a star in the bustling theatre scene in the East End. When he was able to choose roles, his repertoire was ambitious, including Yiddish translations of plays by Ibsen, Gorky, and Strindberg. It also included Shylock, but London's Yiddish audiences found so little merit in the play that they "roared with laughter" during the trial scene. "They were bewildered by the whole piece," writes M. J. Landa, "and could not understand why it had such a hold over people and why it enjoyed its extraordinary reputation in English."[76]

Nevertheless, when Moscovitch was invited to play Shylock in the West End, one contemporary observer remarked that "this crowd was not of the usual first-nighter order. It was composed of small dark people, the men in hats, the women hatless, ceaselessly chatting, arguing, discussing, in rising and falling waves of sound. It was in fact Mile End come West."[77] The Yiddish actor had been "discovered" in 1919 by J. B. Fagan, manager of the Court Theatre, who came to see him in that staple of the repertoire, *Uriel Acosta*. Fagan reportedly prophesied, "A man with your chin can do anything," and handed him a copy of *The Merchant of Venice*.[78] Overcoming his problems learning English was the first challenge, but nothing that "three months of solitude in a corner of Wales" couldn't cure.[79] A more complicated obstacle was the encrustation of decades of English theatre tradition. "Hardly an actor in the cast but had achieved old and prideful glories with Irving or Tree, they'd have you know, and they resented a departure from old routines."[80] But Fagan had given Moscovitch carte blanche to interpret the role as he saw fit, and so he did.

The actor became a sensation as Shylock, first in a nine-month London run at the Court, and later in an extended tour of the north of England, where "In a realistic and elaborately staged three act production, Moskovitch appeared, a six foot, one inch Shylock, whose make-up was praised as being the most repulsive that had ever been seen."[81] His acting was a different story. Critic Desmond MacCarthy's comments could hardly have been more laudatory: "For deprecating movements of the hands, shrugs, dubious slantings of the head, agitated shakings of the wrists, for a certain pervasive subserviency of manner, for effusiveness in cajolery, for homely expansiveness in joy, for childish abandonment to weeping (poor miserable puckered face!), for gusto in *schadenfreude*, his Shylock is perfect."[82] Perfect, perhaps, but indisputably icy: "Other critics were struck by the deliberate *absence* of dignity in Moscovitch's performance, by such cold, businesslike details as the way in which he took off his rings and turned up his sleeves while preparing to cut the pound of flesh. On one point, however, everyone was agreed: the keynote of his interpretation was unyielding hatred."[83] Yet returning to MacCarthy, we find even the hatred of Moscovitch's "Rembrandtesque" Shylock rendered sympathetically: "Shylock's hatred is not a wild passion, it is a tamed passion; it is caged within another — a passion for legality. . . . His Shylock had the first quality it should possess; he was passionate in hate, in business, in family and race-feeling, in revenge and in despair."[84]

A decade later, Moscovitch would bring his unnerving approach to the role across the Atlantic, in a run on Broadway. The plaudits English reviewers had showered on Moscovitch was not lost on their colleagues overseas, but neither was his reputation for fashioning a chilling picture of the moneylender. American Yiddish critics thus anticipated his arrival on Broadway in 1930 with feverish excitement tempered by apprehension at the impact he would make — particularly on Gentile audiences.

In his memoirs, serialized in the *Forverts* a year before his Broadway run in *The Merchant of Venice*, Moscovitch recalled that he had conceived Shylock "not as an ordinary usurer, but as a proud Jew. He does not bow to the wealthy, but demands revenge for insults done to him; he does not beg, he commands."[85] Moscovitch described how his offstage and onstage lives crisscrossed as he performed the role, for he claimed that the actors playing Antonio and Bassanio in the English production had been every bit as anti-Semitic as the characters they portrayed. He then adds, intriguingly, that the insights he gained from creating his Shylock helped him deal with his offstage enemies, who ultimately gained a grudging respect for his unflinching pride.

That same sense of pride disturbed Jewish critics from the outset, and they expressed their reservations about Moscovitch's interpretation even as they marveled at his virtuosity — indeed, *because* of his talents, which helped him convey his interpretation all the more effectively. A correspondent for the *Forverts* attending the initial London run shuddered to imagine what non-Jews in the audience must have been thinking: "Because Moscovitch is Jewish, and because he gave his interpretation of the role with artistic genuineness, with brutal consistency, with true Jewish temperament, he made a colossal impression on the Jewish world. The Gentile theatregoer felt that only a Jew can experience such feelings of revenge and not know what mercy is, for a Gentile could never be so cruel."[86] The critic worried aloud that Moscovitch was confirming Gentiles' worst biases about Jews by portraying Shylock in such a harsh light.

As with earlier reviews of the Shylocks of Adler, Schildkraut, and Schwartz, discussions of Moscovitch's Shylock often noted the public and critical interest in how a skilled Jewish actor would portray the famous moneylender. But uniquely within this quartet of interpreters, Moscovitch did not attempt to make his Shylock sympathetic or pitiable; an English critic wrote, "You might equally well pity a Bengal tiger in mid-spring."[87] Just as the *Forverts* correspondent worried about the message such an interpretation would send to the Gentile world, Alexander Mukdoyni fretted over Moscovitch's Broadway run eleven years later, particularly since he found this Shylock uncomfortably familiar: "Maurice Moscovitch did not seek out a historical Shylock, a Jew who lived in Italy hundreds of years ago. He molded his Shylock after the characteristics of a contemporary Polish Jew. . . . It is no longer a distant historical figure, but one that is quite close by — too close."[88] Moscovitch did not even bother, observes Mukdoyni, to try to make Shylock more sympathetic than Shakespeare meant him to be, but that would not have mattered. While many contemporary actors do, it never works, because the playwright created his character with too much skill to be "fooled." Mukdoyni concludes that one cannot escape the fact that *The Merchant of Venice* is "a terrible, mean, and slanderous old wives' tale."[89]

Abraham Cahan had even less respect for the play than Mukdoyni did. Cahan, a died-in-the-wool socialist realist who never had much patience for Shakespeare in the first place, spends much of his review assuring his readers how overrated the Bard is. The chief weapon in Cahan's arsenal is the business of Portia's disguise, which he picks apart over the course of five paragraphs for being utterly unbelievable. "And this childish nonsense," marvels Cahan, "this silly piece of *purimshpil*, is a literary classic." [90] Beneath the insults, however, lies a sort of acceptance. Mukdoyni's labeling of the play as an "old wives' tale" and Cahan's calling it a *purimshpil* convey an irreverence that Yiddish critics would not have expressed (and probably would not have thought) a generation earlier. The very fact that Yiddish critics no longer place Shakespeare on so high a pedestal indicates the extent to which they have welcomed him as one of their own; contempt implies familiarity.

That familiarity with Shakespeare underscored a major difference between Moscovitch's performance and those of his Yiddish colleagues. The English-Yiddish actor brought to the role an understated quality not usually seen on Yiddish stages:

> Above all, he speaks his longer speeches with a clarity of gesture and mimicry that helps define his character sharply. He does not draw out his words, he does not exaggerate his physical movements, he does not grimace, he does not shout or cry. Even when he discovers that his only daughter, Jessica, the apple of his eye, has robbed him and disappeared, he does not scream, as other actors do. He is dispirited, but quiet. [91]

"As other actors do," or as other *Yiddish* actors do? The writer of this passage, William Edlin of the *Tog*, may well have seen some of each, but he was writing for a Yiddish readership, after all. His readers may well have marveled at a "Yiddish" actor (a Yiddish-trained actor, at any rate) not only turning in such a subdued performance, but managing to convey an eerie ferocity at the same time. [92]

Maurice Schwartz: The Evolution of a Character

Over the course of his long and fruitful career as an actor and director, Maurice Schwartz (1890–1960) would revisit Shylock a number of times, in all cases offering a far gentler interpretation than Moscovitch did. When the Ukrainian-born Schwartz was eleven, his father sailed to America in search of economic opportunity. The patriarch soon sent for the rest of the family, but a ticketing problem forced young Avrom-Moyshe (later Maurice) to stay behind, alone, in Liverpool. The boy spent the next two years in London, working at various jobs, singing in a cantor's choir, and going to the Yiddish theatre, until he was finally able to join his family. After a short time in school, Schwartz left to work in a factory, studying at night with a teacher who read him the German classics and Shakespeare. He soon began acting in New York, where, if the following romanticized account from the *Herald Tribune* can be trusted, he first tried on Shylock's gaberdine: "For his first and rather poignant appearance as Shylock Schwartz has to think back to the age of fourteen. The Williamsburg Bridge was his stage, the sky his proscenium arch, the moon his electrician. The members of a small dramatic club, which he had founded during his first year in this city, were his sole audience at the night interpretations."[93] Schwartz left New York to perform and stage-manage in Baltimore and Chicago. He also worked unofficially as a director, an experience that would serve him well when he returned to New York.

In 1918, Schwartz inaugurated a new era in the Yiddish theatre when he became actor-manager of the Irving Place Theatre, the former German-language house that had already made an impact on New York's Yiddish stages. The Irving Place was the first of a number of venues for the Yiddish Art Theatre, as Schwartz would later name his company. *The Merchant of Venice* would provide the source material for one of the most lucrative plays in the Yiddish Art Theatre's thirty-year history: *Shaylok un zayn tokhter* (Shylock and his daughter, 1947).

Schwartz's Shylock boasted a highly respectable Yiddish pedigree, for as his biographer David Dank writes, "Whenever Maurice Schwartz had the opportunity, he wanted to play Jacob Adler's roles."[94] Adler, in fact, played Shylock at the Yiddish Art Theatre under Schwartz's management on 17 March 1921. Schwartz got his first chance to play Shylock professionally in 1930, when he presented three scenes from *The Merchant of Venice* in English on the R.K.O. vaudeville circuit (fig. 16). The combination of a star of the "legitimate" stage performing serious drama in vaudeville had notable pre-

*16. Maurice Schwartz as Shylock on the R.K.O. vaudeville circuit, 1930.
From the Archives of the YIVO Institute for Jewish Research.*

cedents. Other stars of the regular stage, such as Sarah Bernhardt and Ethel Barrymore, also performed excerpts or one-acts in vaudeville theatres.[95]

The program that featured Schwartz opened at the Franklin Theatre in the Bronx, moved to the Kenmore Theatre in Brooklyn, and wrapped up its run at the Palace Theatre in Manhattan during the week of 19 April 1930. Schwartz felt that he needed to tailor his interpretation to the tastes of the vaudeville audience: "If Shylock underwent a certain humanizing process, he would be more comprehensible to the masses of theatregoers. I was certain that if the Jew of Venice was divested of the stinging avarice and the vituperative bitterness accorded him as a rule, he would be better understood, even by a vaudeville stage." [96] This accommodation to the available theatrical conditions was vintage Schwartz. He made his impact on the Yiddish theatre both as an entrepreneur and as an actor, with a remarkable ability to satisfy his audiences' tastes while still managing to take artistic risks.

This concession to theatrical conditions may have yielded a gentler Shylock than Schwartz would have given otherwise. At the time, he saw Shylock as "a quiet, peace-loving Jew, whose mainstays in life are his learning and religion. The loyalty to the memory of his wife, the abounding love for his daughter and his inner dignity guided his life." [97] Yet if Schwartz muted Shylock's harshness, he still conveyed the power of the character. One critic enjoyed how Schwartz "held in fascinated silence an audience whose risibilities were touched earlier in the program by a female impersonator." [98] John Chapman of the *Daily News* was also struck by the contrasts on the evening's bill: "It is the achievement of Maurice Schwartz that scenes from Shakespeare's 'The Merchant of Venice' do not appear out of place on the current bill at the Palace — the same Palace and the same bill in which Nina Olivette prances through grotesque dances, Horace Heidt's band goes through its jazz rhythms and Ben Blue does his dance of the dying duck." [99] The *New York Times* elaborated on how Schwartz held his own among such disparate offerings: "It is a passionate, furious portrait that he creates, but precise and controlled in diction and held closely to the rhythm of the verse. It leaves no doubt on the part of Mr. Schwartz as to the tragic implications of the character. The 'Hath not a Jew eyes?' speech is delivered in a sort of frenzy, full of despair and a near madness, and the quieter scene with Tubal is likewise replete with revenge and a dark foreboding." [100] Schwartz thus accomplished all that he could have hoped for from his vaudeville appearance: extra revenue for his company, which was struggling at the time, as well as generally favorable reviews. Still, Abraham Cahan was unsatisfied: "This production does not give him a true opportunity to show his talent. The three scenes smack too much of melodrama and he has little opportunity to create something on the stage."[101]

Schwartz would get another, very different, opportunity to interpret Shylock a generation later. In the meantime, the world was changing drastically, and Shylock would inevitably change with it. Anti-Semitic stereotypes had long fueled the fires of periodic accusations, recriminations, and pogroms. Such images would be systematically exploited by the Nazis, and contribute immeasurably to the extermination of six million European Jews. If *The Merchant of Venice* — which presented such stereotypes even as it questioned them — was problematic for Jews before World War II, how could a Jewish theatre company even conceive of producing the play after the Holocaust? On the other hand, the Holocaust might have made Jews examine the play more closely than ever. Previous Yiddish productions had used the play to examine Jewish relations with an often hostile world. The explosion of that hostility to an apocalyptic level called for an extensive reevaluation of Jewish-Gentile relations, and what theatrical classic offered a better opportunity for an onstage reassessment than *The Merchant of Venice*? Besides, if Shylock in any way contributed to the problem of anti-Semitism, perhaps the best way to address that contribution would be to reinvent Shylock from a Jewish perspective.

Such a response came in the form of *Shylock and His Daughter* (also known as *Shylock's Daughter*). Schwartz's adaptation of Ari Ibn Zahav's Hebrew novel, *Shylock, ha'yehudi mi'venetsia* (*Shylock, the Jew of Venice*), opened at the Yiddish Art Theatre on 29 September 1947. The novel grew out of the premise, pointed out by numerous critics of *The Merchant of Venice*, that Shakespeare had little or no personal contact with Jews. Ibn Zahav claimed to have conducted extensive research on "the Shylock problem" and concluded, as Zalmen Zylbercweig wrote in a preview of the play, "that the way in which Shakespeare's plot presents it is a historical lie, a falsehood that has cost Jews very dearly and that must once and for all be erased."[102] Ibn Zahav's novel also offered the opportunity to erase the resistance of Jewish audiences that had hovered over previous Yiddish productions of the play. In 1903, the *New York Times* suggested that no matter how brilliantly Adler performed the role, "to make Shylock fully sympathetic to a

Jewish audience is virtually impossible."[103] Gorin echoed that sentiment while praising Schildkraut's Shylock, concluding that "no matter how much charm a performer showers upon Shylock, he will not be able to make him sympathetic to Jews."[104] Perhaps a different approach to the character would make him more palatable.

It also ran the risk of looking like watered-down Shakespeare, but several critics stressed that the play should be assessed on its own merits rather than compared to its source. The *New York Post*'s Richard Watts insisted, "It would most assuredly be both arrogant and untrue to suggest that this new Yiddish drama sets out to put Shakespeare in his place. It is merely an effort to view the same story and the same set of characters from the standpoint of modern historical knowledge and to right an unintentional wrong."[105] At mid-century, even critics for the Yiddish press felt compelled to deliver such warnings, for their readership, and Schwartz's audience, would for the most part be fully bilingual in Yiddish and English. Younger members of the audience may well have studied the play in their public school classes, and they and their parents may also have encountered the play in English-language productions. Assuming their familiarity with the source of *Shylock and His Daughter*, Nokhem Bukhvald cautioned his readers not to make "the false effort of comparing [the play] with 'The Merchant of Venice' in the literary-dramatic sense. To say that 'the original is better' is simply foolishness."[106]

Such advice remains worth bearing in mind before examining *Shylock and His Daughter* in some detail. Dismissing changes made to the original in the process of adaptation as mere warts on the body Shakespearean can distract us from the task of understanding why *Shylock and His Daughter* was such a commercial success, and what that success tells us about the demands of its audience. The Schwartz/Ibn Zahav adaptation certainly sacrifices some of its source's most potent features; to name just a couple, Jessica's increased presence takes some of the spotlight away from Shylock and Portia, and the casket scenes drop out of the picture altogether (Portia and Antonio — yes, Antonio — are already married). Rather than focusing on what the adaptation gives up, however, we should concentrate on what it accomplishes on its own terms by using a familiar but problematic fable as a palimpsest on which to inscribe a pastiche of the history of anti-Semitism. This achievement clearly struck a chord with an audience that had just lived through Hitler's attempt to find a "Final Solution to the Jewish Problem," for the show ran for most of the 1947–48 season.

Shylock and His Daughter takes place in 1559, with the Jews of Venice living in close contact with their Gentile neighbors. As the play begins, the characters are preparing for the Passover feast, the Seder, and Shylock's servants boast about their skills in preparing Jewish cuisine:

> *Launcelot*: You will be very pleased with our raisin wine. It tastes
> better than the Italian wines. My Passover dishes can be equalled
> only in Paradise.
> *Stephano*: And the matzah balls — the horseradish for the fish —
> *Shylock*: Now, now, enough of self-praise.
> *Launcelot*: And my carrot-pudding! I learned the making of it from
> my mistress, may she rest in peace . . .[107]

Shakespeare's sharp dichotomy between Christian and Jew has been modulated. The adaptation shows a wide spectrum of Jewish-Gentile interaction, from near-familiality to deadly antipathy.

On the more hostile end of the continuum, the play wastes no time establishing an atmosphere of anti-Semitism, as in this catalogue Shylock provides of the Church's acts of persecution: "Already can be seen the writing on the wall. . . . The wicked [Pope] Paolo the Fourth will pay for his hellish decrees. He has burned our Talmud. Debts owed by a Gentile to a Jew are cancelled without payment. A Jew showing himself in the City without the 'hat of shame' is thrown into prison."[108] Such references led Nokhem Bukhvald to remark on the play's use of historical context as dramatic content: "We have before us not a conventional theatre piece, but a tragedy against a real historical background. We receive here Shylock's socio-historical address, so to speak: the Venetian ghetto of the 16th century, with its cruel persecution of Jews, with the Jews' loss of rights that gave Hitler a ready example for the Nuremberg laws."[109] With the play's proximity to World War II, many other audience members would likely have made similar connections between the anti-Semitism of the distant and the very recent past.

In their misery, the Venetian Jews often turn to Shylock, a prosperous banker and moneylender, who has saved a number of his fellow Jews from being burned at the stake. Shylock has lost his wife and three of his four children, and is overjoyed when Samuel Morro, the son of a martyred friend, comes to his home after having escaped the Inquisition. Samuel seems an ideal match for Shylock's only surviving child, Jessica (fig. 17), but Lorenzo, the Gentile manager of Shylock's bank, plans to steal her away. While much more devoted to her father than is her Shakespearean namesake, Jessica also feels stifled by life within the ghetto walls, and thus accepts Lorenzo's invitations to gondola rides and carnival outings. These excursions put Lorenzo in a compromising position. Gratiano and Solanio, who guard the ghetto gate, take him for a wealthy man, and demand three thousand ducats in exchange for keeping his meetings with Jessica a secret. In desperation, Lorenzo turns to his friend Antonio. The latter's assets are all out at sea, but he offers Lorenzo his bond to borrow the money from an ironic source: Shylock's bank.

A reconstructed Shylock is not about to demand a pound of flesh from a potential debtor, as Schwartz explained in the play's program:

> There is no case in history indicating that a Jew ever sought a pound of flesh as security for a loan. This is also psychologically impossible in view of the laws laid down by the Jewish religion according to which Jews must salt the meat of fowl and cattle not only to make it kosher, but in order that not even a drop of blood should remain in the meat. Since Shylock is a very religious man, it is impossible that he could have exacted such terms in his contract with Antonio.[110]

In the Schwartz/Ibn Zahav adaptation, Shylock offers to loan Antonio three thousand ducats without charging interest until Antonio insists upon Shylock's usual terms. Upon Antonio's sarcastic suggestion, Shylock inserts the point about the pound of flesh into the contract as a joke.[111] Bending over backwards to make Shylock a pure victim, Ibn Zahav had to bend logic a bit too. Why would Shylock, whose living comes from charging interest, waive his earnings for any potential debtor, much less an enemy?

Jessica, meanwhile, has caught a severe cold from walking by the sea late at night with Lorenzo. When she recovers, she decides to

17. Charlotte Goldstein as Jessica with Schwartz as Shylock in Shylock and His Daughter, *1947. From the Archives of the YIVO Institute for Jewish Research.*

travel to Rome to intervene on behalf of Jews who have been imprisoned there. With letters of introduction from Antonio and his wife Portia, she meets with Church officials and visits the dungeons where Jews are being tortured. This heightens her empathy for her fellow Jews, but Lorenzo follows her to Rome to try to convince her to convert to Christianity. When he brings her back to Venice to see Antonio's lavish palace, she is dazzled by a scene of greater splendor than she can ever know as a Jew. Antonio and Portia then persuade her to forsake her religion and marry Lorenzo.

Joel Entin found much of the production to be a collage of stock scenes from the Yiddish theatre, but even while noting that the conversion scene was "borrowed from 'historical operas,'" he found it "magical and restrained, and very nicely presented":

> The Cardinal and the nuns march on in white . . . Jessica is also dressed in white, with a white convert's veil on her head. Without the abundance, we would not feel the impact. We also hear sweet, soft church music that comes from the chiming of bells. . . . And all of this is, against the will of the Jewish onlooker, beautiful to the eye and the ear.[112]

The conversion scene, not found in Ibn Zahav's novel, gave audiences a visceral sensation of Jessica's attraction to the Christian world she has long admired, and which she is about to enter.

The pageantry of this scene failed to conceal a problem of character development. As one critic justifiably complained, Jessica's "actions are unmotivated, and we never see into her soul."[113] Richard Yaffe elaborated:

> There is one grave fault in the play — Ibn Zahav's failure to make clear Jessica's motivation. One moment she is another Esther, strong in her will to save her people from the torch and the ghetto; the next moment she accepts weakly the things which are anathema to her. This is not a minor point — on it much of the drama revolves, and a clarification would give the play more stature.[114]

Other critics lamented that the supporting characters were not as fully drawn as Shylock, with one wag going so far as to nickname the production *Shylock's Daughter's Father*.[115]

As in more traditional interpretations, Ibn Zahav/Schwartz's Shylock becomes more vengeful upon losing his daughter, and sets out to collect his gruesome bond. Ibn Zahav took care to attribute such vengefulness to Shylock as an individual rather than as a typical Jew by having the Jews of Venice excommunicate him for seeking un-Jewish revenge in the shedding of another man's blood. Shylock, blinded by his lust for vengeance, takes his debtor to court anyway. He retains Samuel Morro as legal counsel, while Portia, disguised as

Dr. Balthasar, advocates on behalf of Antonio. She upholds Shylock's claim — as she does, technically, in *The Merchant of Venice* — and the Cardinals' pleas for mercy do not deter him any more than the threat of excommunication did. But as he approaches Antonio, carrying the scales to measure the pound of flesh, he breaks down and cries, "I cannot spill blood. I am a Jew." This affirmation of faith is quickly followed by news of a more drastic one by Jessica. Forbidden to return to Judaism, she has drowned herself instead, and Shylock whispers, "Blessed is the true Judge." [116]

Seeing Schwartz play Shylock led many critics to comment on the expansive acting style of the Yiddish Art Theatre. It was a style that *New York Times* reviewer Brooks Atkinson appreciated: "If the acting in Second Avenue is not precisely in the grand manner, it has animation and latitude, with wide gestures and excitement; and you always know that you are not in a library. Without being intolerably flamboyant, Mr. Schwartz acts with boldness, using his hands continuously, waggling an eloquent forefinger and raising shaggy eyebrows to project astonishment." [117] Critics differed in their assessments of just how flamboyant Schwartz's Shylock was, one concluding that his "florid style of acting has never stood him in better stead," [118] another finding him "more subdued and thus more effective than he has ever been in any of his previous Yiddish Art Theatre productions." [119]

It has been a commonplace for reviewers outside the Yiddish community to describe the acting style of the Yiddish theatre as "emotional," "melodramatic," and "exaggerated." Critics well acquainted with the Yiddish theatre were likely to see those terms as relative; applying the same adjectives across the board diluted their power to describe. Schwartz, in fact, was often seen as more controlled than many of his predecessors in the Yiddish theatre, but not throughout *Shylock and His Daughter*, where Bukhvald found him "strong in the quiet moments and superficially 'theatrical' in the 'strong' scenes." [120] Comparable words had been used to describe the Shylock of Jacob Adler, from whom, suggested Joel Entin, Schwartz may have learned how to play the role, and "from whom he may also have learned to shout, and that is a fatal error. When Schwartz shouts, it comes from his stomach — you cannot understand what he is saying." [121]

Schwartz's audience may not have needed to catch every word, for the production vividly reflected its turbulent times. Clearly a product of the Holocaust, the play was also seen by some to relate to even more recent events. C. Gutman divided the audience along the lines of two Jewish organizations active in Palestine at the time: "Those who support the Irgun have almost the whole drama to themselves. Shylock can almost be considered as one of their own: vengeance is the key to his deeds! And those who support the Haganah or who are in general soft Jews who are against bloodshed, can consider Shylock among their ranks at the end: Jewish ethics has triumphed."[122] If the audience as a whole also found parallels between the persecution depicted in the play and other historic Jewish struggles, then the production went a long way toward accomplishing what Schwartz identified as "the national significance of the play, its moral, the mission it leads, the answer to the three-hundred-year-old libel."[123]

Performing in his own adaptation of Ibn Zahav's novel may have had an indelible effect on Schwartz. When he was invited to return to *The Merchant of Venice* in 1959, he refused. "It's definitely an anti-Semitic play," he declared, "and I would not do it."[124] Schwartz's disavowal brought the American Yiddish theatre full circle, in a sense, in its treatment of Shylock. The first recorded professional production, in 1894, failed to find an audience. By 1959, the greatest living Yiddish interpreter of the character refused to play the role at all. The frequent eruptions of anti-Semitism in the intervening decades, exploding into Hitler's Final Solution, finally made the character unbearably problematic. It is fitting that the Shylock that capped the American Yiddish tradition of the role was a revised version, distanced from the sinister mythology that fueled the character's conception and wound its way through the three centuries of his life, onstage and off.

Conclusion

Edelshtein: If you become a Gentile you don't automatically
become a Shakespeare.
Ostrover: Oho! A lot you know. I'll let you in on the facts,
Hershele . . . Now listen — did you ever hear of Velvl
Shikkerparev? Never. A Yiddish scribbler writing romances
for the Yiddish stage in the East End, I'm speaking of London,
England. He finds a translator and overnight he becomes Willie
Shakespeare.
— Cynthia Ozick, "Envy; or, Yiddish in America"

To paraphrase a famous Jewish question, what made Shakespeare different from all other playwrights?[1] In order to answer this question, we need to ask a number of others: How and why did Shakespeare's plays enter American Yiddish culture in the first place? Why did a handful of his dramas succeed with Yiddish audiences, while the rest either failed miserably or were ignored by theatre companies altogether? What do the adaptation, translation, and production of his plays on Yiddish stages in the United States teach us about the development of the American Yiddish theatre: its playwrights, performers, business operations, and audiences? And what do they tell us about the world beyond the Yiddish theatre?

Also in time-honored Jewish tradition, it seems appropriate here to answer a question with another question: so why *not* Shakespeare? The process of reinventing Shakespeare according to a particular culture's aesthetic outlook, theatrical conditions, politics, religious beliefs, and audience expectations has been going on ever since the English Restoration, in English and countless other languages. Even at the dawn of the twenty-first century, as a debate rages over whether various traditional forms of artistic expression are dying a slow death or simply transforming themselves, Shakespeare remains very much alive in the public consciousness. His Globe Theatre has been reconstructed on the South Bank of the Thames, and a steady stream of academic and popular books about his life and work continues to flow. Where his plays were once rewritten to conform to neoclassical standards, they are now filmed to please the "MTV generation." To anyone with an interest in theatre and drama, Shakespeare often seems ubiquitous, even in an era in which film and television pose an ever-present commercial threat to the theatre, and in which it is all but impossible to label any specific actor as a "Shakespearean."

Shakespeare had a more profound hold over American culture in the last quarter of the nineteenth century, when the Jews of eastern Europe began their four-decade mass exodus to the United States. The reputations of many of the most famous American actors of the age — along with distinguished visitors from Europe — rested in large measure on their achievements in Shakespearean roles. Critics debated the relative merits of the great Shakespearean actors and directors. Politicians and essayists quoted liberally from the plays. Comedians and minstrels parodied well-known scenes. Editions of Shakespeare's plays enjoyed a privileged place on readers' bookshelves. The idea of Shakespeare in Yiddish may sound curious to many of us today, based on our combined preconceptions about both Shakespeare and Yiddish culture, but the conditions were ripe for his plays to enter the Yiddish repertoire in the early 1890s.

Plays and Playwrights

The atmosphere in neighboring cultures that proved conducive to the adoption of Shakespeare was further enhanced by the state of the Yiddish theatre at the time. In professional terms, it was a theatrical culture in its infancy — younger, in fact, than most of its audience. Only a tiny number of playwrights had their plays produced in Yiddish until well into the 1890s, and although they often wrote with remarkable speed, there was only so much that the Hurwitzes, Lateiners, Goldfadens, and Shaykevitshes of the world could do to meet the constant demand for new plays. From their earliest works in the mid-1870s, these writers had raided the cupboard of European dramas and operettas for plots and music, which they often blended with character types and issues of immediate interest to their audiences. Students of European drama could find countless familiar passages in these works, including more than a few from Shakespeare himself. The comic doppelgänger scenes of Goldfaden's *Two Kuni Lemls*, for example, bear a strong resemblance to *The Comedy of Errors*. The famous oath scene in the same writer's *Shulamis*, with the heroine in an underground well being urged to "swear" by the soldier who rescues her, feels like an inversion of the ghost scenes in *Hamlet*. Such moments, however, are simply part of the patchwork of early professional Yiddish drama, an intercultural free-for-all in which all plays, all characters, all melodies were there for the taking.

The indiscriminate nature of such borrowing, and the lack of dramatic coherence it tended to breed in the plays that resulted from it, disturbed artistically self-conscious writers like Jacob Gordin. Gordin and like-minded intellectuals took note of the remarkable developments occurring in contemporary European drama, which were yielding not only new dramatic styles, but even new national dramas, as in Ibsen's Norway. The ability to produce works of comparable seriousness of purpose and truthfulness to daily life would help Yiddish drama achieve a legitimacy it hitherto had failed to earn. Without a "better drama," such critics contended, the Yiddish theatre would continue to be little more than a circus, where talented but coarse performers pandered to the basest impulses of the audience. Among the devices the Gordinites developed in their attempt to raise the aesthetic level of Yiddish drama was the adaptation of classic plays to Jewish life.

While Gordin claimed to despise what his contemporaries were writing for the Yiddish stage, he realized that he could not jettison their techniques completely. His actors demanded their lines of business, and his audiences wanted comic scenes and songs to relieve them from two hours of unmitigated tension. Unsatisfied with what he felt were the haphazard ways in which his predecessors combined such elements, Gordin devised a dramatic structure that provided a logical place for expository monologues, emotional exchanges, comic figures, and even song. Shakespeare, himself a master at pulling together disparate elements of entertainment into what the Romantic critics championed as a cohesive whole, provided Gordin with a perfect vehicle for translating classic works into the Yiddish vernacular.

Gordin and the playwrights who followed him in Judaizing the classics combined several ingredients into a successful formula. They would begin by working with a time-honored play from the Western canon, often already translated into an intermediary language, such as Russian or German. Dramas revolving around a family conflict, especially an intergenerational one, tended to be most effective. They set most of the action in the "Old Country," eastern Europe, which had already acquired a mythic aura made grander by the journey across the Atlantic and the striking contrast with the fast-paced American city. The Jewish content of the plays was enhanced by rituals such as weddings, funerals, and holidays, drawing the viewer into the emotions of the onstage participants. The music itself often quoted Jewish liturgy. Comic figures provided a foil to the main action, and often satirized well-known character types in the community. These ingredients were stirred vigorously with passionate performances, usually accompanied by seltzer and peanuts, and voilá! Judaized Classic Gordinaise. The recipe served millions.

The most popular of these plays became embedded in the consciousness of America's Yiddish-speaking Jews, for they helped audiences come to terms with the challenges of immigrant life. The Jews who had come to America from eastern Europe did not always find their religious beliefs helpful in adapting to their new homeland. Often, in fact, new immigrants felt that they had to forgo certain religious practices in order to succeed in America. By depicting the most outwardly pious characters as the most destructive, adaptations such as *The Jewish King Lear*, *The Yeshiva Boy*, and *The Oath on the Torah* reassured recent Jewish immigrants to the United States that being a good Jew depended on adherence to the spirit rather than the letter of Jewish laws and customs.

Judaizing Shakespeare's plays may have made them more accessible, but keeping the Shakespearean plot and characters intact provided benefits as well. Particularly as audiences grew more acclimated to America and more aware of Western culture, Shakespearean authorship signified global recognition of artistic achievement. Even if a Yiddish playwright had penned the greatest work of dramatic literature ever written, who outside of the ghetto would know? Conversely, the most lackluster production of Shakespeare still had that magical name attached to it. Yiddish translators thus applied themselves to rendering Elizabethan dialogue into Yiddish, which often meant the stilted, Germanized Yiddish known as *daytshmerish*. Even so-called straight translations rarely meant turning the English into Yiddish line by line. The writers streamlined complicated plots, combined and cut secondary characters, bowdlerized sexually suggestive language, and exchanged metaphor for literal meaning. Most important of all, they subordinated all other characters to the leading roles, thus pleasing the stars and enabling themselves to live to write another translation.

The fact that Yiddish translators and adaptors all but disregarded Shakespeare's comedies should not come as a complete surprise. The great tragedies, more than the comedies, were regarded as touchstones of both dramatic literature and of performers' prowess, and thus a more reliable route to conferring distinction on the Yiddish theatre. The stories the tragedies told may also have moved audiences to tears more effectively than the comedies would have moved them to laughter. The Shakespeare plays that enjoyed the greatest success with Yiddish audiences are all, to a significant extent, dramas of family conflict — an emotive issue for new immigrants confronting multiple challenges to the integrity and happiness of their own families.

The tragedies also lend themselves to melodrama; that is, the adaptors could amplify the virtues and minimize the character flaws of heroes and heroines, thus satisfying the desire of the immigrant Jewish audience for clear-cut moral lines in its entertainment. If not only the evil deeds of Macbeth and Richard III, but even the steely virtue of Coriolanus were hard to accept, one can imagine the Yiddish theatregoer being baffled by the amorality of comic figures like Petruchio and Falstaff. Much of the appeal of Shakespeare's comedies also lies in the richness of their language. Surely this would have suffered at the hands of Yiddish adaptors, who mined Shakespearean's works for situations and characters more than for verbal nuance. Besides, for comic repartee in their own language, built upon a riotous linguistic mixture of Yiddish with German, *daytshmerish*, Hebrew and Aramaic, and speech impediments like lisping and stuttering, Yiddish audiences already had a popular body of work produced by writers who had proved their ability to elicit gales of laughter.

These observations notwithstanding, there were precedents for adaptating classic European comedies into Yiddish, and contemporary reasons for doing so. Molière, for example, had proved highly adaptable, in such works as Wolfssohn's *Tartuffe*-like *Silliness and Sanctimony*, or Shaykevitsh's *Coquettish Ladies*, which updates *L'école des femmes* to spoof the pretensions of assimilated Jews in late nineteenth-century Europe. And Shakespearean comedy could boast a distinguished performance tradition that was alive and well in America. New Yorkers in the late nineteenth and early twentieth centuries could have seen the much-heralded performances of Ada Rehan as Rosalind, E. H. Sothern as Benedick to Julia Marlowe's Beatrice, or their Malvolio and Viola, among many others. If it occurred to Thomashefsky to emulate Booth's Hamlet or Adler to mimic Irving's Shylock, it hardly seems out of the question for Yiddish comedians to test their mettle as Shakespearean clowns.

Yet we are left merely to speculate as to how David Kessler's Falstaff cavorting with Keni Liptzin's Mrs. Ford, or Sigmund Mogulesco's Benedick doing verbal battle with Bertha Kalish's Beatrice, might have fared with Yiddish audiences. Such ideas, if they ever tickled the fancies of Yiddish adaptors at the time, never saw the light of day. Shakespeare's comedies were not entirely absent from American Yiddish culture; several of them were summarized in a series running in *Di yidishe gazeten* in 1893–1894, and in Hermalin's 1908 borrowing of the Lambs' *Tales From Shakespeare*. Onstage offerings of Shakespeare's comedies, however, were limited to one adaptation. Boris Thomashefsky's *The Pretty American* (1910), a version of *The Taming of the Shrew* with music by Arnold Perlmutter and Herman Wohl, would be the only American Yiddish play based on a Shakespearean comedy.[2]

Over time, both the translators and adaptors of Shakespeare gained more than merely new titles to place on the marquee, or a few rays of the poet's reflected glory shining on the Yiddish stage. Even when the motives for translating classic plays were purely commercial, they contributed to at least one plank of the more ambitious didactic program of the theatrical reformers: to expose audiences largely unfamiliar with secular culture to many of the most noteworthy titles in Western drama. This made them more aware of the breadth, if not always the depth, of the dramatic repertoire. The best of the translations achieved distinction in their own right. These include Joseph Bovshover's translation of *The Merchant of Venice*, Y. Y. Shvarts's versions of *Hamlet* and *Julius Caesar*, Mark Schweid's unpublished script for *Othello*, and Berl Lapin's treatment of the *Sonnets*, in addition to versions produced in Europe by such translators as Y. Goldberg, Shmuel Halkin, and Aaron Tseytlin.[3]

Sadly, the audience able to appreciate the achievements of such translators has dwindled to nearly nothing, but these works deserve a place of honor in Yiddish literary history. So, in different ways, do the most noteworthy adaptations of Shakespeare into Yiddish, which helped navigate a road between very different theatrical cultures. Playwrights like Gordin, Zolatarevsky, Rakov, and Kobrin found often ingenious ways to superimpose situations, themes, and characters onto the prevailing theatrical conditions of the turn-of-the-century American Yiddish stage. In doing so, they made the work of any non-Yiddish playwright potentially viable in a manner more immediately accessible to the audience. Yiddish theatregoers would become acquainted with many familiar characters from Western drama in Jewish form: not only the Jewish King Lear and the Jewish Hamlet, but also the Jewish Medea, the Jewish Nora, and countless others. The pattern of failures of straight Shakespearean translations during the same period teaches us how crucial it was for the playwrights to find Jewish idioms for these works. Yiddish audiences showed little interest in Lear the pagan British king, but Dovid Moysheles was someone they would gladly invite into their homes.

Actors and Performances

Most of the Yiddish versions of Shakespeare's works matter less as examples of literary translation than as vehicles for performance. On days and evenings off, Yiddish actors could see the performances of the great American actors and the most notable visitors from Europe, and it was only natural to wish themselves in the shoes of colleagues who could be applauded by more heterogenous crowds in more glamorous venues. The names of the leading fin-de-siècle Shakespearean actors frequently appear, like mantras, in Yiddish commentary on the theatre from actors and critics alike. Yiddish performers hoped to add to their own prestige by calling themselves Shakespeareans as well. They may have enjoyed godlike status in the Jewish community, but their egos were swelling at a pace that made them soon tire of dining merely on Jewish ambrosia. The Yiddish actors had caught a terminal case of classical influenza.

From the start, some critics found this notion laughable. Who were these tyros — these *pishers*, to use the Yiddish vernacular — to try on the roles created by the most esteemed playwright in the English language? How could they expect to succeed? They not only dared to perform Shakespeare's plays, but made exaggerated claims for their work in the spirit of nineteenth-century American theatrical puffery. The poster claiming that Shakespeare wrote the role of Hamlet especially for Boris Thomashefsky may have been an extreme example, but superlatives were the stock in trade of almost every ad. One Shakespeare play after another was billed as "the greatest masterpiece of all time," just as each company contained "the greatest artists in the world." Such boasts had a necessarily short shelf life; as American Yiddish audiences gained familiarity with both Shakespeare and the contemporary theatre scene, they became less susceptible to being bamboozled by promoters.

The inflated advertising rhetoric eventually died down, but some critics continued to view the production of Shakespeare in Yiddish as nothing more than a gimmick. In a 1909 essay, Moyshe Zeifert returned to the theme of Yiddish actors' alleged mangling of Shakespeare:

> People who have been brought up on Lateiner's, Hurwitz's, and Shaykevitsh's plays; people who not only have never attended a dramatic school, but have never even had a real drama teacher; people who cannot distinguish between Zolatarevsky and Shakespeare . . . have the *chutzpah* to appear on the Yiddish stage in *Shylock*, in *Hamlet*, in [Hauptmann's] *The Sunken Bell*, in [Sudermann's] *Heimat* and the like — plays in which mediocre Gentile actors would never dare to perform. What is the result of such productions? The ordinary theatregoer sleeps soundly through them, and the intelligent one, who has seen real artists in the same plays, gets appendicitis or nervous dyspepsia from them, and will not come to the theatre a second time.[4]

Zeifert was particularly rough on the Yiddish actors, but other critics would have agreed with the general tenor of his remarks.

The productions often provided skeptics like Zeifert with no shortage of ammunition. The language often failed to capture any of the poetry of the original, and at times confused the meaning of the dialogue. Cuts and changes resulted in unmotivated actions and abrupt endings. These flaws undoubtedly appear more glaring on the page than they did in performance, but every textual shortcoming had its onstage counterpart. The same conditions that forced playwrights to turn out hastily written scripts made actors learn several roles at once, and many an awkward moment made the prompter the most important person in the theatre. Emphasis on the stars often came at the expense of the quality of the ensemble. Some of the most lauded Shakespearean performances, in Yiddish as in many other languages, were supported by indifferent acting.

Yet a broader view of the productions and a closer look at Zeifert's critical standards paint a more flattering picture. English-speaking American critics would have taken issue with the observation that "mediocre Gentile actors would never dare to perform" Shakespeare's plays. The Yiddish theatre was by no means alone in producing some laughably awful Shakespearean efforts; it is no accident that two of the nineteenth century's greatest humorists, Dickens and Twain, caricatured inept productions of Shakespeare's plays in *Great Expectations* and *Huckleberry Finn*. Zeifert also seems to assume that his readers intuitively know the difference between "ordinary" and "intelligent" theatregoers, just as his fellow critics peppered their reviews with loaded but vague terms such as "art," "the better plays," "*shund.*" Such hierarchies focused more on texts than on productions, so that a lackluster staging of a Gordin play would still qualify as "better drama," whereas even a solidly acted Lateiner melodrama that left the audience in tears could not escape the *shund* label inevitably placed on any of his works. In fact, the more emotional the audience's reaction, the more it piqued the reviewers from the Yiddish press, who described Jewish spectators as simpletons, barbarians, children, even barnyard animals — creatures who did not know what was good for them.

In disregarding the validity of the audience's taste, these critics overlooked a great deal of what made the American Yiddish theatre so remarkable. Theatregoers got passionately involved with what happened onstage. Women watching Jacob Gordin's *Siberia* in 1891 were said to have thrown their shawls onto the stage for the shivering inmates of a Siberian prison camp. Critics scoffed at such naiveté, but the fervor of Yiddish audiences impressed outsiders accustomed to more reserved responses. When Jacob Adler performed Shylock, for example, reviewers from the English-language press marveled at the spectacular reception that met him: "He made his entrance into the streets of Venice treading upon a path of roses. It is thus that an east side favorite makes his transit, for as Mr. Adler walked on in the first act there was a shower of rose leaves from an upper box which literally covered the stage. At the same moment what seemed to be the best trained claque that New York has yet known made itself heard from all parts of the house."[5] Even when these stars performed outside the Yiddish theatre, their stalwarts remained faithful.

Naysayers like Zeifert did not give the actors enough credit, overlooking how far the Yiddish theatre had come in such a short time. Those who first performed Shakespeare's plays in Yiddish had neither formal training (as Zeifert is quick to point out) nor mentors who spoke their mother tongue. Whether they had been civil servants-turned-prizefighters, like Jacob Adler, or choirboys, like Boris Thomashefsky, or worked their way through the ranks in more traditional ways, like Bertha Kalish, awareness of the international Shakespearean tradition helped Yiddish performers raise their sights, and probably made them better actors in the long run. In rare cases — a Schildkraut having been trained in German and Austrian theatres, or a Thomashefsky hiring a German director — outside influences flowed directly into Yiddish performance practice. But Yiddish actors were also influenced simply by seeing the performances of their American and European colleagues. Thomashefsky clearly exaggerated when he claimed to have seen Edwin Booth's Hamlet fifty times, but he may well have seen it on several occasions. By doing so, he would have witnessed that era's gold standard of Shakespearean performance, a level to which he claimed to aspire.

One of the most remarkable aspects of the story of Shakespeare in Yiddish is how quickly the actors began being able to hold their own with non-Yiddish counterparts. Within a decade of the first translations, the best of the Yiddish Shakespeareans would attract comparisons to some of the most celebrated artists of their day. Critics would favorably compare Bertha Kalish's Hamlet to that of Sarah Bernhardt and Jacob Adler's Shylock to Henry Irving's — and it is worth noting that the English-language reviewers were often more appreciative than their colleagues from the Yiddish press. Shakespeare gave the Yiddish actors exactly what they had wanted from him all along: a mark of legitimacy and a means of measuring their talent against that of actors who performed in English, French, Italian, and German.

Those languages offered a much wider audience than Yiddish did. The eastern European Jewish immigrants to the United States established a community that would support a host of Yiddish newspapers, journals, and theatres, but this was dwarfed by the larger world outside the Jewish neighborhoods. For fame-hungry artists, simple demographic facts created what writer Cynthia Ozick calls "the prison of Yiddish";[6] those who were kings and queens of the Jewish quarter were invisible to most American spectators, and would remain so unless and until they could make themselves understood in English. Shakespeare's plays provided a cultural bridge between Yiddish actors and English-speaking theatregoers and critics. Anyone familiar with *Hamlet* did not need to know Yiddish to evaluate a Bertha Kalish's performance, and success in such a role could be the ticket to a Broadway (or later, Hollywood) contract.

Yet the very boundaries that made Yiddish a prison made it liberating in other ways. It might keep actors and writers from achieving more widespread recognition, but it also freed them from having to please a wider audience, who would undoubtedly bring a different set of expectations to the theatre or cinema. A glimpse at the range of Jewish roles available to actors appearing on the English-language stage and screen at the time offers a case in point. One survey of American Jewish characters from 1860 to 1910 concludes that female performers had but two outlets: "Outside the passionate intensity of the belle juive, the only other performance commonly allowed Jewish women on stage during this period was that of a masculinized hag."[7] Meanwhile, in the first wave of silent films in the teens, "Jews mostly occupy lower-class positions, with several occupations recurring in the early films: pawnshop owners, clothing merchants, money brokers, sweatshop workers, peddlers, tailors, grocery store/delicatessen owners."[8] No such shackles bound actors on the Yiddish stage, where Bertha Kalish could play a Danish prince and Boris Thomashefsky the "Crown Prince of Jerusalem." The Yiddish theatre gave Jewish writers, actors, and audiences room to imagine themselves in any guise they wanted, from royalty to ragamuffins, statesmen to soldiers, heroines to whores.

The Business of Theatre

While some actors were attempting to break out of the Yiddish prison, demographic changes were interacting with prevailing business practices to help bring about a decline in Shakespearean productions. The financial organization of Yiddish troupes in late nineteenth-century America fostered a rapid turnover of plays and foregrounded the stars. Company members of each company were paid according to the mark system; with each mark representing a percentage of the take. The more vital one's place in the company was deemed to be, the more marks one earned. Bit players earned a salary instead, which sometimes worked to their advantage, as actor Boaz Young learned when he joined Jacob Adler's company:

> I would receive a dollar a performance (seven dollars a week, Saturday afternoons included; Sunday performances were forbidden), and would also have to sing in the choir. I understood that I was not considered a member of the company, because only the choristers earned salaries. The actors worked on the "mark" system, cooperatively. There were weeks when in fact I earned more than an actor would, but I had still not achieved my goal: to become a full-fledged actor.[9]

Since shareholders had to shoulder the burden of paying the operating costs, their pay structure entailed a certain amount of risk, but for many, the status of full membership compensated for any potential loss of income.

It did not take long for the actors to band together to protect their interests, and during the 1887–1888 season, they formed Hebrew Actors Union Local No. 1: the first actor's union in the United States. Nahma Sandrow describes a number of pressures that led to the need for a strong union:

The mark system had degenerated. Payment by marks or salaries was often desperately low — though unionizing was never to bring much improvement on that score. Employment was uncertain from one season . . . to the next. As stars controlled the companies, lower actors had fewer chances to try different roles. . . . Another reason for organizing was that with time these actors seem to have been developing a growing consciousness of themselves as professionals, even as artists. Unionizing was one expression of that feeling.[10]

At times, though, unionization seemed to do more harm than good. Members of the Hebrew Actors Union often preserved their turf by keeping out new talent; Maurice Schwartz, for example, failed his union audition several times. The union often supported indifferent actors at the expense of more talented ones, and made prohibitive demands on producers to pay a bloated contingent of support staff. Such demands made it difficult for companies to take any artistic risks, and contributed to the emphasis on long runs rather than the rotating repertory that dominated before World War I.

Another key element of the financial structure of the Yiddish theatre that was designed to fill seats but was widely criticized for hampering creativity, was the tradition of benefit performances. Guilds, clubs, and fraternal support organizations "bought blocks of tickets at discounts of between 50 percent and 80 percent. They would then sell the tickets to members, friends, and the public. The benefits took place primarily on week nights, when an audience was more difficult to attract, but there were some on weekends as well."[11] Companies performed the warhorses of the repertoire for benefits, and tried out new material on weekends, when business was more brisk. A successful season would balance these two aspects of the business; companies sought new productions that would keep running for numerous weekends in a row, but before the 1920s, even the most popular of these would run side by side with the old repertory on weekdays.

This system always had both artistic and commercial pitfalls, but both worsened over time. In many ways, the United States proved so welcoming that the new immigrants rapidly moved away from their own languages and traditions. Yet as long as the Yiddish audience was replenished with a steady stream of new immigrants, this was not fatal to Yiddish culture. This influx was eventually all but cut off by a series of increasingly restrictive immigration laws passed by Congress beginning in 1917 and culminating in the Johnson-Reed Act of 1924. Whereas some 190,000 Jews had immigrated to the United States in 1920, only 10,000 were admitted in the fiscal year 1924–1925. The number would continue to decline, and with it, the Yiddish theatre's perennial revitalization.[12] *New York Times* critic Brooks Atkinson noted the interlocking demographic and cultural change with a sense of sadness: "Ever since the restrictions upon immigration went into effect the Yiddish-speaking audiences have declined, and the younger generation are constantly drifting toward Broadway. They are missing something satisfying and native. For the Yiddish stage preserves the pungent tradition of imaginative plays and the acting is contagiously excitable."[13]

The trend was irreversible. By the time of Atkinson's remarks, in the early 1930s, the leading Jewish talent was working in English, as writers, directors, performers, composers, and producers in American theatre and film. With declining immigration, new competition from motion pictures and radio, and the audience gravitating to English-language entertainment, Yiddish theatres found that the critical mass needed to sustain the benefit system was disappearing. Companies like Schwartz's Yiddish Art Theatre relied more and more on productions that would run for an entire season, and as Sandrow observes, "This attrition of the repertory system, in its turn, reduced playwrights' opportunities to see their works produced and weakened the Yiddish actors' traditional flexibility in switching from role to role and type to type."[14] Roles that had been darlings of the old repertoire thus became little more than museum pieces, so Dovid Moysheles, Mirele Efros, Avigdor in *The Yeshiva Boy*, and other favorites were dusted off and trotted out for display only rarely, sometimes in gimmicky formats like the 1940 production featuring a different star actress for each act of *Mirele Efros*.

The Journey of the Yiddish-Speaking Audience

Initially, though, benefits had helped to establish a broadly based audience for the American Yiddish theatre, and that audience would become the stuff of legend. In order to be able to introduce

Shakespeare into the repertoire, theatre companies would have to satisfy "Moyshe," who was famously opinionated, vocal, and capricious. It could not be taken for granted that just because playwrights wanted to adapt the plays of Shakespeare, Goethe, Schiller, and Ibsen, and the actors wanted to perform them, audiences would oblige by filling the auditoriums. After all, the bulk of the American Yiddish audience at the turn of the century, to borrow the words of a Philistine capitalist depicted in a satirical newspaper sketch, would not have known "Shakes-beer" from lager beer;[15] if they had, early translators like Zeifert, Hermalin, and Goldberg might have been pilloried for their efforts. The prestige of Shakespeare's name would thus have a minimal impact on ticket sales. A better strategy would be to offer the same delights that could be found in the operettas and melodramas that were so popular: spectacular stage effects, stirring music, exotic locations, and the pleasure of seeing their favorite actors in new heroic exploits.

The manner in which Shakespeare or any other playwright was performed in the Yiddish theatre often came down to what Moyshe wanted — or at least what the playwrights, actors, and theatre managers thought he wanted. Between the lines of American Yiddish versions of Shakespeare emerges a portrait of the audience for whom they were performed. What that audience demanded was to be moved: to weep over recognizable sorrows, to erupt in gales of laughter, to be stirred by a pretty melody. That is not to say that it sought entertainment devoid of ideas — just that those ideas needed to be clear, relevant, and superbly stimulating. Of course, the same could be said for Shakespeare's own audience, and more than one visitor to an American Yiddish theatre made the connection between the spontaneity of Moyshe's reactions and the rambunctiousness of the groundlings who had occupied the pit of the Globe three centuries earlier:

> Many of the early Elizabethan and early Yiddish plays were short-lived and hastily written combinations of genres and styles. The rivalry between acting companies, the boisterousness of the audience, the postludes of jigs and songs and prayers, even the high productivity and generally low literary merits of men like Peele, Greene, and Dekker, with their heroes full of bombast and rodo-

montade, remind one of the early Yiddish theatre on the East Side. The Elizabethan and the Yiddish theatre clearly had both actors and audiences delighting in what Bottom was hoping for, a part to tear a cat in.[16]

Many of the most sympathetic observers seemed to find in Moyshe a sort of *bête sauvage*; here was a being sufficiently unladened with the encrustations of bourgeois society to enjoy Shakespeare's theatricality on a more visceral level than his more worldly — or was it more jaded? — uptown neighbors. Never mind that the Yiddish texts may have been much further from Shakespeare's than were those used for Broadway productions; in its spontaneity, bombast, and rowdiness, perhaps the Yiddish theatre was closer to the Elizabethan spirit.

Tales of latter-day Jewish groundlings calling for Shakespeare to take a bow or trying to rescue the Jewish King Lear from his daughters may sound too good to be true, but they are certainly plausible. There was little reason for most of the audience in the early 1890s to have known that Shakespeare was not their contemporary and their *landsman* (granted, the name "Shekspir" doesn't *sound* Jewish, but he could have changed his name while being processed through Ellis Island). The same spectators would have had only slightly more familiarity with the theatrical fourth wall than they did with Shakespeare, and the annals of Western theatre are filled with naive spectators who break the actor/audience barrier when their emotions get the better of them. What is clear about these legends is that they could have happened only up to a certain point in the development of the Yiddish theatre. Within a generation, the Yiddish audience would see Shakespeare as a symbol of varied and sometimes contradictory ideas.

By World War I — roughly the dividing line between the first and second "Golden Ages" of the American Yiddish theatre — America's Yiddish speakers had encountered Shakespeare and his work in many different forms and contexts. At least ten of his plays had been translated and/or adapted for the Yiddish stage, most of those in multiple versions. Translations of *Julius Caesar* and *The Merchant of Venice* had been published. Many of the plays were discussed individually or serially in the press, and Yiddish commentators had gotten into the practice so common in other Western cultures of sprinkling their writings on all manner of subjects with apt Shakespearean quotations. And when Dovid Moyshe Hermalin published a book of synopses of the plays in 1908, he sought "to give the Yiddish reader a conception of Shakespeare. We say a conception and not a study, because in order to study Shakespeare . . . we must turn to the original, or at least to the famous German translation, which is almost as good as the original. It is highly doubtful whether there will ever be a comparable Yiddish translation of Shakespeare, but meanwhile, we think that the following work will be a great service to our poor Yiddish literature." [17] The program of validating Yiddish via Shakespeare — and particularly via Shakespeare in German — was still going strong. Whether or not Hermalin achieved his purpose, his book clearly proved popular, being issued in second and third printings in 1909 and 1912. [18]

In short, Shakespeare's presence in the culture had moved beyond the theatre alone. When Europe and America commemorated the tercentenary of Shakespeare's death, for example, America's Yiddish speakers took an active part. Much of the commentary that filled Yiddish newspapers and journals in the spring of 1916 was as derivative as it was earnest, but humorists used the occasion as an opportunity for lighthearted commentary. For the socialist *Forverts*, Shakespeare's iconic status underscored incongruities bred by the commodification of high culture. One cartoon shows a peddler smiling from behind a pushcart loaded with busts of the poet and bearing a sign reading, "Cheap! Cheap! Shakespeares cheap! A quarter apiece!" (fig. 18). Holding out a sample of his wares to an obese, scowling, well-dressed boss — and a parvenu to boot, we are told — the peddler encourages him to buy "the best Shakespeare in the market." "Who is he, this Shakespeare?" snarls the boss. "Must be that Kaleh Mox, ha?" When the peddler assures him that Shakespeare is *not* Karl Marx, the boss concludes, "In that case, they can both go to hell. . . . They should both be shipped out of America, those miligants, those anchorists, those radicanals!" [19] The capitalist's ignorance, as well as his butchery of the English language, show his unfitness for coping with anything that falls outside the narrow sphere of his shop.

The journal *Der groyser kundes* made much of the fact that the tercentenary coincided with the first anniversary of the death of Polish Yiddish writer Yitskhok Leybush Peretz, one of the pioneers of modern Yiddish literature. The cover of the April 21 issue showed the

18. *"The Best Shakespeare in the Market." From* Der forverts, *30 April 1916.*

muses of world literature and Yiddish literature in mourning (fig. 19), while another drawing placed the two winged writers in the clouds, where they amiably compared notes on literary immortality (fig. 20). Elsewhere in the same issue, contributors poked fun at the adoration of Shakespeare, which they juxtaposed with comic effect to contemporary Yiddish theatrical practice. The cartoon "If Shakespeare Had to Sell a Play Today" (fig. 21) traces the playwright's fruitless attempt to sell his latest play to a Yiddish theatre. Jacob Adler, David Kessler,

19. The muses of world literature and Yiddish literature mourn Shakespeare and Peretz on the anniversaries of the writers' deaths. From Der groyser kundes, *21 April 1916.*

Boris Thomashefsky, and Bessie Thomashefsky all turn him away, each finding that his play lacks some key ingredient, be it artistry, "punch," "national fervor," or some undefined quality found in Gordin's dramas. The cartoonist implies that the Yiddish theatre would reject even the world's greatest dramas to make room for the pap that constitutes its customary fare. A similar situation arises in a sketch in which Moyshe Nadir[20] (Isaac Reiss) imagines himself approaching Shakespeare's grave, "à la Zolatarevsky's 'Yeshiva Boy,'" and coaxing the writer out of his tomb for an interview. This time, Shakespeare gets Nadir's advice before trying to write for the Yiddish stage, and is told that whatever he writes must have "some kind of girl, you understand; and bastards; and someone should say Kaddish in the third act; and some pale woman, you understand, should carry 'the fruit of her love under her heart' and should sing a little duet with the comedian . . . and in the last act the lover should fall back in love with his beloved and the music should come in with a happy melody, and it should thunder and snow and a torrential rain should fall, and

20. "In Paradise": Shakespeare and Peretz in Heaven.
From Der groyser kundes, *21 April 1916.*

21. *"If Shakespeare Had to Sell a Play Today." Shakespeare is rejected, clockwise from top left, by David Kessler, Jacob Adler, Boris Thomashefsky, and Bessie Thomashefsky (who is busy writing her memoirs, her pen guided by her ghostwriter). From* Der groyser kundes, *21 April 1916.*

two suns with five giant moons should shine through the window, and — "[21] But Shakespeare has had enough, and returns to his grave.

These writings and cartoons also belong to a particular historical moment, just as the legends of uninitiated theatregoers were the product of an earlier era. As of 1916, Shakespeare has gone from being a one-dimensional icon to being many things to many people: worthy of serious commentary, but also emblematic of many of the ironies of American Yiddish culture. As the audience for Shakespeare in Yiddish began to dwindle, such occasions for humor became less and less frequent. It is telling in this regard to fast-forward to the quadricentennial of Shakespeare's birth, in 1964. This time, the Yiddish press pays little attention. In place of the hullaballoo of 1916, we find the *Forverts* reviewer giving a less than tepid endorsement of a production of *Hamlet* starring Richard Burton. "The truth is," he yawns, "'Hamlet' today is almost entirely literature . . . [and] is throughout a philosophical drama. If you are not interested in philosophy, there is nothing left for you in the production."[22]

Shakespeare's presence in Yiddish in the previous couple of decades would not have challenged the critic's conclusion that Shakespeare's plays were "almost entirely literature." Steadfast fans could undoubtedly find revivals of old warhorses like *Mirele Efros*, but these had become more an exercise in nostalgia than a way of communicating vital messages to throngs of avid spectators. After World War II, the Yiddish Shakespeare often seemed more alive on the page than on the stage, with new versions of the *Sonnets* in 1944 and 1953, *King Lear* in 1947,[23] and the only Yiddish monograph on Shakespeare in 1946. In his introduction to *William Shakespeare*, Avrom Taytlboym noted that "the richness of a language and the importance of its literature are assessed by its important translations of the Bible and of the works of William Shakespeare."[24] *Plus ça change*: still the old project of turning to Shakespeare for some measure of cultural legitimacy.

That project could become esoteric at times, such as a debate in the pages of a Yiddish linguistic journal in 1941 over the proper Yiddish transcription of Shakespeare's name. Leybush Lerer called for Yiddish orthography to "throw off the yoke of languages that were only intermediaries, particularly Russian and German, and reckon with the sounds of the language from which the name comes."[25] Thus, "Shakespeare" would be transcribed phonetically as "Sheykspir," not "Shekspir." Esoteric as the question may sound, the journal printed a dissenting opinion in the following issue, even though the respondent himself wondered whether it made sense to explore such minutiae "at a time when the American Jew has no desire to pick up a Shakespeare book in Yiddish."[26] Lerer would have disagreed: "The higher our cultural growth develops, the more it grates on the ears when people mispronounce a name as famous as William *Shakespeare*."[27] The very vowels in Shakespeare's name become imbued here with talismanic power, making them a key to a Yiddish speaker's ability to navigate Western culture.

It is hard to imagine any American Jew mispronouncing Shakespeare's name today. Many would be unaware that there was ever a time when their grandparents and great-grandparents called him "Shekspir." Ironically, this development stems in part from the same agenda that helped bring Shakespeare into Yiddish in the first place, by using him as a bridge from the provincial Jewish milieu to the surrounding culture. Yiddish speakers crossed that bridge so quickly that their grandchildren are hardly aware it existed, and thus risk losing a sense of where they come from. In contemporary American Jewish letters, Shakespeare in Yiddish has returned as a symbol, this time of the loss of identity: artistic as well as ethnic.

Tony Kushner's two-part epic drama, *Angels in America* (1991), begins with a eulogy for an old Jewish woman that doubles as a paean to the voyages undertaken by generations of Jewish immigrants to America. Addressing the mourners, a rabbi comments on the intimate connection between America and the "Old Country": "You do not live in America. No such place exists. Your clay is the clay of some Litvak shtetl, your air the air of the steppes — because she carried the old world on her back across the ocean, in a boat, and she put it down on Grand Concourse Avenue, or in Flatbush, and she worked that earth into your bones, and you pass it to your children, this ancient, ancient culture and home." [28] The descendants of this woman and others like her have all but forgotten their ancestors' journeys; hence the need for a eulogy that pays tribute to a community even more than it does to an individual. After the funeral, the rabbi chides the woman's grandson Louis for having neglected her:

> *Louis*: I pretended for years that she was already dead. When they called to say she had died it was a surprise. I abandoned her.
> *Rabbi Isidor Chemelwitz*: "Sharfer vi di tson fun a shlang iz an umdankbar kind!"
> *Louis*: I don't speak Yiddish.
> *Rabbi Isidor Chemelwitz*: Sharper than the serpent's tooth is the ingratitude of children. Shakespeare. *Kenig Lear.*[29]

Scolding Louis in the didactic spirit of Jacob Gordin, the rabbi seems to be implicitly castigating the young man for walking away from his Jewishness as well.

The distance from the Jewish past can come in many forms. Cynthia Ozick spins a more extended conceit out of *The Jewish King Lear* in her short story "Actors" (1998), which intertwines artistic concerns with issues of Jewish identity. When Sephardic actor Matt Sorley (né Mose Sadacca) lands his first major role in years, it comes from an unexpected source: a "Lear of the Upper West Side" written by the recently deceased daughter of an old Yiddish actor. The director, a Yale-educated prodigy named Ted Silkowitz, wants to "restore the old lost art of melodrama. People call it melodrama to put it down, but what it is is open feeling, you see what I mean? . . . The old Yiddish theatre kept it up while it was dying out everywhere else. Killed by understatement. Killed by abbreviation, downplaying. Killed by sophistication, modernism, psychologizing, Stanislavsky, all those highbrow murderers of the Greek chorus, you see what I mean? The Yiddish Medea. The Yiddish Macbeth! Matt, it was *big!*"[30] This *Lear*, Silkowitz believes, will help the modern theatre find its future in its forgotten past.

Although Matt, "who worshipped nuance, tendril, shadow, intimation, instinct" (83), is skeptical at first, he becomes seduced by the grandeur of the role. The "pursuit of his grand howl" (89) that dominated the rehearsal process seems to pay off on opening night, when "no one laughed, no one coughed. It was Lear all the same, daughter-betrayed, in a storm, half mad, sported with by the gods, a poor, bare, forked animal, homeless, shoeless, crying in the gutters of a city street on a snowy night. . . . Matt's throat let out its unholy howl; it spewed out old forgotten exiles, old lost cities, Constantinople, Alexandria, kingdoms abandoned, refugees ragged and driven, distant ash heaps . . . the wild, roaring cannon of a human heartbeat" (92). A moment later, however, the spell is broken by ninety-six-year-old veteran Yiddish actor Eli Miller, the late playwright's father. Making his way down the aisle, he attacks the production as a fraud, calling it "charlatanism! Pollution!" He dismisses Matt's vocal gymnastics as "rotten" next to the "thunder" of Jacob Adler's voice, and the audience gives the old man a standing ovation. "Many in the audience," Matt later learns, "laughed until they wept" (92).

Matt had seemed to be on his way to capturing an ethnotheatrical Golden Fleece. Ozick's eloquent descriptions of his acting seem to suggest a power in declamatory performance that has become all but lost to our era; the director's unlikely vision was on its way to becoming a reality through Matt's pursuit of the howl. Yet a more authentic voice insists that this was no epiphany at all, but rather a misguided attempt to bring back what is gone in all but memory — the memory of a near-centenarian, no less. Matt and Silkowitz try to evoke the spirit of the Golden Age of Yiddish theatre, but Eli Miller tells us quite emphatically that ours is at best an age of bronze.

Rabbis and old actors chide today's younger generations for having lost their way. The grandchildren do not speak Yiddish, much less understand Shakespeare's dialogue in Yiddish. The artistic grandchildren of Jacob Adler, no matter how long they grow their beards or how hard they work at deepening their voices, cannot approach the majesty of his acting. It seems in retrospect to be easier to cross the bridge from Yiddish to American culture than to return in the other direction — or perhaps even to remember where the bridge was in the first place. America offered the immigrant Jews and their descendants a dizzying degree of freedom to be themselves, but perhaps even more freedom to be something else. To change their names, shave their beards, dispose of their wigs, get new wardrobes, lose their accents, forget their language, adopt another. Once all these and many other concessions had been made to the "Golden Land," the old stories, the old plays, changed their meaning too.

The lost world of Shakespeare in Yiddish can still have meaning, though we would do well to take Eli Miller's warnings seriously. He is right to suggest that such a world is difficult to recover, but the effort is worth making, for the Yiddish theatre serves as a powerful tool to help us understand the world of eastern European Jewry and its legacy. During its most fruitful period, the American Yiddish theatre had been one of the most vital outlets of self-expression for more than two million American Jews. Shakespeare and his dramas, as both sources and symbols, played an important role throughout this era. Their ubiquity in European and American theatre helped American Yiddish culture feel that it belonged to something larger. And for a critical historical moment, Yiddish audiences found new meaning in their own experience through Shakespearean characters refashioned in their image.

Notes

PREFACE

1. Exactly how one defines *daytshmerish*, and the purposes for which it is used, are complicated matters. Dror Abend offers a detailed discussion of both these questions in "'Scorned My Nation': A Comparison of Translations of *The Merchant of Venice* into German, Hebrew, and Yiddish (Ph.D. diss., New York University, 2001), 85 ff.

2. Sanders, "Shakespeare in Yiddish," *Cleveland Plain Dealer Sunday Magazine*, 25 January 1903, 5.

3. Quoted in Nahma Sandrow, *Vagabond Stars* (New York: Harper and Row, 1977), 262.

INTRODUCTION

1. Boris Thomashefsky, *Mayn lebns-geshikhte* (New York: Trio Press, 1937), 332. All translations from the Yiddish are my own unless noted otherwise.

2. Esther Cloudman Dunn, *Shakespeare in America* (1939; rpt. New York: Benjamin Blom, 1968), 274.

3. C. W. Sanders, "Shakespeare in Yiddish," 5.

4. Gerald Sorin, *A Time for Building: The Third Migration, 1880–1920* (Baltimore: Johns Hopkins University Press, 1992), 38. See also Moses Rischin, *The Promised City* (Harvard University Press, 1962; rpt. Harper & Row, 1970), 20 and 33.

5. Historian Arthur Hertzberg, *The Jews in America* (New York: Columbia University Press, 1986), 141, elaborates on this phenomenon:

   The dominant cause of mass migration [of Jews from eastern Europe] was poverty. Almost all middle-class Jews managed to find ways of reestablishing themselves elsewhere in Russia; it was the peddlers and the tailors who left for America. . . . Anti-Semitism did indeed limit the economic possibilities for Jews in [Russia, Austro-Hungary, and Romania], but the middle class found ways of surviving. It was the poor who were most affected by the lack of opportunity; they were the people who emigrated.

6. Leonard Dinnerstein, *Antisemitism in America* (New York: Oxford University Press, 1994), 35–57.

7. Sorin, 52.

8. Naomi W. Cohen, *Encounter With Emancipation* (Philadelphia: Jewish Publication Society of America, 1984), 325.

9. Sorin, 56.

10. Abraham Cahan, *Yekl* (New York: D. Appleton, 1896; rpt. New York: Dover, 1970), 33–4.

11. For English overviews of the *purimshpil*, see Nahma Sandrow, 1–20; and Israel Zinberg, *A History of Jewish Literature*, 12 vols., trans. Bernard Martin (Cincinnati: Hebrew Union College / Ktav, 1975), 7:301–44. More detailed history and analysis can be found in B. Gorin, *Di geshikhte fun yidishn teater* (New York: Literarisher Farlag, 1923), 1:19–63; J. Shatzky, "An akhashveyresh-shpil mit 100 yor tsurik," in *Arkhiv far geshikhte fun yidishn teater un drame*, ed. J. Shatzky (Vilna: YIVO, 1930), 159–74; J. Shatzky, "Di ershte geshikhte fun yidishn teater," *Filologishe shriftn* 2 (Vilna, 1928), 215–64; I. Shiper, *Geshikhte fun yidisher teater — kunst un drame*, 3 vols. (Warsaw: Kultur Lige, 1923–28); Khone Shmeruk, *Makhazot mikrayim b'yidish, 1697–1750* (Jerusalem: Academy of Sciences and Humanities, 1979); Max Weinreich, "Tsu der geshikhte fun der elterer akhashveyresh-shpil," *Filologishe shriftn* 2 (Vilna, 1928), 425–52; and Zalmen Zylbercweig, *Leksikon fun yidishn teater* (New York, 1963), 4:3610–29.

12. Basic information on the *batkhn* can be found in I. Lifschitz, "Batkhonim un leytsim bay yidn," in Shatzky, *Arkhiv*, 38–74; Shiper, 1:66–80, 3:20–42; and Zylbercweig, 1:132–44. For a more extensive account, see Ariela Krasni, *Habadkhan* (Ramat Gan: Bar Ilan University, 1998).

13. Sandrow, 36. For more on Broder singers, see Gorin, 1:132–49; Shatzky, *Arkhiv*, 455; Zylbercweig, 1:216–36 and 1:508–15; and Shloyme Prizament, *Broder-zinger* (Buenos Aires, 1960).

14. Avrom Goldfaden, "Fun 'Shmendrik' biz 'Ben-Ami,'" *Amerikaner*, 29 March 1907.

15. Goldfaden probably saw Ira Aldridge perform while a rabbinical student in Zhitomir, Ukraine. In their biography of the tragedian, Herbert Marshall and Mildred Stock write that Aldridge went on several long tours of the Russian provinces between 1861 and 1866, and list Zhitomir (where Goldfaden was based throughout this period) as a place where Aldridge performed. Aldridge's sojourn, according to a Russian theatre historian, "was a whole epoch in the cultural life of each town." See Herbert Marshall and Mildred Stock, *Ira Aldridge: The Negro Tragedian* (London: Rockliff, 1958), 275–6.

16. Goldfaden, "Fun 'Shmendrik' biz 'Ben Ami.'"

17. Ibid. Goldfaden alludes here to a popular song from the Passover Seder, in which Jews recall having been slaves to Pharaoh in Egypt.

18. See, for example, Gorin, 1:167–256 and Sandrow, 40–90.

19. The history of the Yiddish theatre in Russia until the October Revolution is chronicled in N. Oyslender's *Yidisher teater, 1887–1917* (Moscow: Emes, 1940). For coverage of interwar European Yiddish theatre, see *Yidisher teater in eyrope tsvishn beyde velt-milkhomes*, 2 vols. (New York: Congress for Jewish Culture, 1968 and 1971).

20. Mark Slobin, *Tenement Songs* (Urbana: University of Illinois Press, 1982), 3.

21. Boaz Young, *Mayn lebn in teater* (New York: YKUF, 1950), 62.

22. Ibid., 63.

23. Tashrak, *Etikete* (New York: Hebrew Publishing Company, 1912), 87.

24. Bessie Thomashefsky, *Mayn lebns-geshikhte* (New York: Varhayt, 1916), 178.

25. Hutchins Hapgood, *The Spirit of the Ghetto* (New York, 1902; rpt. Cambridge, Mass.: Harvard University Press, 1967), 117−8.

26. For more on Hurwitz, see *Leksikon fun der nayer yidisher literatur*, 3:112−14; Perlmutter, 66−72; and Zylbercweig, 1:591−605. On Lateiner, see *Leksikon fun der nayer yidisher literatur*, 4:414−16; Perlmutter, 61−5; and Zylbercweig, 2:964−90. Gorin assesses the two playwrights' dramaturgy in 2:72−93, while a summary of the work of these writers and their contemporaries appears in Sandrow, 104−14. For a detailed assessment of the competition between Hurwitz and Lateiner in New York, see Marvin Leon Seiger, "A History of the Yiddish Theatre in New York City to 1892" (Ph.D. diss., Indiana University, 1960), 196−310.

27. Jacob Shatzky, ed., "Goldfadens a statut far a yidisher dramatisher shul in nyu-york, in 1888," in *Arkhiv*, 287.

28. Seiger, 201−2.

29. This mini-performance and others are described in Gorin, 1:96−98. Similar experiences are described in Leon Kobrin, *Erinerungen fun a yidishn dramaturg* (New York: Committee for Kobrin's Writings, 1925), 1:28−29; Boris Thomashefsky, *Thomashefsky's teater shriftn* (New York, 1908), 23−27.

30. Seiger, 314.

31. Ibid., 321.

32. For a discussion of playwright and theatre manager John F. Poole, see Walter Meserve, "Our English-American Playwrights of the Mid-Nineteenth Century," *Journal of American Drama and Theatre* 1 (Spring 1989), 16−17.

33. Gorin, 2:74.

34. B. Vaynshteyn, "Di ershte yorn fun yidishn teater in odes un in nyu-york," in *Arkhiv far geshikhte fun yidishn teater un drame*, ed. Jacob Shatzky (Vilna: YIVO, 1930), 251.

35. Ibid., 253.

36. Seiger, 202.

37. Young, 59.

38. "A Quaint Hebrew Drama," *N.Y. Sun*, 22 February 1885.

39. Seiger, 236.

40. Addresses and seating capacity for the People's, Thalia, and Windsor are taken from Diane Cypkin, "Second Avenue: The Yiddish Broadway" (Ph.D. diss., New York University, 1986), 12−18.

41. Thomas Postlewait, "The Hieroglyphic Stage: American Theatre and Society, Post-Civil War to 1945," in *The Cambridge History of American Theatre*, vol. 2, ed. Don B. Wilmeth and Christopher Bigsby (Cambridge: Cambridge University Press, 1999), 113.

42. Hapgood, 133.

43. Henry James, *The American Scene* (London: Chapman and Hall, 1907), 198.

44. Ibid., 196.

45. Boris Thomashefsky, *Mayn lebns-geshikhte*, 279.

46. Bessie Thomashefsky, 208.

47. John H. James, "The Theatre of the Ghetto." *New York Dramatic Mirror* (28 July 1900), 3. Quoted in Seiger, 296.

48. Hapgood, 130.

49. Lawrence Levine, *Highbrow/Lowbrow: The Emergence of Cultural Hierarchy in America* (Cambridge, Mass.: Harvard University Press, 1988), 31.

50. Ibid., 21.

51. Cary Mazer, *Shakespeare Refashioned: Elizabethan Plays on Edwardian Stages* (Ann Arbor: UMI Research Press, 1980), 5.

52. Michael Dobson, "Improving on the Original: Actresses and Adaptations," in *Shakespeare: An Illustrated Stage History*, ed. Jonathan Bate and Russell Jackson (Oxford: Oxford University Press, 1996), 50.

53. Gary Taylor, *Reinventing Shakespeare* (London: Weidenfeld & Nicolson, 1989), 47–8.

54. Quoted in Marvin Carlson, *Theories of the Theatre* (Ithaca: Cornell University Press, 1984), 146.

55. Victor Borovsky, "The Organisation of the Russian Theatre, 1645–1763," in *A History of Russian Theatre*, ed. Robert Leach and Victor Borovsky (Cambridge: Cambridge University Press, 1999), 51.

56. Zdeněk Stříbrný, *Shakespeare and Eastern Europe* (Oxford: Oxford University Press, 2000), 29–30.

57. Simon Williams, *Shakespeare on the German Stage*, vol. 1: 1586–1914 (Cambridge: Cambridge University Press, 1990), 151.

58. John McCormick, *Popular Theatres of Nineteenth-Century France* (London: Routledge, 1993), 141.

59. Ania Loomba, "Shakespearian Transformations," in *Shakespeare and National Culture*, ed. John J. Joughin (Manchester: Manchester University Press, 1997), 119–21.

60. B. Gorin, "Tsien besere shtiker hayzer?" *Teater zhurnal* 1 (15 November 1901), 2.

61. Levine, 38.

62. Gorin, 2:116.

63. Nokhem Bukhvald, *Teater* (New York: Farlag-Komitet Teater, 1943), 297.

64. Henry Feingold, *A Midrash on American Jewish History* (Albany: State University of New York Press, 1982), 87.

1. "GORDIN IS GREATER THAN SHAKESPEARE":
THE JEWISH KING AND QUEEN LEAR

1. Quoted in Zalmen Zylbercweig, *Vos der yidisher aktyor dertseylt* (Vilna: B. Kletzkin, 1928), 31–2.

2. Bessie Thomashefsky, *Mayn lebns-geshikhte* (New York: Varhayt Publishing Company, 1916), 198–9.

3. S. Niger, *Dertseylers un romanistn* (New York: Central Yiddish Culture Organization, 1946), 1:198.

4. Ibid., 203.

5. Jacob Gordin, "Erinerungen fun Yankev Gordin: vi azoy bin ikh gevorn a dramaturg?" *Idishe bine*, ed. Chanon Minikes (New York, 1897), 166.

6. Ibid., 167.

7. Jacob Gordin, "Der suzhet fun mayn tsukunftige [*sic*] drame," *Arbeter tsaytung*, 20 May 1892. Gordin had previously read at a benefit at the Romania Opera House.

8. *Folksadvokat*, 20 April 1894.

9. Jacob Gordin, *Yokl der opern-makher*, in *Yankev Gordins eyn-akters* (New York: Tog, 1917), 185.

10. Shlemiel's catalogue of ingredients for a Yiddish spectacle would be echoed in a review of a production of *Julius Caesar* staged by Boris Thomashefsky in 1895: "How did you forget," the reviewer scolded Shakespeare, "to give the costumer a chance [to make] 120 Turkish hats, 200 Spanish boots, 150 Portuguese trousers, 270 uhlans' shirts, and a few thousand African spears?" Similarly, the critic argued, Shakespeare denied the director the chance to "make a few dozen heavens and hells" and other exotic settings, and to fill the stage with sheep, donkeys, horses, and oxen; "without them, the Yiddish stage certainly cannot exist." See Dr. Kritikus, "Yulius Tsezar," *Der yidisher pok*, 8 February 1895, 171.

11. Irving Howe, *World of Our Fathers* (New York: Harcourt Brace Jovanovich, 1976), 461.

12. Quoted in Leon Kobrin, *Erinerungen fun a idishn dramaturg* (New York: Committee for Kobrin's Writings, 1925), 1:123.

13. Zalmen Zylbercweig, *Di velt fun Yankev Gordin* (Tel Aviv: Elisheva, 1964), 406.

14. B. Gorin, *Di geshikhte fun yidishn teater* (New York: Max N. Mayzel, 1923), 2:111.

15. Jacob Gordin, *Der yidisher kenig Lir*, unpaginated manuscript of 1894 in Jacob Gordin Papers, YIVO Archives. All subsequent quotations from the play come from this text. Although it cannot be traced directly to the original production script of the play, this manuscript was copied from an earlier script less than a year and a half after the first production; the title page reads: "Written for Sam Engelman . . . by Mr. Jules Firer . . . the 24th of May 1894." The action in this version barely differs from the version published in Warsaw in 1907 without Gordin's permission, and all the characters are the same. The dialogue in the published text, however, diverges in a number of places, especially by significantly watering down Shamay's sardonic commentary.

16. Boaz Young, *Mayn lebn in teater* (New York: YKUF, 1950), 89.

17. The dynamics among Dovid's children ring true historically. Initially, the *misnagdim* saw the Hasidim as such a threat that writs of excommunication were issued against Hasidic leaders. Once the Haskalah began gathering force, though, the former two groups found a common enemy in the latter.

18. Arthur Hertzberg, *The Jews in America* (New York: Simon & Schuster, 1989), 171.

19. The examples Shamay uses to express this idea are noteworthy. He begins the passage with a Jewish variation upon Edmund's comment, "The wheel has come full circle, I am here." (V.iii.175) In lieu of using the Christian image of the wheel of fortune, Gordin illustrates life's ups and downs in terms of the *dreydl*, a spinning top associated with Hanukkah. *Peysekh* [Passover], *Shvues* [Shavuot], and *Sukes* are the Jewish harvest festivals. *Kharoyses* is a dish made of chopped apples, walnuts, wine, and cinnamon, and eaten on matzoh to symbolize the mortar with which the Jews in Egypt were made to build the pyramids. The vegetables eaten on *Shvues* indicate the holiday's agricultural connection. Such an association also informs Shamay's mention of the *esreg* and *lulev*, the citron and branches central to the celebration of *Sukes* (or Sukkot). The Sabbath is not only the day of rest, but the holiest of Jewish holidays. Jews would scrimp and even borrow in order to mark it with a special meal, often including fish and meat. *Havdole* marks the end of the Sabbath and the beginning of the working week.

20. Leonard Prager, "Of Parents and Children: Jacob Gordin's *The Jewish King Lear*," *American Quarterly* 18 (1966), 510.

21. Celia Adler, 1:173.

22. "Drama," *Harper's Weekly*, 18 March 1899.

23. Prager, 516.

24. Kritikovsky, "Klasishe trern," *Yidishe gazeten*, 11 November 1892.

25. *Harper's Weekly*, 18 March 1899.

26. Young, 79.

27. Joseph Rumshinsky, *Klangen fun mayn lebn* (New York: Farlag Biderman, 1944), 264–5.

28. *Forverts*, 20 October 1903.

29. *King Lear*, in *The Arden Shakespeare*, ed. Kenneth Muir (London: Methuen, 1972), 180.

30. *Kenig Lir*, trans. Mikhl Goldberg. Typescript in the Thomashefsky Collection, New York Public Library Jewish Division, #3.

31. Ibid.

32. A theatrical anecdote, for which I am indebted to Michael Morrison, reinforces this point. The story is told of an actor, renowned on both Yiddish- and English-language American stages, who gets into a cab at Kennedy Airport and asks to be taken to a Broadway theatre. The Jewish cab driver, thrilled to be carrying such an important passenger, excitedly

asks the actor what part he will be playing. "King Lear," responds the star. The driver ponders this, then asks a moment later, "Do you think it will work in English?"

33. Zylbercweig, *Di velt fun Yankev Gordin*, 158.

34. Ibid., 157.

35. Jacob Gordin, *Mirele Efros* (New York, 1898), 12. All subsequent quotations from the play will be cited in the text, as will multiple citations after the first one from primary sources throughout the book.

36. Irving Howe, *World of Our Fathers* (New York: Harcourt Brace Jovanovich, 1976), 495.

37. Leon Kobrin, "Di idishe kenigin Lir," *Arbeter tsaytung*, 21 August 1898.

38. Moyshe Katz, "'Di idishe kenigin Lir' oder 'Mirele Efros'" (conclusion), *Forverts*, 4 September 1898.

39. B. Feygenboym, "Di 'kenigin' fun ale idishe drames." *Abend-blat*, 22 August 1898.

40. Katz, "'Di idishe kenigin Lir' oder 'Mirele Efros,'" 4 September 1898.

41. Ibid.

42. Kobrin, "Di idishe kenigin Lir."

43. Katz, "'Di idishe kenigin Lir' oder 'Mirele Efros,'" 4 September 1898.

44. Kobrin, "Di idishe kenigin Lir."

45. B. Feygenboym, "Di 'kenigin' fun ale idishe drames."

46. Ibid.

47. Katz, "'Di idishe kenigin Lir' oder 'Mirele Efros.'" *Forverts*, 28 August 1898.

48. Morris Rosenfeld, "Kuni leml un der idisher kenig lir," reprinted in *Arkhiv far geshikhte fun yidishn teater un drame*, ed. Jacob Shatzky (Vilna: YIVO, 1930), 448.

49. Ibid.

50. Poet Joseph Bovshover had penned a verse tribute in honor of *The Jewish King Lear*. See "Tsu Yankev Gordin" in *Amerike in yidishn vort*, ed. Nakhmen Mayzel (New York: YKUF, 1955), 169.

51. Morris Vintshevski, Prologue to *Mirele Efros* (New York, 1898), 3.

52. Ibid.

53. Ibid., 4.

54. The tenth-anniversary celebration was capped by Gordin's own tribute to himself: a one-act sketch called "The Character Gallery," in which seventeen characters from nine different Gordin plays appear, one by one, and deliver speeches designed to elicit applause for the characters and their creator. Berl Bernstein and Jacob P. Adler appeared as Shamay and Dovid Moysheles, respectively, and the parade was anchored by Keni Liptzin as Mirele Efros. See *Yankev Gordins eyn-akters* (New York: Tog, 1917), 205–20.

55. Zalmen Libin, *Geklibene skitsn* (New York: Forverts, 1902), 56.

56. Ibid., 58.

57. A. Hart, "Kenig lir alts border." Unpaginated, undated manuscript in Perlmutter Play Collection, YIVO Archives, #353. This manuscript contains two versions of the sketch. The apparent original is described here; a variant follows essentially along the same lines, but with some additional jokes and the final stage direction, "Finish up as you wish." The same play collection also contains a similar sketch by Hart, "Kenig lir's probe" [King Lear's rehearsal, #356], another variation on the same theme.

58. B. Gorin, "Zelde geyt in teater," in *Di idishe bine*, ed. Khonen Y. Minikes (New York: J. Katzenelenbogen, 1897), n.p. Subsequent quotations will be cited in the text.

59. "A Moving Picture," *Groyser kundes* 1 (15 September 1909), 9.

60. *Groyser kundes* 3 (17 November 1911), 7.

61. Zylbercweig, *Leksikon*, 2:1116.

62. Abraham Cahan, "Ver iz a besere 'Mirele Efros,' Madam Liptzin oder Madam Kaminska?" *Forverts*, 9 December 1911.

63. Feygenboym, "Di 'kenigin' fun ale idishe drames."

64. L. Fogelman, "Di role fun Mirele Efros in fir farsheydene geshtaltn," *Forverts*, 11 December 1936.

65. A. Mukdoyni, "Teater notitsn," *Morgen zhurnal*, 20 December 1936.

66. Ibid.

67. A. Mukdoyni, "Parodye un komedye," *Morgen zhurnal*, 9 December 1932.

68. Ibid.

69. In fact, *Mirele Efros* had been given two screen adaptations at the dawn of the Yiddish cinema: Andrzej Marek's version, produced in Warsaw in 1912 and starring Esther-Rokhl Kaminska, and V. Krivtsov's Moscow adaptation the following year. See Eric A. Goldman, *Visions, Images, and Dreams: Yiddish Film Past and Present* (Ann Arbor: UMI Research Pres, 1979), 175 and 177.

70. Goldman, 77; J. Hoberman, *Bridge of Light: Yiddish Film Between Two Worlds* (New York: Museum of Modern Art, 1991), 210.

71. Goldman, 124.

72. Alter Epshteyn, "Di barimte 'Mirele Efros' vet bald gezen vern als a film," *Tog*, 21 August 1939.

73. Nokhem Bukhvald, "'Mirele Efros' in a film," *Morgen frayhayt*, 23 October 1939.

2. CLASSICAL INFLUENZA, OR, HAMLET LEARNS YIDDISH

1. Boris Thomashefsky, *Mayn lebns-geshikhte* (New York: Trio Press, 1937), 295–6.

2. Moyshe Zeifert, "Di geshikhte fun idishn teater," in *Di idishe bine*, ed. Khonen Jacob Minikes (New York, 1897), 44–5.

3. Dan Miron, "Folklore and Antifolklore in the Yiddish Fiction of the *Haskala*," in *Studies in Jewish Folklore*, ed. Frank Talmage (Cambridge, Mass.: Association for Jewish Studies, 1980), 219.

4. Alexander Harkavy, "Iz yidish a shprakh fir drame?" *Di fraye yidishe folks-bine* 1 (1897), 16.

5. Ibid.

6. "Unzer platform," *Di fraye yidishe folksbine* 1 (1897), 2.

7. Harkavy was hardly the first activist of a minority language to co-opt Shakespeare as an instrument of cultural legitimation. A century earlier, similar efforts had been made in Czech and Hungarian. The first Czech translator of Shakespeare, K. H. Thám, was also the author of *A Defence of the Czech Language*; he and his compatriots, in the words of one historian, "wanted to prove to the whole nation and the world that the Czech language was capable of expressing the highest achievements of European dramatic art, even if they had to use inadequate or clumsy prose and some equally clumsy rhymes." Similarly, the first translator of Shakespeare into Hungarian, Ferenc Kazinczy, was "a poet, critic, translator, and ardent organizer of a nationalist rehabilitation of the Hungarian language and literature." See Zdeněk Stříbrný, *Shakespeare and Eastern Europe* (Oxford: Oxford University Press, 2000), 60–61.

8. Boris Thomashefsky, "Hinter di kulisn," *Teater velt* 1 (November 1908), 18.

9. Ibid.

10. Thomashefsky, *Mayn lebns-geshikhte*, 297–8.

11. Ibid., 299–300.

12. Bessie Thomashefsky, *Mayn lebns-geshikhte* (New York: Varhayt Publishing Company, 1916), 222–3.

13. Boris Thomashefsky, *Mayn lebns-geshikhte*, 298–9.

14. Ibid., 300–1.

15. Zeifert portrays Shakespeare as ironically intoning the opening lines of the *Al kheyt*, the long confessional prayer said twice at each of the four services on Yom Kippur, the Day of Atonement.

16. Moyshe Zeifert, "Geshikhte fun idishn teater," 45.

17. Ibid., 46–8.

18. *Arbeter tsaytung*, 8 December 1893.

19. Pasekh shin: sha, "Teater kritik: Hamlet prints fun denemark," *Yidishe gazeten*, 15 December 1893. Zalmen Zylbercweig calls Zeifert's *Hamlet* a "free adaptation," probably from German; if so, Zeifert probably adapted *Othello* in a similar manner. See "Shekspir af der yidisher bine un literatur," *Hundert yor yidish teater* (London: Jewish Cultural Society, 1962), 27.

20. Pasekh shin: sha, "Teater kritik."

21. Thomashefsky, "Hinter di kulisn," 17.

22. Gordin undoubtedly would have concurred with this distinction between adaptation and original work. A document in Gordin's handwriting found among his papers in the YIVO Archives lists all of his plays, breaking them down into four categories: "translated and adapted," "borrowed subjects," "one-acters," and "original." He includes both *The Jewish King Lear* and *Mirele Efros* in the latter group.

23. Thomashefsky chose it as the play for a benefit performance for himself

at the Thalia on 21 December 1893. It was staged four more times in January 1894, but then may have started to lose its luster, for it did not reappear until March 31.

24. *Yidishe gazeten*, 26 January 1894.

25. None of the books on Edwin Booth makes any mention of a William Booth. Neither do Edwin Booth's obituaries, which do mention surviving immediate family members. See, for example, Stanley Kimmel, *The Mad Booths of Maryland* (New York: Bobbs-Merrill, 1940); L. Terry Oggel, *Edwin Booth: A Bio-Bibliography* (Westport, Conn.: Greenwood Press, 1992); and Eleanor Ruggles, *Prince of Players: Edwin Booth* (New York: Norton, 1953). Furthermore, Raymond Wemmlinger, librarian of the Hampden-Booth Library at The Players, has never come across a similar phenomenon in the English-speaking American theatre (telephone communication with the author, 30 November 1993). Various obituaries can be found in the clippings file on Edwin Booth at the Billy Rose Theatre Collection, New York Public Library at Lincoln Center. That same collection makes note of the obituary of one William E. Booth in the *New York Dramatic Mirror* of 17 September 1904, which reads in its entirety: "William E. Booth, an actor who was this season a member of an Uncle Tom's Cabin company playing in the Middle West, died in St. Francis Hospital, Columbus, O., on September 10. The remains will be buried by the Actors' Fund in the Fund plot in the Cemetery of the Evergreens." Any connection between this William Booth and that of the Yiddish performance seems purely coincidental.

26. Mark Twain, *The Adventures of Huckleberry Finn* (1884; rpt. New York: Penguin Books, 1966), 200.

27. Ibid., 213.

28. "Odler" (in German, "adler") is Yiddish for eagle, and "der groyser odler" [The great eagle] became a nickname for Jacob Adler. This nickname was sometimes Hebraicized as "nesher hagodl."

29. Moyshe Zeifert, "Alts tsulib parnose," *Idishe bine*, 17 December 1909.

30. Mikhl Goldberg's *King Lear* is discussed in chapter 1, his *Othello* in chapter 3, his *Romeo and Juliet* and *Coriolanus* in chapter 4.

31. *Hamlet*, trans. Mikhl Goldberg. Perlmutter Play Collection, YIVO Archives, 1300, p. 15. Slight variants of this speech appear in two other extant scripts of Goldberg's translation: number 1300A in the same collection, and a typescript in the Thomashefsky Collection, Jewish Division, New York Public Library.

32. Ibid., n.p.

33. Mark Slobin, *Tenement Songs: The Popular Music of the Jewish Immigrants* (Urbana: University of Illinois Press, 1982), 4.

34. *Abend-blat*, 30 January 1899. A similar ad appears in *Der teglekher herald* starting on the same day.

35. Zylbercweig, *Leksikon*, 1:736–7. By giving himself an acting job, the

playwright could significantly increase his income. At that time, American Yiddish playwrights sold their work for a flat fee (in New York, fifty dollars seems to have been a common rate in the 1890s), but if they participated as actors too, would be paid an additional amount (around five dollars) for each night they appeared on stage.

36. Isidore Zolatarevsky, *Der yeshive bokher*. Unpaginated manuscript in Thomashefsky Collection, New York Public Library Jewish Division, 22. The Thomashefsky Collection also owns a typescript with the following in English on the title page: "Keshover Cleveland Ohio 11.2. Election Eve 1920"; and an undated manuscript without a title page. All further citations will come from the former.

37. Joseph Rumshinsky, *Klangen fun mayn lebn* (New York: Biderman, 1944), 811. Both Zolatarevsky and composer Louis Friedsel would be remembered in death, as they had been famed in life, for their contributions to *The Yeshiva Boy*. At Friedsel's funeral in 1923, Joseph Rumshinsky led a chorus assembled from the Cantors' Union, the Actors' Union, and the Choral Union in singing the play's closing melody, which had become famous as a death march. And although he went on to write dozens of melodramas, many of them commercially successful, Zolatarevsky's tombstone commemorates his legendary Jewish *Hamlet*: "Here lies Yitskhok Zolatarevsky, the creator of *Yeshive bokher*." See Sholem Perlmutter, *Yidishe dramaturgn un teater-kompozitors* (New York: YKUF, 1952), 349 and 184.

38. The Sound Archives at YIVO contain recordings of Friedsell's *kaddish* by Meyer Goldin (1905), David Kessler (1905 and 1913), Hyman Adler (1911), Joseph Feldman and Morris Goldstein (1921), and Boris Thomashefsky (1927).

39. Israel Zangwill, *Ghetto Comedies* (New York: Macmillan, 1923), 297.

40. These figures are provided by Zylbercweig, *Leksikon fun yidishn teater*, 4:2426.

41. *The Kreutzer Sonata*, Gordin's loose adaptation of Tolstoy's story, was also adopted by the English-language American stage, though Bertha Kalish was not the first to star in the English version. Blanche Walsh originated the role of Miriam (the English version's equivalent of Ettie) in an adaptation by Langdon Mitchell in 1906.

42. Jill Edmonds, "Princess Hamlet," in *The New Woman and Her Sisters*, ed. Vivien Gardner and Susan Rutherford (Ann Arbor: University of Michigan Press, 1992), 60.

43. The date is according to Bernard Grebanier, *Then Came Each Actor* (New York: David McKay Company, Inc., 1975), 254. Edmonds dates Sarah Siddons's debut as Hamlet at 1776; see "Princess Hamlet," 59.

44. A. H. Fromenson, "Kalish as Hamlet." Undated clipping from unidentified newspaper in Scrapbook, Bertha Kalich Papers, Billy Rose Theatre Collection, New York Public Library at Lincoln Center.

45. "The Theatres," *Commercial Advertiser*, 23 February 1901.

46. *New York Dramatic Mirror*, 9 February 1901.

47. *Abend-blat*, 7 November 1898. Actually, the Yiddish translation was billed as *Féodora*, a perhaps unintentional conflation of two similarly titled Sardou plays, *Fédora* and *Théodora*, both of which became Bernhardt vehicles. Although Kalish was not mentioned in the initial advertisements, she later told a reporter that she had played the role. See "Yiddish Duse, About to Make Her Debut on the English Stage in 'Fedora,' Discusses Her Art and Her Ambitions," *New York Times*, 14 May 1905, III, 5.

48. Cornelia Otis Skinner, *Madame Sarah* (Boston: Houghton Mifflin, 1967), 261.

49. Max Beerbohm, "Hamlet, Princess of Denmark," reprinted in Beerbohm, *Around Theatres* (London: Rupert Hart-Davis, 1953), 36.

50. These details are provided by William Winter, *Shakespeare on the Stage* (1911; rpt. New York: Benjamin Blom, 1969), 1:433–5.

51. Robert Speaight, *Shakespeare on the Stage* (London: Collins, 1973), 96.

52. Winter, 1:432.

53. "The Theatres," *Commercial Advertiser*, 23 February 1901.

54. Alan Dale, "Bertha Kalisch, the Yiddish Favorite, Plays Hamlet," *New York Morning Journal*, 31 January 1901.

55. "The Theatres," *Commercial Advertiser*, 23 February 1901.

56. Dale, "Bertha Kalisch, the Yiddish Favorite."

57. For a brief biographical sketch, see "Alan Dale," *The American Jewish Year Book*, 5665 (1904/1905), ed. Cyrus Adler and Henrietta Szold (Philadelphia: Jewish Publication Society, 1904), 74.

58. Dale, "Bertha Kalisch, the Yiddish Favorite."

59. Ibid.

60. Dale, "Bertha Kalisch, the Yiddish Favorite."

61. *New York Dramatic Mirror*, 9 February 1901.

62. Fromenson, "Kalish as Hamlet."

63. "The Theatres," *Commercial Advertiser*, 23 February 1901. The critic added that Kalish carried out this bit of business "after the Wilson Barrett manner." Towards the end of Edwin Booth's career in the mid-1880s, Booth "was too old, of course, to fit anyone's notion of what Hamlet ought to look like. Unluckily an English actor named Wilson Barrett . . . was Hamletizing in America and persuading newspaper writers far and wide that the true Hamlet was a bouncing juvenile." Eminent critic William Winter was not persuaded, however: "In Wilson Barrett's performance of *Hamlet* the manifestation of filial love was conspicuous for fervency and zeal. But filial love is not the sovereign charm of *Hamlet* nor is it the dominant impulse of his character." See Shattuck, *Shakespeare on the American Stage* (Washington, D.C.: Folger Shakespeare Library, 1987), 1:39; and Winter, 1:374.

64. In the manuscript of the Vilenski translation, the "Wilson Barrett" end-

ing has been crossed out and a new one, much closer to Shakespeare's, inserted in different handwriting. The new ending eliminates Hamlet's threat with his sword, and ends the act with Hamlet saying, "Good night, mother, good night. Come sir, I must make an end of you." (73) Kalish clearly used the more sentimental ending in January of 1901, but apparently reverted to Shakespeare's at some later point in the translation's stage life.

65. *New York Dramatic Mirror*, 9 February 1901.

66. Dale, "Bertha Kalisch, the Yiddish Favorite."

67. *New York Dramatic Mirror*, 9 February 1901.

68. *Commercial Advertiser*, 23 February 1901; *New York Dramatic Mirror*, 9 February 1901.

69. Dale, "Bertha Kalisch, the Yiddish Favorite."

70. *Commercial Advertiser*, 23 February 1901.

71. Fromenson, "Kalish as Hamlet."

72. See chapter 5.

73. Looking back on the production three years later, Kalish told journalist Hutchins Hapgood, "I think Hamlet was my greatest artistic success." She also told him of her plans to star in *Cymbeline* and *As You Like It*. This would have added two new works to the Yiddish Shakespearean repertoire, but she never appeared in those plays in any language. See Hutchins Hapgood, "Star of Yiddish Stage: Bertha Kalisch," *The Sunday Telegraph*, 27 March 1904.

74. *Hamlet*. Unpaginated, undated manuscript (translator unknown) in the YIVO Archives, Play Collection, #17.2.1. The title page reads, "*Hamlet*, property of Josef Kessler."

75. K. Retsenzent, "Hamlet," *Idisher ekspres*, 28 June 1922.

76. "Hamlet," *Velt*, 25 October 1917.

77. Ibid.

78. K. Retsenzent, "Hamlet."

3. AN *OTHELLO* POTPOURRI

1. *Di arbeter tsaytung*, 27 May 1892. It has been difficult to substantiate any of the advertisement's claims. The *New York Times Index* makes no reference whatsoever to Morrison in the late 1880s and early 1890s. A review of Schiller's *Maria Stuart* in April 1892, just before the *Arbeter tsaytung* ad appeared, provides a cast list that does not include Morrison ("Maria Stuart," *New York Times*, 9 April 1892). He may well have been a member of Saxe-Meiningen's company, but if so, he seems to have left the troupe before the spring of 1892.

2. Boris Thomashefsky, *Mayn lebns-geshikhte*, 245–60; Bessie Thomashefsky, *Mayn lebns-geshikhte* (New York: Varhayt Publishing Company, 1916), 166–70.

3. "*Lamed-vovnik*" derives from the Hebrew letters *lamed* and *vov*, whose nu-

merical equivalent totals thirty-six: twice the value of the word *"khay,"* meaning "life."

4. Bessie Thomashefsky, 168.

5. Gorin, 2:169.

6. Abraham Cahan, "Morits Morison's role af der idisher bine," *Forverts*, 29 August 1917.

7. Boris Thomashefsky, "Tomashevski bashraybt vi azoy er hot zikh bakent mit Morison'en," *Forverts*, 30 August 1917.

8. Rudolph Schildkraut would come to be one of the most important Yiddish-speaking interpreters of Shylock. See chapter 5.

9. Thomashefsky commissioned several Shakespeare translations in the mid-1890s from Dovid Moyshe Hermalin, who is thus a likely candidate for translator of the 1894 *Othello*, starring Thomashefsky and Sigmund Feinman. After putting the play aside for several years, Thomashefsky returned to it in 1899 at the Windsor Theatre, with Rosa Karp as his Desdemona. Since Mikhl Goldberg was by this point Thomashefsky's Shakespeare translator of choice, this is likely when his *Othello* was first used. My dating is based on my own survey of New York Yiddish theatre advertisements throughout this period.

10. *Othello*, trans. Mikhl Goldberg. Unpaginated manuscript in Perlmutter Play Collection, YIVO Archives, #1303.

11. Zylbercweig, *Leksikon*, 4:2962.

12. Leon Kobrin, *Erinerungen fun a idishn dramaturg* (New York: Committee for Kobrin's Writings, 1925), 1:13–20.

13. For slightly different recollections of Gordin's response to Kobrin's first play, see Kobrin, *Erinerungen*, 1:83–9; and Joel Entin, "Leon Kobrin der dramaturg," in Leon Kobrin, *Dramatishe shriftn* (New York: Leon Kobrin Book Committee, 1952), xv–xviii.

14. Entin, "Leon Kobrin der dramaturg," xix–xx.

15. Korolenko's novel appeared in *Der emes* starting with the first issue on 3 May 1895 and running until 16 August of the same year. The same translation was reprinted in the *Forverts* from 11 April to 10 May 1903.

16. Noah Prilutski, *Yidish teater*, vol. 2 (Bialystok: Farlag A. Albek, 1921), 43.

17. Shmuel Niger, *Dertseylers un romanistn* (New York: Central Yiddish Culture Organization, 1946), 218.

18. Leon Kobrin, *Der blinder muzikant, oder der yidisher Otelo*. The YIVO Institute has a manuscript copy, "specially written for Boris Thomashefsky," in its Perlmutter Collection. The Jewish Division of the New York Public Library has two copies of the play in the Thomashefsky Collection: an unpaginated manuscript (17) and a typescript (7). The manuscript's title page reads, "Der blinder muzikant oder der yidisher Otelo! Family drama in 4 acts by Leon Kobrin, written especially for Mr. Boris Thomashefsky. Staged by D. Grolts NY November 9 — 1904 People's Theatre." The typescript's provenance is not as clear; written in pencil on the title page

are the words, "11/2/28 Harry Sherman Hollywood Calif." I will base my analysis on the two manuscript versions (the YIVO manuscript being essentially a slightly longer version of the NYPL manuscript).

19. See Harry Carpenter, *Boxing: A Pictorial History* (Glasgow: Collins, 1975), 28 – 32; and Claude Droussent, *L'Encyclopédie de la Boxe* (Paris: Editions Ramsay, 1990), 35 – 46. In the Thomashefsky Collection manuscript, "Fitz" is crossed out and "Willard" penciled in. Jesse Willard was most famous for stripping the world heavyweight title from Jack Johnson in a controversial fight on 5 April 1915. The name change in the script probably indicates that Fitzsimmons, who was prominent when *Der blinder muzikant* premiered, was referred to in the initial production, but the reference was changed to Willard when the same script was used in a revival years later. In the typescript, Bessie initially refers to Johnson, whose name is crossed out and replaced by [Jack] Dempsey.

20. Prilutski, 44.

21. Ronald Sanders, *Shores of Refuge* (New York: Schocken Books, 1988), 183.

22. By the late teens, while *The Blind Musician* was being revived at the Lennox Theatre, blindness had become so prevalent in American Yiddish plays that a commentator from the *Groyser kundes* moaned, "Please, people, call in an eye doctor for the Yiddish drama!" See Pif-paf, "Teater koyln," *Groyser kundes* 11 (7 February 1919), 5.

23. D. M., "Der blinder muzikant," *Fraye arbeter shtime*, 14 November 1903.

24. The YIVO manuscript contains a scene, cut from the Thomashefsky Collection scripts, that starts with a soliloquy of several pages in which Yozef concludes that Rosa loved not him, but the idea of his future success. Michael unwittingly provokes Yozef much more than in the Thomashefsky Collection scripts by rambling on about how he has done nothing to disabuse his friends of their misconception that he is married to Rosa.

25. D. M., "Der blinder muzikant," *Fraye arbeter shtime*, 21 November 1903.

26. Entin later recalled that Kobrin took the review personally, a reaction that brought a temporary halt to their friendship. See "Leon Kobrin der dramaturg," xxv.

27. Joel Entin, "Der blinder muzikant," *Forverts*, 13 November 1903.

28. Ibid.

29. D. M., "Der blinder muzikant."

30. Prilutski, 44.

31. Entin, "Der blinder muzikant."

32. See Joel Berkowitz, "The *Tallis* or the Cross?: Reviving Goldfaden at the Yiddish Art Theatre." *Journal of Jewish Studies* 50 (Spring 1999), 120 – 38.

33. Schwartz staged revivals of Gordin's *The Jewish King Lear* and *Mirele Efros* on 17 January 1919 and 1 February 1919, respectively. He also wrote (under the pseudonym M. Charnoff) and starred in a play called *Shekspir un kompani* [Shakespeare and company], which premiered at the Nora

Bayes Theatre on 19 October 1925. The title is deceiving, however. The pseudo-Pirandellian situation comedy follows the results of a business-man's decision to write a play about a love triangle and to insist that his wife, a retired actress, play the part of the wife opposite her former real-life paramour. The husband, of course, gets extremely jealous, and ulti-mately resolves never to attempt playwriting again. Shakespeare's name in the title sets up a play on the word "company" in its dual meanings as theatre troupe and business, but the play's content has nothing to do with Shakespeare. One critic concluded that "not only does *Shakespeare and Company* do no honor to Shakespeare's name; it does not even do so for Maurice Schwartz's." See Pompador, "Drame-ayn, drame-oys," *Groy-ser kundes* 17 (30 October 1925), 6.

   Besides *Shylock and His Daughter* (discussed in chapter 5), the Yiddish Art Theatre staged one other Judaized adaptation of Shakespeare. *Di legende fun yidishn kenig Lir* [The Legend of the Jewish King Lear], about a troupe of actors performing Gordin's play, premiered on 30 November 1932, but ran for only one weekend.

34. *Othello*, trans. Mark Schweid, 14. Incomplete typescript in Maurice Schwartz Papers, YIVO Archives. The script lacks a title page and goes only up to the middle of Shakespeare's III.iii. Yet besides its location in the Maurice Schwartz Papers, other characteristics signal that the script is the Schweid translation. First is the overall quality of the translation in such matters as following Shakespeare's rhyme and meaning. Second is the script's treatment of Iago; cuts in the character's speeches agree with the critics' interpretation of the character. Finally and most idiosyncrati-cally is the greatly expanded role of the Clown, who is added to a number of scenes in the text, again corresponding to the critics' observations.

35. Nokhem Bukhvald, "'Otelo' in idishn kunst teater," *Morgen frayhayt*, 7 Feb-ruary 1929.

36. Stephen Rathbun, "In and Out of the Theater," *New York Sun*, 4 Febru-ary 1929.

37. N. Bukhvald, "'Otelo' in idishn kunst teater."

38. Rathbun, "In and Out of the Theater."

39. Bukhvald, "'Otelo' in idishn kunst teater."

40. "Schwartz to Act Iago," *New York Times*, 28 January 1929.

41. "Yiddish Art Theatre Gives 'New' Othello," *New York Times*, 4 February 1929.

42. Ibid.

43. A. Glants, "Di Shekspir oyffirung in kunst teater," *Tog*, 8 February 1929; Rathbun, "In and Out of the Theater."

44. "Yiddish Art Theatre Gives 'New' Othello," *New York Times*, 4 February 1929.

45. Abraham Cahan, "'Otelo' in Shvarts's kunst teater," *Forverts*, 8 Febru-ary 1929.

46. Ibid.

47. Bukhvald, "'Otelo' in idishn kunst teater."
48. Ibid.
49. Ibid.
50. B. Y. Goldshteyn, "Af der teater evenyu," *Di fraye arbeter shtime*, 15 February 1929.
51. M. V. S., "New Iago Shown in the Yiddish Art Theater's 'Othello,'" *Herald Tribune*, 4 February 1929.
52. Cahan, "'Otelo' in Shvarts's kunst teater."
53. Ibid.
54. Dr. A. Mukdoyni, "Shekspir-oyffirungen," *Morgen zhurnal*, 17 February 1929.
55. Goldshteyn, "Af der teater evenyu."

4. "PARENTS HAVE HEARTS OF STONE": *ROMEO AND JULIET*

1. *Teglekher herald*, 11 September 1894.
2. *Teglekher herald*, 19 September 1894.
3. Five manuscript versions of *Romeo and Juliet* can be found in the Perlmutter Play Collection, YIVO Archives. Two are by Mikhl Goldberg, #1302 being a slightly abridged version of 1302B. 1302A is by Mendl Teplitski, "For B. Thomashefsky, Lessee and manager of Peoples Theatre, New York, September 16, [??]." 1302C, by D. M. Hermalin, purports to be "completely reworked" by B. Vilenski (who translated *Hamlet* for Bertha Kalish). No translator is mentioned in the manuscript numbered 1302D, though that text does include a cast list, with Thomashefsky as Romeo and Keni Liptzin as Juliet.

   The following sequence seems likely for several of the texts: since Keni Liptzin played Ophelia to Thomashefsky's Hamlet in 1894 — the same season that *Romeo and Juliet* premiered at the Thalia — it seems likely that MS 1302D came first. (Liptzin also would have been unlikely to play Juliet as of 1898, when the success of *Mirele Efros* made her almost exclusively an interpreter of Gordin.) After the 1894–1895 season, Thomashefsky put the play aside until 1899, when he played Romeo to Sophia Karp's Juliet at the Windsor Theatre. At this point, he may well have commissioned a new translation: probably either by Mikhl Goldberg or by Hermalin / Vilenski. Thomashefsky did not perform *Romeo and Juliet* at the People's Theatre until 1904; this was almost certainly the Teplitski translation, which specifically mentions that theatre.

   Subsequent references will identify the manuscripts by number in the body of the text.
4. Jacob Mestel, *Unzer teater* (New York: YKUF, 1943), 38.
5. Only one of the translations discussed here — Mendl Teplitski's [1302A] — includes Romeo's reluctant duel with Paris, though even that seems to have been cut in production at some point, since it is crossed out in the manuscript.
6. Bessie Thomashefsky, *Mayn lebns-geshikhte* (New York: Varhayt, 1916), 191.

7. Ibid.

8. Ibid.

9. *Teglekher herald*, 30 October 1894.

10. *Julius Caesar* was staged at the Thalia Theatre for four evenings in February 1895, after which it seems to have dropped out of the production repertoire of the Yiddish theatre, though translations made more for reading than for performance were published in 1918 and 1933. *Julius Caesar* was, in fact, the first known example of a Shakespeare translation into Yiddish, in a version by Betsalel Vishnipolski (Warsaw: Ginz, 1886). See Leonard Prager, "Shakespeare in Yiddish," *Shakespeare Quarterly* 19 (1968), 149–63; and Dahlia Kaufman, "The First Yiddish Translation of *Julius Caesar*," trans. Elinor Robinson, in *The Field of Yiddish*, 5th Collection, ed. David Goldberg (New York: YIVO and Northwestern University Press, 1993), 219–42.

11. Dovid Moyshe Hermalin's translation of *Macbeth* (no longer extant) was produced at the Thalia on 3 and 4 May 1895.

12. Boris Thomashefsky, *Mayn lebns-geshikhte* (New York: Trio Press, 1937), 334.

13. Ibid., 333.

14. Ibid.

15. Ibid., 334.

16. Ibid.

17. Kobrin, *Erinerungen fun a yidishn dramaturg*, (New York: Committee for Kobrin's Writings, 1925), 2:125–7.

18. William Kaiser, "Der toes af der bine," in *Di idishe bine*, ed. Khonen Y. Minikes (New York: J. Katzenelenbogen, 1897), n.p.

19. Gordin biographer Kalmen Marmor posits that Gordin may have been influenced by Shakespeare in creating Reb Shraga, and says that with his sympathetic portrait of a religious figure, the playwright "set out on the road toward artistic objectivity." Marmor, *Yankev Gordin* (New York: YKUF, 1953), 83.

20. Bessie Thomashefsky, *Mayn lebns-geshikhte* (New York: Varhayt, 1916), 239.

21. Jacob Gordin, *Di litvishe brider Luriye* (Warsaw: Edelshteyn, 1907), 24.

22. Marmor, 82.

23. Y. L. Peretz, "Di Luriyes," 1906. Rpt. in *Ale verk* (New York: CYCO, 1947), 6:203.

24. Ibid., 202.

25. Joseph Groper, *Romeo un Zhulyete*. Undated, unpaginated MS in Perlmutter Play Collection, YIVO Archives, #253. The play was probably first performed either at the Windsor Theatre, where Groper worked upon his arrival in the United States in 1899, or some time after that at the People's Music Hall, where he wrote, directed, and performed in sketches. See Zalmen Zylbercweig, *Leksikon fun yidishn teater*, 1:527–8.

26. For plays up to 1892, see the chronology provided by Marvin Seiger in

"A History of the Yiddish Theatre in New York City to 1892" (Ph.D. diss., Indiana University, 1960), 528–63. Subsequent titles and dates are based on my own survey of Yiddish theatre advertisements in the New York Yiddish press.

27. Sam Shneyer, *Yehudis*. Undated, unpaginated MS in Perlmutter Play Collection, YIVO Archives, #1739. The first page of the script bears the penciled inscription, "Perry St. Theatre, Cleveland. Max Gabel, manager."

28. Ibid., 185.

29. According to both Zylbercweig's *Leksikon* (4:2498) and the *Leksikon fun der nayer yidisher literatur* (8:402). Perlmutter places Rakov in the United States as early as 1900.

30. Some confusion over the premiere of this play clouds the secondary sources. Perlmutter says that the play had its 1903 debut in Boston, then played elsewhere in New England before coming to New York, where he says it did not open until several years later. Zylbercweig puts the New York debut at 10 April 1907 rather than 10 April 1903, the date announced in the Yiddish newspapers. Zylbercweig and Perlmutter may be correct in stating that the play was first presented in Boston, but if so, it was weeks, not years, before the New York premiere. Incidentally, *Der batlen* [The idler] has generated its share of confusion as well. Perhaps Perlmutter's remark that this play was inspired by *Der yeshive bokher* led the *Leksikon fun der nayer yidisher literatur* to write incorrectly that *Der batlen* was "better known as *Der yeshive bokher*" (8:402).

31. Nokhem Rakov, *Di shvue baym seyfer-toyre, oder, di yidishe Romeo un Yulia.* Unpaginated, undated MS, Vilner Archive, YIVO.

32. "Shakespeare in Yiddish," *New York Evening Post*, 3 June 1903.

33. John Corbin, "Topics of the Drama," *New York Times*, 26 April 1903.

34. Joshua Kohn, *The Synagogue in Jewish Life* (New York: Ktav, 1973), 193.

35. "Shakespeare in Yiddish," *New York Evening Post*.

36. Avrom Goldfaden, *Oysgeklibene shriftn*, ed. Shmuel Rozhanski (Buenos Aires: Literary Society of YIVO in Argentina, 1963), 51.

37. Corbin, "Topics of the Drama."

38. Rakov does not provide the text for Sheyndele's song, but merely the stage direction, "She sings from the Song of Songs." The "literal translation" the *New York Evening Post* reporter claims to provide is far more chaste:

> My beloved one spake and said unto me,
> Rise up, my love, my fair one, come away,
> For, lo! the winter is past and rain is over and gone;
> The flowers appear on the earth, the time of the singing bird is come.
> Tell me, O thou whom my soul loveth,
> Where thou feedest, where thou makest the flock to rest at noon;
> For why should I be as one that turneth aside from the flocks of my
>   companions?

39. Maurice Lamm, *The Jewish Way in Love and Marriage* (San Francisco: Harper & Row, 1980), 231.

40. Ninety years later, this line conjures up the guilt trip that serves as the punch line to so many Jewish mother jokes, but beside the fact that the context for the remark is quite somber, such jokes had not yet come into fashion at the time, according to William Novaks and Moshe Waldoks, editors of *The Big Book of Jewish Humor* (New York: Harper & Row, 1981), 268: "Jokes about the Jewish mother — the biggest cliché in contemporary Jewish humor — are a relatively recent phenomenon. Traditional Jewish humor had no such jokes . . . it was not until the mass arrival of Jewish immigrants to America that the Jewish mother was transformed into an object of humor — and even then, only after several decades."

41. Chaver-Paver, *Romeo un Dzhuliet. Yidishe kultur* (1956), 60.

5. "A TRUE JEWISH JEW": A SHYLOCK QUARTET
Material from this chapter was previously published in *Theatre Survey* 37 (May 1996), 75–98.

1. B. Gorin, "Shaylok," *Amerikaner*, 3 March 1911.

2. The American Yiddish theatre's only other nineteenth-century encounter with the play came in 1899, with the publication of poet Joseph Bovshover's translation.

3. Joseph Bovshover, *Shaylok oder der koyfman fun venedig* (New York: Katzenellenbogen, 1899).

4. Bertha Kalish, "A brodveyer kholem," *Tog*, 12 November 1925.

5. Jacob Adler, "Mayn lebn," *Naye varhayt*, 2 May 1925.

6. William Winter, *Shakespeare on the Stage* (1911; reprint, New York: Benjamin Blom, 1969), 1:175.

7. Alan Hughes, *Henry Irving, Shakespearean* (Cambridge: Cambridge University Press, 1981), 229.

8. Quoted in Henry Tyrrell, "Jacob Adler — The Bowery Garrick," *Theatre* 2 (November 1902), 19.

9. Ibid.

10. "Mr. Adler's Shylock," *Jewish Exponent*, 15 May 1903.

11. Ibid.

12. "Mr. Adler Scores in Shylock Role," *New York Herald*, 15 May 1905.

13. L., "The True Shakespeare's Jew," *American Hebrew*, 15 May 1903.

14. "Plays and Players," *Globe and Commercial Advertiser*, 16 May 1905.

15. A review in the *American Hebrew* on 8 May 1903 claimed that Adler used poet Joseph Bovshover's translation as his performance text, but other critics' descriptions suggest that this could have been the case only if Adler had significantly cut Bovshover's text. Numerous cuts and stage directions in the typescript in the Jacob Adler Papers in the YIVO Archives, on the other hand, precisely match the descriptions given in the reviews. This typescript was undoubtedly the text Adler used for his productions.

16. George C. D. Odell, *Shakespeare from Betterton to Irving* (1920; rpt. New York: Dover Publications, 1966), 2:423.

17. "Mr. Adler's Shylock," *Jewish Exponent*, 15 May 1903.

18. *Shaylok*, anonymous typescript, Jacob Adler Papers, YIVO Archives, 9.

19. "Plays and Players," *Globe and Commercial Advertiser,* 16 May 1905.

20. Ibid.

21. Ibid.

22. Quoted in Tyrrell, 19.

23. L., "The True Shakespeare's Jew," *American Hebrew*, 15 May 1903.

24. Ibid.

25. Morris Vintshevski, "Shaylok, a idisher id," *Forverts*, 28 December 1901.

26. Kh. Aleksandrov, "Shaylok af der idisher bine," *Abend blat*, 28 December 1901.

27. B. Gorin, "'Shaylok' oder 'Der koyfman fun venedig,'" *Teater zhurnal*, 15 December 1901.

28. Ibid.

29. Aleksandrov, "Shaylok af der idisher bine."

30. Gorin, "'Shaylok' oder 'Der koyfman fun venedig.'"

31. Bernard Gorin, "The Yiddish Theatre in New York," *Theatre* 2 (January 1902), 18.

32. Lulla Rosenfeld, in Jacob Adler, *A Life on the Stage* (New York: Alfred A. Knopf, 1999), 344.

33. "Adler in Shylock at Academy of Music," *Jewish Exponent*, 8 May 1903. On Augustin Daly's production — his last major venture — see Charles Shattuck, *Shakespeare on the American Stage* (Washington, D.C.: Folger Shakespeare Library, 1987), 1:90–2.

34. "Shaylok der id," *Di yidishe gazeten*, 15 May 1903.

35. Philadelphia's *Jewish Exponent*, writes Murray Friedman, was "created by the older elite in 1887 to help in the Americanizing process." See the Introduction to *Jewish Life in Philadelphia, 1830–1940*, ed. Murray Friedman (Philadelphia: ISHI Publications, 1983), 10.

36. Louis Lipsky, "Acting and Jacob P. Adler," *Jewish Exponent*, 8 May 1903.

37. "Always in Good Humor," *New York Evening Mail*, 16 May 1905.

38. Ibid.

39. "Plays and Players," *Globe and Commercial Advertiser*, 16 May 1905.

40. "The Yiddish Shylock," *New York Times*, 26 May 1903.

41. "Mr. Adler in New York," *American Hebrew*, 29 May 1903.

42. "Plays and Players," *Theatre Magazine* 3 (July 1903), 160.

43. "Mr. Adler's Shylock," *Jewish Exponent*, 15 May 1903.

44. "Jacob Adler Gives a Masterful Shylock," *New York American*, 16 May 1905.

45. *New York Evening Post*, 13 May 1905.

46. "Idisher Shaylok," *Di idishe velt*, 26 May 1903.

47. "Mr. Adler's Shylock," *Jewish Exponent*, 15 May 1903.

48. "Mr. Adler Scores in Shylock Role," *New York Herald*, 15 May 1905.

49. Moyshe Katz, "Shaylok's tip revolutsyonirt," *Idishe velt*, 28 May 1903.
50. "Shaylok der id," *Di yidishe gazeten*, 15 May 1903.
51. Alexander Harkavy, "Iz yidish a shprakh fir drame?" *Fraye yidishe folksbine* 1 (1897), 17. See chapter 2 for a more detailed discussion of this article.
52. "Der nayer Shaylok," *Yidishe gazeten*, 29 May 1903.
53. John Gross, *Shylock: A Legend and Its Legacy* (New York: Simon & Schuster, 1992), 240.
54. Hermann Sinsheimer, *Shylock: The History of a Character* (1947; reprint New York: Benjamin Blom, 1963), 142.
55. *Groyser kundes* 3 (19 May 1911), 5.
56. "Erev peysekh vokh in idishn teater," *Varhayt*, 18 March 1911.
57. "Shildkroyt als Shaylok," *Yidishes tageblat*, 26 March 1911.
58. Joel Entin, "Dos teater," *Tsukunft* 16 (October 1911), 584.
59. Ibid.
60. "Irving Place — The Merchant of Venice," *New York Mirror*, 29 March 1911.
61. D. C., "In teater," *Fraye arbeter shtime*, 20 May 1911.
62. Leon Kobrin, "Shildkroyt in Shaylok," *Idisher kemfer*, 7 April 1911.
63. Jacob Milkh, "Gedanken iber Shaylok," *Tsukunft* 16 (October 1911), 546.
64. Ibid.
65. A. Epshteyn, "'Shaylok' in nayem idishn teater," *Varhayt*, 18 March 1911.
66. Kobrin, "Shildkroyt in Shaylok."
67. *New York Mirror*, 29 March 1911.
68. Quoted in Stephen Rathbun, "New Apollo Theatre, Mary Nash and Ben Ami Start Their Season Next Week," *New York Sun*, 13 November 1920.
69. B. Gorin, "Shildkroyt als Shaylok," *Morgen zhurnal*, 17 November 1920.
70. Ibid.
71. "Schildkraut Plays 'Merchant of Venice,'" *New York Mail*, 12 November 1920.
72. Rathbun, "New Apollo Theatre."
73. "Schildkraut Plays 'Merchant of Venice.'"
74. Rathbun, "New Apollo Theatre."
75. Ibid.
76. M. J. Landa, *The Shylock Myth* (London: W. H. Allen, 1942), 38.
77. "Moscovitch, a New Shylock in London," *Christian Science Monitor*, 4 November 1919.
78. "And So He Came to Star on Broadway," *New York Times*, 11 January 1930.
79. Ibid.
80. Ibid.
81. Toby Lelyveld, *Shylock on the Stage* (London: Routledge & Kegan Paul, 1961), 107.
82. Desmond MacCarthy, *Drama* (London: Putnam, 1940), 15.

83. Gross, 186.

84. MacCarthy, 20.

85. Maurice Moscovitch and Y. L. Fayn, "Di lebns geshikhte fun dem idish-englishn shoyshpiler Moris Moskovitsh," *Forverts*, 27 December 1929.

86. A shtendiger oyrekh, "Moris Moskovitsh in der role fun 'Shaylok' af der englisher bine," *Forverts*, 4 November 1919.

87. W. A. Darlington, *Through the Fourth Wall* (London, 1922), 20.

88. Dr. A. Mukdoyni, "Moskovitsh-Shaylok," *Morgen zhurnal*, 4 December 1930.

89. Ibid.

90. Ab. Cahan, "Moris Moskovitsh in zayn barimter Shekspir role," *Forverts*, 4 December 1930.

91. William Edlin, "Vi Moris Moskovitsh shpilt 'Shaylok,'" *Tog*, 7 December 1930.

92. For more on Moscovitch's Shylock, see John Gross, *Shylock* (New York: Simon & Schuster, 1992), 184–6.

93. "Schwartz First Did Shylock Under Williamsburg Bridge," *New York Herald Tribune*, 20 April 1930, VIII, 5.

94. David Dank, *Shvarts af vays* (New York, 1963), 28.

95. I am grateful to Thomas Postlewait for pointing out this connection.

96. Maurice Schwartz, "Shylock in Vaudeville," *Tog* English supplement, 27 April 1930.

97. Ibid.

98. "Vaudeville," *New York World*, 20 April 1930.

99. John Chapman, "Maurice Schwartz Plays Shylock for Palace Fans," *New York Daily News*, 22 April 1930.

100. "Maurice Schwartz a Fervid Shylock," *New York Times*, 21 April 1930.

101. Abraham Cahan, "Moris Shvarts hot groysn erfolg af der amerikaner vodvil steydzh," *Forverts*, 25 April 1930.

102. Zalmen Zylbercweig, "Moris Shvarts zogt 'Shayloks tokhter' hot groyse idish-natsyonale misye," *Morgen zhurnal*, 25 July 1947.

103. "The Yiddish Shylock," *New York Times*, 26 May 1903.

104. Gorin, "Shildkroyt als Shaylok."

105. Richard Watts, Jr., "Yiddish Art Company Offers Shylock Play," *New York Post*, 7 October 1947.

106. N. Bukhvald, "'Shaylok un zayn tokhter' in idishn kunst-teater," *Morgen frayhayt*, 10 October 1947.

107. Maurice Schwartz, *Shylock and His Daughter*, trans. Abraham Regelson (New York: Yiddish Art Theatre, 1947), 27.

108. Schwartz, *Shylock and His Daughter*, 28.

109. Bukhvald, "'Shaylok un zayn tokhter.'" Ibn Zahav certainly intended audiences to see this connection. In a short essay entitled "Shylock the Jew" that prefaces the English translation, he claims that "Paul IV's period was a small-scale precursor of Hitler's time, and the Nuremberg laws

were practically a copy of Paul's roman edicts against the Jews. See Schwartz, *Shylock and His Daughter*, n.p.

110. Theatre program, *Shaylok un zayn tokhter*, Israel Theatre Archive, Tel Aviv University.

111. William Edlin, "'Shaylok un zayn tokhter' efnt sezon fun kunst teater," *Tog*, 3 October 1947.

112. Joel Entin, "Der alter Shaylok af a nayem untershlag," *Idisher kemfer*, 24 October 1947.

113. C. Gutman, "'Shaylok un zayn tokhter' in idishn kunst teater,'" *Morgen zhurnal*, 3 October 1947.

114. Richard A. Yaffe, "'Shylock and Daughter' Sets Record Straight," *P. M.*, 6 October 1947.

115. David Lifson, *The Yiddish Theatre in America* (New York: Thomas Yoseloff, 1965), 384. This wisecrack came from Amos Hirshbayn, son of playwright Perets Hirshbayn.

116. Schwartz, *Shylock and His Daughter*, 146. Readers may recall that *The Yeshiva Boy* ended with the chorus pronouncing this same traditional formula.

117. Brooks Atkinson, "On Second Avenue," *New York Times*, 30 November 1947, II, 1.

118. Jeanette Wilken, "Schwartz an Authentic New 'Shylock,'" *New York Daily News*, 1 October 1947.

119. Yaffe, "'Shylock and Daughter' Sets Record Straight."

120. Bukhvald, "'Shaylok un zayn tokhter.'"

121. Entin, "Der alter Shaylok."

122. Gutman, "'Shaylok un zayn tokhter.'"

123. Quoted in Zylbercweig, "Moris Shvarts zogt."

124. Quoted in Lifson, 320.

CONCLUSION

1. At the Passover Seder, the youngest child present traditionally leads the *fir kashes* (four questions), beginning with, "Why is this night different from all other nights?"

2. The title of this play presents a historical puzzle, for the Thomashefsky Collection contains a manuscript by the same name, "adapted from the German by Leon Kobrin." This script is clearly not the *Sheyne amerikanerin* first produced by Thomashefsky in January 1910. Aside from the play's not being attributed to Kobrin in advertisements and reviews and the Kobrin MS having no apparent connection to *The Taming of the Shrew* — inconclusive evidence, as earlier discussions in this chapter show — Kobrin's script is not a musical, and its characters' names have nothing in common with the names in the director's score of Thomashefsky's play (in the Perlmutter Collection, YIVO). All of these factors combined indicate that the Kobrin script was not the same as the

Thomashefsky musical; they do not, however, establish what it was. Standard sources on Kobrin mention no such play. If it ever was produced, it must have been under another name.

3. *Shaylok oder der koyfman fun venedig*, trans. Joseph Bovshover (New York: Katzenellenbogen, 1899, rpt. New York: Hebrew Publishing Co., 1911); *Hamlet* and *Julius Caesar*, trans. Y. Y. Shvarts (New York: Forward, 1918); *Othello*, trans. Mark Schweid, 1929 (Maurice Schwartz Collection, YIVO Archives); B. Lapin, *Sonetn* (New York: Bloch, 1953). During a six-year sprint in the mid-thirties, Y. Goldberg's translations of *Julius Caesar*, *Hamlet*, *Macbeth*, *Othello*, *Romeo and Juliet*, *Richard III*, both parts of *Henry IV*, and *The Tempest* were published in Minsk.

4. Moyshe Zeifert, "Der groyser mes," in *Amerike*, ed. Y. Vortsman (New York: Farlag "Natsyonale Bibliotek," 1909), 40.

5. "The Yiddish Shylock of Jacob P. Adler," *New York Times*, 16 May 1905.

6. Cynthia Ozick, "Envy; or, Yiddish in America," in *The Pagan Rabbi and Other Stories* (New York: E. P. Dutton, 1983), 47.

7. Harley Erdman, *Staging the Jew* (New Brunswick: Rutgers University Press, 1997), 41.

8. Lester D. Friedman, *Hollywood's Image of the Jew* (New York: Frederick Ungar, 1982), 10.

9. Boaz Young, *Mayn lebn in teater* (New York: YKUF, 1950), 78–9.

10. Nahma Sandrow, *Vagabond Stars* (New York: Harper & Row, 1977), 296.

11. Daniel Soyer, *Jewish Immigrant Associations and American Identity in New York, 1880–1939* (Cambridge, Mass.: Harvard University Press, 1997), 108.

12. On American immigration restrictions, see, *inter alia*, Leonard Dinnerstein, *Antisemitism in America* (New York: Oxford University Press, 1994), 96; Henry Feingold, *A Time for Searching: Entering the Mainstream, 1920–1945* (Baltimore: Johns Hopkins University Press, 1992), 24–30; and Howard Sachar, *A History of the Jews in America* (New York: Knopf, 1992), 319–24.

13. Brooks Atkinson, "Theatrical Drama," *New York Times*, 18 December 1932.

14. Sandrow, 295.

15. Der Lakhediger, "Halt Shekspir a hoyzn shop?" *Forverts*, 23 April 1916.

16. Irving Howe, *World of Our Fathers* (New York: Routledge, 1976), 467.

17. D. M. Hermalin, *Shekspir's oysgeveylte verk* (New York: Drukerman, 1908), v. The book was reissued in 1909 and 1912.

18. Hermalin based the idea for his work on Charles and Mary Lamb's *Tales from Shakespeare* (1813), which included prose retellings of twenty of Shakespeare's plays. Hermalin included eighteen in his collection, for some reason leaving out *Measure for Measure* and *Pericles*. He added a summary of "The Rape of Lucrece," and in the second and third editions added *Julius Caesar* as well.

19. "Der bester Shekspir in market," *Forverts*, 30 April 1916.

20. The pseudonym, pronounced "na-deer" and not to be confused with

the English word "nadir," means something along the lines of "here, take this."

21. *Groyser kundes* 8 (21 April 1916), 5.

22. D. S., "Ritshard Burton in Shekspir's 'Hamlet,'" *Forverts*, 24 April 1964.

23. Dr. A. Asen published Yiddish translations of the *Sonnets* (New York: Bellemir Press, 1944) and *King Lear* (New York: Grenich Printing, 1947). See also B. Lapin translation of the *Sonnets* (New York: Bloch, 1953).

24. Avrom Taytlboym, *Vilyam Shekspir* (New York: Yidisher Kultur Farband, 1946), 7.

25. Leybush Lerer, "Shekspir oder Sheykspir?" *Yidishe shprakh* 1 (May–June 1941), 87.

26. Borukh Glazman, "Take Shekspir un nit Sheykspir," *Yidishe shprakh* (September–October 1941), 153.

27. Lerer, 89.

28. Tony Kushner, *Angels in America, Part One: Millennium Approaches* (New York: Theatre Communications Group, 1992), 10.

29. Ibid., 24–25.

30. Cynthia Ozick, "Actors," *New Yorker* (5 October 1998), 83–84.

Bibliography

PRIMARY SOURCES

Published

Asen, Avrom. *King Lear*. New York, 1947.
———. *Sonnets*. New York: Bellemir Press, 1944.
Bovshover, Joseph. *The Merchant of Venice (Shaylok oder der koyfman fun venedig)*. New York: Katzenellenbogen, 1899. Rpt. New York: Hebrew Publishing Co., 1911.
Chaver-Paver [Gershon Aynbinder]. "Romeo un Dzhuliet." *Yidishe Kultur* 1 (1956), 59–63.
Goldberg, I. *Hamlet*. Minsk, 1934.
———. *Julius Caesar*. Minsk, 1933.
———. *Macbeth*. Minsk, 1938.
———. *Othello*. Minsk, 1935.
———. *Romeo and Juliet*. Minsk, 1935.
———. *Richard III*. Minsk, 1936.
———. *Henry IV, Parts 1 and 2*. Minsk, 1936.
———. *The Tempest*. Minsk, 1937.
Gordin, Jacob. *The Jewish King Lear* (English synopsis). New York: George Jessel Lodge No. 566, December 1905.
———. *Di litvishe brider Luria*. Warsaw, 1907.
———. *Der yidisher kenig Lir*. Warsaw: Jewish Theatre Library, 1907.
———. *Mirele Efros, di yidishe kenigin Lir*. New York, 1898. Rpt. New York: Hebrew Publishing Company, 1911.
Hermalin, D. M. *Shekspir's oysgevelte verk*. New York: Druckerman, 1908.
Lapin, B. *Sonnets*. New York: Bloch, 1953.
Shvarts, Y. Y. *Hamlet* and *Julius Caesar*. Serially in *Tsukunft*. Rpt. New York: Forward, 1918.
Schwartz, Maurice. *Shylock and His Daughter*. Trans. Abraham Regelson. New York: Yiddish Art Theatre, 1947.
———. *Shaylok un zayn tokhter*. New York: Yiddish Art Theatre, 1947.
Zolatarevsky, Isidore. *Der yeshive-bokher*. Warsaw, 1922.

Unpublished

Der blinder muzikant, oder der yidisher Otelo, by Leon Kobrin. Boris Thomashefsky Collection, New York Public Library (NYPL), Jewish Division.

Der blinder muzikant, "specially written for Boris Thomashefsky," 1904. Perlmutter Play Collection, YIVO Archives.

Coriolanus, translated by Mikhl Goldberg. Thomashefsky Collection, NYPL.

Esther fun eyn gedi. Thomashefsky Collection, NYPL.

Hamlet, translated by Mikhl Goldberg. Perlmutter Play Collection, YIVO Archives, and Thomashefsky Collection, NYPL.

Hamlet, translated by D. M. Hermalin. Perlmutter Collection, YIVO.

Hamlet, Prince of Denmark, translated for Boris Thomashefsky by Leon Kobrin. Thomashefsky Collection, NYPL.

Hamlet, Prince of Denmark, translated by I. J. Schwartz, 1918. Jacob Ben-Ami Papers, YIVO Archives.

Hamlet, "specially adapted from the German for Madame Bertha Kalish by B. Vilenski." Perlmutter Play Collection, YIVO Archives.

Hamlet, translated by Moyshe Zeifert, 1892. Thomashefsky Collection, NYPL.

Hamlet, translator unknown. YIVO Archives.

Julius Caesar, translated by D. M. Hermalin. MS of 1895, Perlmutter Play Collection, YIVO Archives.

Kenig Lir als border, by A. Hart. Perlmutter Play Collection, YIVO Archives.

King Lear, translated by Mikhl Goldberg. YIVO Archives.

King Lear, translator unknown. Thomashefsky Collection, NYPL.

Di litvishe brider Luria. Jacob Gordin Papers, YIVO Archives.

Macbeth, translated by S. Mentsher. YIVO Archives.

Macbeth. Maurice Schwartz Collection, YIVO Archives.

The Merchant of Venice, translator unknown. YIVO Archives.

The Merchant of Venice. Maurice Schwartz Collection, YIVO Archives.

The Merchant of Venice [under the title *Shaylok*], translated by M. Goldberg. Perlmutter Play Collection, YIVO Archives.

The Merchant of Venice [*Shaylok*], translated by Moyshe Shor. Moyshe Shor Collection, YIVO Archives.

The Merchant of Venice [*Shaylok*], translator unknown. Typescript in Jacob Adler Papers, YIVO Archives.

The Merchant of Venice [*Shaylok, der koyfman fun venedig*], translated by Joseph Schwartzberg, 1921. YIVO Archives.

Mirele Efros, by Jacob Gordin. Jacob Gordin Papers, YIVO Archives.

Mirele Efros, by Jacob Gordin. English translation by A. J. Gordin. Jacob Gordin Papers, YIVO Archives.

Othello, translated by Yaakov Bilder, 1893. Perlmutter Play Collection, YIVO Archives.

Othello, translated by Mikhl Goldberg. Perlmutter Play Collection, YIVO Archives.

Othello. Maurice Schwartz Collection, YIVO Archives.

Othello, translated by Mark Schweid, 1929. Maurice Schwartz Collection, YIVO Archives.

Richard III, translated by Eva Hurwitz. Thomashefsky Collection, NYPL.
Romeo and Juliet, translated by Mikhl Goldberg (two versions). Perlmutter Play Collection, YIVO Archives.
Romeo and Juliet, translated by D. M. Hermalin. "Completely new adaptation, and in scenes set by B. Vilenski." Perlmutter Play Collection, YIVO Archives.
Romeo and Juliet, translated by Mendl Teplitski. Perlmutter Play Collection, YIVO Archives.
Romeo and Juliet, translator unknown. Perlmutter Play Collection, YIVO Archives.
Romeo un Zhulyete, by Joseph Groper. Perlmutter Play Collection, YIVO Archives.
Di sheyne amerikanerin, a comedy in five acts, adapted from the German by Leon Kobrin. Thomashefsky Collection, NYPL.
Di shvue baym seyfer-toyre, oder di yidishe Romeo un Yuliye, by Nokhem Rakov. Vilner Archives, YIVO.
Yehudis, by Sam Shneyer. Perlmutter Play Collection, YIVO Archives.
Der yeshive bokher, by Isidore Zolatarevsky. Thomashefsky Collection, NYPL.
Der yidisher kenig Lir, by Jacob Gordin. Jacob Gordin Papers, YIVO Archives.
Der yidisher kenig Lir. MS of 1894 in Jacob Gordin Papers, YIVO Archives.

SECONDARY SOURCES

Abend, Dror. "'Scorned My Nation:' A Comparison of Translations of *The Merchant of Venice* into German, Hebrew, and Yiddish." Ph.D. diss., New York University, 2001.
"Adler in Shylock at Academy of Music." *Jewish Exponent*, 8 May 1903.
Adler, Jacob. "Mayn lebn." *Naye varhayt*, 2 May 1925.
———. *My Life on the Stage*. Trans. Lulla Adler Rosenfeld. New York: Knopf, 1999.
Adler, Lulla Rosenfeld. *Bright Star of Exile: Jacob Adler and the Yiddish Theatre.* New York: Thomas Y. Crowell, 1977.
Adler, Tsili [Celia], with Yakov Tikman. *Tsili Adler dertseylt.* 2 vols. New York: Tsili Adler Foundation un Bukh-Komitet, 1959.
"Adler's Shaylok." *Yidishe gazeten*, 19 May 1905.
"Adler's Shylock in Harlem." *New York Times*, 19 June 1906.
Akselrod, Ida. "Shekspir un zayn tsayt." *Tsukunft* 21 (May 1916), 421–5.
"Alan Dale." *The American Jewish Year Book*, 5665 (1904/5), ed. Cyrus Adler and Henrietta Szold (Philadelphia: Jewish Publication Society, 1904), 74.
Aleksandrov, Kh. "Shaylok af der idisher bine." *Abend-blat*, 28 December 1901.
Alter, Iska. "When the Audience Called 'Author! Author!': Shakespeare on New York's Yiddish Stage." *Theatre History Studies* 10 (1990), 141–62.

"Always in Good Humor." *New York Evening Mail*, 16 May 1905.

"And So He Came to Star on Broadway." *New York Times*, 11 January 1930.

Atkinson, Brooks. "On Second Avenue." *New York Times*, 30 November 1947, II, 1.

———. "Theatrical Drama." *New York Times*, 18 December 1932.

Bate, Jonathan, and Russell Jackson, eds. *Shakespeare: An Illustrated Stage History*. Oxford: Oxford University Press, 1996.

Beerbohm, Max. *Around Theatres*. London: Rupert Hart-Davis, 1953.

Ben-Avuye, Elisha [Yitskhok-Ayzik Gonsher]. "In idishn teater." *Tog*, 12 and 26 November 1920.

Berkowitz, Joel. "The *Tallis* or the Cross?: Reviving Goldfaden at the Yiddish Art Theatre." *Journal of Jewish Studies* 50 (Spring 1999), 120–38.

Bernheimer, Charles, ed. *The Russian Jew in the United States*. Philadelphia: J. C. Winston, 1905.

"Der bester Shekspir in market." *Forverts*, 30 April 1916.

Bialik, Ilana. "Audience Response in the Yiddish 'Shund' Theatre." *Theatre Research International* 13 (Summer 1988), 91–105.

Bialin, A. H. *Moris Shvarts un der yidisher kunst teater*. New York: Itshe Biderman, 1934.

Biancolli, Louis. "Shylock as the Victim of Venice." *New York World-Telegram*, 30 September 1947.

Bloom, Harold, ed. *Shylock*. New York: Chelsea House, 1991.

Boraisha-Fogel, Adah. "Shakespeare Translations in Yiddish." *Jewish Book Annual* 14 (1956–57), 32–37.

Bordman, Gerald. *American Musical Theatre*. 2nd ed. New York: Oxford University Press, 1993.

———. *American Theatre*. 3 vols. New York: Oxford University Press, 1994–96.

Borovsky, Victor. "The Organisation of the Russian Theatre, 1645–1763." In *A History of Russian Theatre*, ed. Robert Leach and Victor Borovsky, 41–56. Cambridge: Cambridge University Press, 1999.

Bristol, Michael. *Big-time Shakespeare*. London: Routledge, 1996.

———. *Shakespeare's America/America's Shakespeare*. London: Routledge, 1990.

Bukhvald, Nokhem. "'Mirele Efros' in a film. *Morgen frayhayt*, 23 October 1939.

———. "'Otelo' in idishn kunst teater," *Morgen frayhayt*, 7 February 1929.

———. "'Shaylok un zayn tokhter' in idishn kunst-teater." *Morgen frayhayt*, 10 October 1947.

———. *Teater*. New York: Farlag-Komitet Teater, 1943.

Cahan, Abraham. *The Education of Abraham Cahan*. Trans. Leon Stein, Abraham P. Conan, and Lynn Davison. Philadelphia: The Jewish Publication Society of America, 1969.

———. "Gordin's *Mirele Efros*." *Forverts*, 10 March 1908.

———. "Moris Moskovitsh in zayn barimter Shekspir role." *Forverts*, 4 December 1930.

————. "Moris Shvarts hot groysn erfolg af der amerikaner vodevil steydzh." *Forverts*, 25 April 1930.

————. "Morits Morison's role af der idisher bine." *Forverts*, 29 August 1917.

————. "'Otelo' in Shvarts's kunst teater." *Forverts*, 8 February 1929.

————. "Ver iz a besere 'Mirele Efros,' Madam Liptzin oder Madam Kaminski?" *Forverts*, 9 December 1911.

————. *Yekl*. New York: D. Appleton, 1896. Rpt. New York: Dover, 1970.

Carlson, Marvin. *The Italian Shakespearians: Performances by Ristori, Salvini, and Rossi in England and America*. Washington, D.C.: Folger Shakespeare Library, 1985.

————. *Theories of the Theatre*. Ithaca: Cornell University Press, 1984.

Carpenter, Harry. *Boxing: A Pictorial History*. Glasgow: Collins, 1975.

Cassedy, Stephen. *To the Other Shore: The Russian Jewish Intellectuals Who Came to America*. Princeton: Princeton University Press, 1997.

Chapman, John. "Maurice Schwartz Plays Shylock for Palace Fans." *New York Daily News*, 22 April 1930.

Cohen, Derek. "Shylock and the Idea of the Jew," in *Jewish Presences in English Literature*, ed. Derek Cohen and Deborah Heller, 25–39. Montreal: McGill-Queen's University Press, 1990.

Cohen, Naomi W. *Encounter With Emancipation: the German Jews in the United States, 1830–1914*. Philadelphia: Jewish Publication Society of America, 1984.

Cohen, Sarah Blacher, ed. *From Hester Street to Hollywood: The Jewish-American Stage and Screen*. Bloomington: Indiana University Press, 1983.

Corbin, John. "How the Other Half Laughs." *Harper's New Monthly Magazine* (1898), 41.

————. "Topics of the Drama." *New York Times*, 26 April 1903.

Cypkin, Diane. "Second Avenue: The Yiddish Broadway." Ph.D. diss., New York University, 1986.

D. C. "In teater." *Fraye arbeter shtime*, 20 May 1911.

D. M. "Der blinder muzikant." *Fraye arbeter shtime*, 14 and 21 November 1903.

D. S. "Ritshard Burton in Shekspir's 'Hamlet.'" *Forverts*, 24 April 1964.

Dale, Alan. "Bertha Kalisch, the Yiddish Favorite, Plays Hamlet." *New York Morning Journal*, 31 January 1901.

Dank, David. *Shvarts af vays*. New York, 1963.

Darlington, W. A. *Through the Fourth Wall*. London: Chapman and Hall, 1922.

Dawidowicz, Lucy, ed. *The Golden Tradition: Jewish Life and Thought in Eastern Europe*. Boston: Beacon, 1967.

Dimov, Osip. "Boris Thomashefsky — a fartseykhenung." *Der tog*, 22 December 1955.

Diner, Hasia R. *A Time for Gathering: The Second Migration, 1820–1880*. Baltimore: Johns Hopkins University Press, 1992.

Dinnerstein, Leonard. *Antisemitism in America*. New York: Oxford University Press, 1994.

Dobson, Michael. "Improving on the Original: Actresses and Adaptations."

In *Shakespeare: An Illustrated Stage History*, ed. Jonathan Bate and Russell Jackson, 45–68. Oxford: Oxford University Press, 1996.

"Drama." *Harper's Weekly*, 18 March 1899.

Dr. Kritikus [pseud.]. "Yulius Tsezar," *Der yidisher pok*, 8 February 1895, 171.

Droussent, Claude. *L'Encyclopédie de la Boxe*. Paris: Editions Ramsay, 1990.

Dunn, Esther Cloudman. *Shakespeare in America*. 1939. Rpt. New York: Benjamin Blom, 1968.

Durham, Weldon B., ed. *American Theatre Companies, 1888–1930*. Westport, Conn.: Greenwood Press, 1987.

Eastman, Arthur M. *A Short History of Shakespearean Criticism*. New York: Random House, 1968.

Edlin, William. "In der velt fun drame un muzik." *Morgen zhurnal*, 27 March, 10 April 1911.

———. "'Shaylok un zayn tokhter' efnt sezon fun kunst teater." *Tog*, 3 October 1947.

———. "Vi Moris Moskovitsh shpilt 'Shaylok.'" *Tog*, 7 December 1930.

Edmonds, Jill. "Princess Hamlet." In *The New Woman and Her Sisters: Feminism and Theatre, 1850–1914*, ed. Vivian Gardner and Susan Rutherford. Ann Arbor: The University of Michigan Press, 1992.

Eisen, Arnold. "In the Wilderness: Reflections on American Jewish Culture." *Jewish Social Studies* 5 (Fall 1998/Winter 1999), 25–39.

"Elaborate Revival of the 'Merchant of Venice.'" *Jewish Comment* (Baltimore), 8 and 15 May 1903.

Engle, Ron and Tice L. Miller, eds. *The American Stage*. Cambridge: Cambridge University Press, 1993.

Entin, Joel. "Der alter Shaylok af a nayem untershlag." *Idisher kemfer*, 24 October 1947.

———. "Der blinder muzikant." *Forverts*, 13 November 1903.

———. "Leon Kobrin der dramaturg," in Leon Kobrin, *Dramatishe shriftn*, xv–xviii. New York: Leon Kobrin Book Committee, 1952.

———. "Di shrek fun leben in Shekspir's tragedyes." *Varhayt*, 9 May 1916.

Epshteyn, Alter. "Di barimte 'Mirele Efros' bet bald gezen vern als a film." *Tog*, 21 August 1939.

———. "'Shaylok' in nayem idishn teater." *Tog*, 19 November 1920.

Erdman, Harley. *Staging the Jew: The Performance of an American Ethnicity, 1860–1920*. New Brunswick: Rutgers University Press, 1997.

Erens, Patricia. *The Jew in American Cinema*. Bloomington: Indiana University Press, 1984.

"Erev peysekh vokh in idishn teater." *Varhayt*, 18 March 1911.

Feingold, Henry L. *A Midrash on American Jewish History*. Albany: State University of New York Press, 1982.

———. *A Time for Searching: Entering the Mainstream, 1920–1945*. Baltimore: Johns Hopkins University Press, 1992.

Feygenboym, B. "Di 'kenigin' fun ale idishe drames." *Abend-blat*, 22 August 1898.

Fogelman, L. "Di role fun Mirele Efros in fir farsheydene geshtaltn." *Forverts*,
11 December 1911.

———. "'Shaylok un zayn tokhter' in idishn kunst teater." *Forverts*, 3 October
1947.

Fogl, Ada. "Y. Goldbergs yidishe iberzetsung fun *Hamlet*." *Yidishe shprakh* 12
(January–March 1952), 1–11.

Foulkes, Richard, ed. *Shakespeare and the Victorian Stage*. Cambridge: Cambridge
University Press, 1986.

Friedman, Lester D. *Hollywood's Image of the Jew*. New York: Frederick Ungar
Publishing Co., 1982.

Friedman, Murray, ed. *Jewish Life in Philadelphia, 1830–1940*. Philadelphia: ISHI,
1983.

Friesel, Evyatar. "The 'Americanization' of American Jewry: Old Concept,
New Meanings." *American Jewish History* 81 (Spring–Summer 1994), 321–30.

Fromenson, A. H. "Adler's Shylock." *Yidishe gazeten* English supplement,
26 May 1905.

———. "Kalish as Hamlet." Clipping from unidentified newspaper.
Scrapbook, Bertha Kalich Papers. Billy Rose Theatre Collection, New
York Public Library at Lincoln Center.

Gabler, Neil. *An Empire of Their Own: How the Jews Invented Hollywood*. New
York: Crown Publishers, 1988.

Gardner, Herb. *Conversations with My Father*. New York: Samuel French, 1994.

Girzdanski, Dr. M. "Der funt fleysh." *Teater zhurnal* 2 (15 February 1902).

Glants, A. "Di Shekspir oyffirung in kunst teater." *Tog*, 8 February 1929.

Glazman, Borukh. "Take Shekspir un nit Sheykspir," *Yidishe shprakh*
(September–October 1941), 151–4.

Goldberg, I. *Unzer dramaturgye*. New York: YKUF and Yekhiel Levenstein
Bukh-Komitet, 1961.

Goldfaden, Avrom. "Fun 'Shmendrik' biz 'Ben-Ami.'" *Amerikaner*, 29 March
1907.

———. *Oysgeklibene shriftn*, ed. Shmuel Rozhanski. Buenos Aires: Literary
Society of YIVO in Argentina, 1963.

Goldman, Eric A. *Visions, Images, and Dreams: Yiddish Film Past and Present*.
Ann Arbor: UMI Research Press, 1979.

Goldshteyn, B. Y. "Af der teater evenyu." *Fraye arbeter shtime*, 15 February
1929.

Goldstein, Rebecca. *Mazel*. New York: Penguin, 1995.

Gordin, Jacob. *Yokl der opern-makher*. In *Yankev Gordins eyn-akters*. New York:
Tog, 1917.

Gorin, B [Yitskhok Goydo]. *Di geshikhte fun yidishn teater (tsvey toyznt yor teater
bay iden)*. 2 vols. New York: Max N. Mayzel, 1923.

———. "Goyishkayt in idishn teater." *Tsukunft* 23 (December 1918), 741.

———. "Shaylok." *Amerikaner*, 3 March 1911.

———. "Shaylok oder der koyfman fun venedig." *Teater zhurnal* 1
(15 December 1901).

———. "Shildkroyt als Shaylok." *Morgen zhurnal*, 17 November 1920.

———. "Tsien besere shtiker hayzer?" *Teater zhurnal* 1 (15 November 1901), 1–2.

———. "The Yiddish Theatre in New York." *Theatre Magazine* 2 (January 1902), 18.

———. "Zelde geyt in teater." In *Di idishe bine*, ed. Khonen Y. Minikes. New York: J. Katzenelenbogen, 1897.

"Der goyisher Shaylok vos Shekspir hot megayer geven." *Varhayt*, 1 April 1911.

Grebanier, Bernard. *Then Came Each Actor*. New York: David McKay, 1975.

Grimsted, David. *Melodrama Unveiled: American Theatre and Culture, 1800–1850*. Chicago: University of Chicago Press, 1968.

Gross, John. *Shylock: A Legend and Its Legacy*. New York: Simon & Schuster, 1992.

Gutman, C. "'Shaylok un zayn tokhter' in idishn kunst teater." *Morgen zhurnal*, 3 October 1947.

Halpern, Richard. *Shakespeare Among the Moderns*. Ithaca: Cornell University Press, 1997.

Handlin, Oscar. *The Uprooted: The Epic Story of the Great Migrations that Made the American People*. Boston: Little, Brown, 1951.

Hapgood, Hutchins. *The Spirit of the Ghetto*. 1902. Rpt. Cambridge: Harvard University Press, 1967.

———. "Star of Yiddish Stage: Bertha Kalisch." *Sunday Telegraph*, 27 March 1904.

Harkavy, Alexander. "Iz yidish a shprakh fir drame?" *Di fraye yidishe folksbine* 1 (1897), 13–7.

Hawkins, William. "Long Hours Keep Maurice Schwartz Youthful." *New York World-Telegram*, 7 December 1946.

Heilman, Samuel. *The People of the Book: Drama, Fellowship, and Religion*. Chicago: University of Chicago Press, 1983.

Heinze, A. R. *Adapting to Abundance: Jewish Immigrants, Mass Consumption, and the Search for American Identity*. New York: Columbia University Press, 1990.

Hertzberg, Arthur. *The Jews in America: Four Centuries of an Uneasy Encounter*. New York: Simon & Schuster, 1989.

Heylprin, L. "A idisher Shekspir?" *Tog*, 28 April 1916.

Higham, John. *Send These to Me: Jews and Other Immigrants in Urban America*. New York: Atheneum, 1975.

———. *Strangers in the Land: Patterns of American Nativism 1860–1925*. New Brunswick: Rutgers University Press, 1955. Rpt. Rutgers University Press, 1988.

Hoberman, J. *Bridge of Light: Yiddish Film Between Two Worlds*. New York: Museum of Modern Art and Schocken Books, 1991.

Horowitz, Mayer. "Bibliography of Yiddish Translations of English Literature." *Jewish Book Annual* 11 (1952–53), 136–53.

Howe, Irving. *World of Our Fathers*. New York: Harcourt Brace Jovanovich, 1976.

Hughes, Alan. *Henry Irving, Shakespearean*. Cambridge: Cambridge University Press, 1981.

"Idisher Shylock." *Idishe velt*, 26 May 1903.

"Irving Place — King Lear." *New York Mirror*, 22 March 1911.

"Irving Place — The Merchant of Venice." *New York Mirror*, 29 March 1911.

"Jacob Adler as Shylock." *Sun*, 16 May 1905.

"Jacob Adler Gives a Masterful Shylock," *New York American*, 16 May 1905.

James, Henry. *The American Scene*. London: Chapman and Hall, 1907.

James, John A. "The Theatre of the Ghetto." *New York Dramatic Mirror*, 28 July 1900.

Johnson, Paul. *A History of the Jews*. New York: Harper & Row, 1987.

Joselit, Jenna Weissman. "Telling Tales: Or, How a Slum Became a Shrine." *Jewish Social Studies* 2 (Winter 1996), 54–63.

———. *The Wonders of America: Reinventing Jewish Culture, 1880–1950*. New York: Hill and Wang, 1994.

Joughin, John, ed. *Shakespeare and National Culture*. Manchester: Manchester University Press, 1997.

K. Retsenzent [pseud.]. "Hamlet." *Idisher ekspres*, 28 June 1922.

Kadison, Luba, and Joseph Buloff. *On Stage, Off Stage: Memories of a Lifetime in the Yiddish Theatre*. Cambridge, Mass.: Harvard University Press, 1992.

Kagan, Berl. *Leksikon fun yidish-shraybers*. New York: Ilman-Cohen, 1986.

Kaiser, William. "Der toes af der bine." In *Di idishe bine*, ed. Khonen Y. Minikes, n.p. New York: J. Katzenelnbogen, 1897.

Kalish, Bertha. "A brodveyer kholem." *Tog*, 12 November 1925.

Kaminska, Ida. *My Life, My Theater*. Trans. Curt Leviant. New York: Macmillan, 1973.

Katz, M. "Herr Yankev Adler in Shaylok." *Idishe velt*, 28 May 1903.

———. "Shaylok's tip revolutsyonirt." *Idishe velt*, 29 May 1903.

Kaufman, Dahlia. "The First Yiddish Translation of Julius Caesar," *The Field of Yiddish*, 5th Collection, ed. David Goldberg (YIVO and Northwestern University Press, 1993), 219–42.

Kaufman, Rhoda Helfman. "The Yiddish Theatre in New York and the Immigrant Community: Theatre as Secular Ritual." Ph.D. diss., University of California, Berkeley, 1986.

Kimmel, Stanley. *The Mad Booths of Maryland*. New York: Bobbs-Merrill, 1940.

"'King Lear' in Hebrew." *New York Times*, 13 August 1899.

Kobrin, Leon. *Dramatishe shriftn*. New York: Leon Kobrin Book Committee, 1952.

———. *Erinerungen fun a yidishn dramaturg*. 2 vols. New York: Committee for Kobrin's Writings, 1925.

———. "Di idishe kenigin Lir." *Arbeter tsaytung*, 21 August 1898.

———. *Mayne fuftsik yor in amerike*. Buenos Aires: Yidbukh, 1955.

———. "Shildkroyt in Shaylok." *Idisher kempfer*, 7 April 1911.

Kohansky, Mendel. "The Curtain Comes Down: A Hundred Years of the Yiddish Stage." *Forum* (1976), 112.

Kohn, Joshua. *The Synagogue in Jewish Life*. New York: Ktav, 1973.

Koralnik, A. "Der 'nar' bay Shekspir'n." *Tog*, 23 April 1916.

———. "Shekspir un di englishe literatur." *Tsukunft* 21 (May 1916), 429–32.

Kornblit, Z. *Di dramatishe kunst*. New York: Itshe Biderman, 1928.

———. "Di sheyne amerikanerin." *Yidishe bine*, 21 January 1910.

Kott, Jan. *Shakespeare Our Contemporary*. London: Methuen, 1964.

Krasni, Ariela. *Habadkhan*. Ramat Gan; Bar Ilan University, 1998.

Kritikovsky [pseud.]. "Klasishe trern." *Yidishe gazeten*, 11 November 1892.

Kushner, Tony. *Angels in America, Part One: Millennium Approaches*. New York: Theatre Communications Group, 1992.

L. "The True Shakespeare's Jew." *American Hebrew*, 15 May 1903.

L. B. "Schwartz Gives Shylock to Yiddish Stage." *New York Times*, 30 September 1947.

Der Lakhediger [pseud.]. "Halt Shekspir a hoyzn shop?" *Forverts*, 23 April 1916.

Lamb, Charles and Mary. *Tales From Shakespeare*. Philadelphia: Bradford and Inskeep, 1813.

Lamm, Maurice. *The Jewish Way in Death and Mourning*. New York: Jonathan David, 1969.

———. *The Jewish Way in Love and Marriage*. San Francisco: Harper & Row, 1980.

Landa, M. J. *The Jew in Drama*. London: P. S. King & Son, 1926.

———. *The Shylock Myth*. London: W. H. Allen, 1942.

Lawrence, Jerome. *Actor: The Life and Times of Paul Muni*. New York: Putnam, 1974.

Leach, Robert, and Victor Borovsky, eds. *A History of Russian Theatre*. Cambridge: Cambridge University Press, 1999.

Lederhendler, Eli. "Historical Reflections on the Problem of American Jewish Culture." *Jewish Social Studies* 5 (Fall 1998/Winter 1999), 40–51.

Leksikon fun der nayer yidisher literatur. 8 vols. New York: Congress for Jewish Culture, 1958–1981.

Lelyveld, Toby. *Shylock on the Stage*. London: Routledge & Kegan Paul, 1961.

Lerer, Leybush. "Shekspir oder Sheykspir?" *Yidishe shprakh* 1 (May–June 1941), 86–9.

Levine, Lawrence. *Highbrow/Lowbrow: The Emergence of Cultural Hierarchy in America*. Cambridge, Mass.: Harvard University Press, 1990.

Lewison, Ludwig. "The Homeless Muse." *The Nation* 111 (1 December 1920), 623.

Libin, Zalmen [Israel Zalmen Hurwitz]. *Geklibene skitsn*. New York: Forverts, 1902.

Lifson, David S. *The Yiddish Theatre in America*. New York: Thomas Yoseloff, 1965.

Lipsky, Louis. "Acting and Jacob P. Adler." *Jewish Exponent*, 8 May 1903.

Liptzin, Sol. *A History of Yiddish Literature*. New York: Jonathan David Publishers, 1972.

Loomba, Ania. "Shakespearian Transformations." In *Shakespeare and National Culture*, ed. John J. Joughin, 109–41. Manchester: Manchester University Press, 1997.

Luriye, Esther. "Shekspir un di daytshe literatur." *Tsukunft* 21 (May 1916), 433–7.

M. V. S. "New Iago Shown in the Yiddish Art Theater's 'Othello.'" *Herald Tribune*, 4 February 1929.

MacCarthy, Desmond. *Drama*. London: Putnam, 1940.

"Madame Kalisch as Hamlet." *New York Dramatic Mirror*, 9 February 1901.

Madison, Charles A. *Jewish Publishing in America*. New York: Sanhedrin Press, 1976.

Marmor, Kalmen. *Yankev Gordin*. New York: YKUF, 1953.

Marshall, Herbert, and Mildred Stock. *Ira Aldridge: The Negro Tragedian*. London: Rockliff, 1958.

Matis, Dovid. "'Mirele Efros' in moderne kleyder." *Morgen frayhayt*, 25 August 1939.

"Maurice Schwartz a Fervid Shylock." *New York Times*, 21 April 1930.

"Maurice Schwartz — Shylock in Vaudeville." *Day*, 27 April 1930.

Mazer, Cary M. *Shakespeare Refashioned: Elizabethan Plays on Edwardian Stages*. Ann Arbor: UMI Research Press, 1980.

McCormick, John. *Popular Theatres of Nineteenth-Century France*. London: Routledge, 1993.

Meersman, Roger. "The Meininger in America." *Speech Monographs* 33 (March 1966), 40–9.

Meserve, Walter. "Our English-American Playwrights of the Mid-Nineteenth Century." *Journal of American Drama and Theatre* 1 (Spring 1989), 5–18.

Mestel, Jacob. *Unzer teater*. New York: YKUF, 1943.

———. *Zibetsik yor teater repertuar*. New York: YKUF, 1954.

Milkh, Jacob. "Gedanken iber Shaylok." *Tsukunft* 16 (October 1911), 545–50.

Miller, James. *The Detroit Yiddish Theater, 1920 to 1937*. Detroit: Wayne State University Press, 1967.

Minikes, Khonen Jacob, ed. *Di idishe bine*. New York, 1897.

Miron, Dan. "Folklore and Antifolklore in the Yiddish Fiction of the *Haskala*." In *Studies in Jewish Folklore*, ed. Frank Talmage. Cambridge, Mass.: Association for Jewish Studies, 1980.

———. *A Traveler Disguised: The Rise of Modern Yiddish Fiction in the Nineteenth Century*. New York: Schocken Books, 1973.

Mor, Y. "Idish teater a la brodvey." *Tsukunft* 30 (December 1925), 715–6.

Morevski, Avrom. *Shaylok un Shekspir*. Vilna, 1937.

———. "Shekspir on shtivl." *Tsukunft* 34 (April 1929), 273–6.

"Moscovitch, a New Shylock in London." *Christian Science Monitor*, 4 November 1919.

Moscovitch, Maurice, and Y. L. Fayn, "Di lebns geshikhte fun dem idish-englishn shoyshpiler Moris Moskovitsh," *Forverts*, 27 December 1929.

"Mr. Adler in New York." *American Hebrew*, 29 May 1903.

"Mr. Adler as Shylock." *American Hebrew*, 8 May 1903.

"Mr. Adler Scores in Shylock Role." *New York Times*, 15 May 1905.

"Mr. Adler's Shylock." *Jewish Exponent*, 15 May 1903.

Mukdoyni, Alexander [Alexander Kapel]. "Moskovitsh-Shaylok." *Morgen zhurnal*, 4 December 1930.

———. "Parodye un komedye." *Morgen zhurnal*, 9 December 1932.

———. "Shekspir-oyffirungen." *Morgen zhurnal*, 17 February 1929.

———. *Teater*. New York: A. Mukdoyni Yubiley-Komitet, 1927.

———. "Teater-notitsn." *Morgen zhurnal*, 20 December 1936.

Nadir, Moyshe [Isaac Reiss]. "An intervyu mit Vilyam Shekspir." *Groyser kundes* 8 (21 April 1916), 5, 10.

Nahshon, Edna. *Yiddish Proletarian Theatre: The Art and Politics of the Artef, 1925–1940*. Westport, Conn.: Greenwood Press, 1998.

"Dos naye idishe teater." *Yidishes tageblat*, 12 November 1920.

"Der nayer Shaylok." *Yidishe gazeten*, 29 May 1903.

Niger, Shmuel. *Dertseylers un romanistn*. New York: CYCO, 1946.

Nomberg, H. D. "Romeo un Yulia." *Teater velt* 2 (29 January–19 March 1909).

"Notitsn." *Teater zhurnal*, 15 February 1902.

Novaks, William, and Moshe Waldoks, ed. *The Big Book of Jewish Humor*. New York: Harper & Row, 1981.

Nyuman, H. "Shekspir als poet un psikholog." *Tsukunft* 21 (May 1916), 426–9.

"The Observer." *Jewish Gazette English Supplement*, 22 February 1901.

Odell, G. C. D. *Annals of the New York Stage*, vols. 12–15. New York, 1940–1949.

———. *Shakespeare from Betterton to Irving*. 3 vols. New York, 1920.

Oggel, L. Terry. *Edwin Booth: A Bio-Bibliography*. Westport, Conn.: Greenwood Press, 1992.

Osherovitsh, M. *Dovid Kesler un Muni Vayzenfraynd*. New York, 1930.

Oyslender, N. *Yidisher teater, 1887–1917*. Moscow: Emes, 1940.

Ozick, Cynthia. "Actors." *New Yorker* (5 October 1998), 80–92.

———. "Envy; or, Yiddish in America." In *The Pagan Rabbi and Other Stories*. New York: E. P. Dutton, 1983.

Pasekh shin: sha [pseud.]. "Teater kritik: Hamlet prints fun denemark." *Yidishe gazeten*, 15 December 1893.

Pechter, Edward, ed. *Textual and Theatrical Shakespeare: Questions of Evidence*. Iowa City: University of Iowa Press, 1996.

Peretz, Y. L. *Ale verk*. New York: CYCO, 1947.

Perlmuter, Sholem. *Yidishe dramaturgn un teater-kompozitors*. New York: YKUF, 1952.

Perlzon, Y. "Mit hundert yor tsurik." *Der Forverts*, 10 April 1975.

Pif-paf [pseud.]. "Teater koyln." *Groyser kundes* 11 (7 February 1919), 5.

"Plays and Players." *Globe and Commercial Advertiser*, 16 May 1905.

"Plays and Players." *Theatre Magazine* 3 (July 1903), 160.

Pompador [pseud.]. "Drame-ayn, drame-oys." *Groyser kundes* 17 (30 October 1925), 6, 12.

Postlewait, Thomas. "The Hieroglyphic Stage: American Theatre and Society, Post-Civil War to 1945." In *The Cambridge History of American Theatre*, vol. 2, ed. Don B. Wilmeth and Christopher Bigsby, 107–95. Cambridge: Cambridge University Press, 1999.

Prager, Leonard. "Of Parents and Children: Jacob Gordin's *The Jewish King Lear*." *American Quarterly* 18 (1966), 506–16.

———. "Shakespeare in Yiddish." *Shakespeare Quarterly* 19 (1968), 149–63.

Prilutski, Noah. *Yidish teater*, vol. 2. Bialystok: A. Albek, 1921.

"A Quaint Hebrew Drama." *N.Y. Sun*, 22 February 1885.

Raphael, Marc Lee. "From Marjorie to Tevya: The Image of the Jews in American Popular Literature, Theatre and Comedy, 1955–1965." *American Jewish History* 74 (September 1984), 66–72.

Rathbun, Stephen. "In and Out of the Theater." *New York Sun*, 4 February 1929.

———. "New Apollo Theatre, Mary Nash and Ben Ami Start Their Season Next Week." *New York Sun*, 13 November 1920.

Retsenzent, K. [pseud.] "Hamlet." *Idisher ekspres*, 28 June 1922.

Rischin, Moses. *The Promised City: New York's Jews, 1870–1914.* Cambridge, Mass.: Harvard University Press, 1962.

Rogoff, Hillel. "Vilyam Shekspir, zayn leben un virken." *Tsukunft* 21 (April 1916), 299–302.

Rosenfeld, Morris. "Kuni leml un der idisher Kenig Lir." Reprinted in *Arkhiv far geshikhte fun yidishn teater un drame*, 1:448. Ed. Dr. Jacob Shatsky. Vilna: YIVO, 1930.

Ruggles, Eleanor. *Prince of Players: Edwin Booth.* New York: Norton, 1953.

Rumshinsky, Joseph. *Klangen fun mayn lebn.* New York: Itshe Biderman, 1944.

Sachar, Howard M. *A History of the Jews in America.* New York: Alfred A. Knopf, 1992.

Sanders, C. W. "Shakespeare in Yiddish." *Cleveland Plain Dealer Sunday Magazine*, 25 January 1903, 5.

Sanders, Ronald. *The Downtown Jews: Portraits of an Immigrant Generation.* New York: Harper & Row, 1969.

———. *Shores of Refuge.* New York: Schoken Books, 1988.

Sandrow, Nahma. *Vagabond Stars: A World History of Yiddish Theater.* New York: Harper & Row, 1977.

Sarna, Jonathan. "The Cult of Synthesis in American Jewish Culture." *Jewish Social Studies* 5 (Fall 1998/Winter 1999), 52–79.

Sayler, Oliver M., ed. *Max Reinhardt and His Theatre.* New York: Brentano's, 1924.

Schauss, Hayyim. *The Jewish Festivals.* Trans. Samuel Jaffe. New York: Union

of American Hebrew Congregations, 1938. Rpt. New York: Schocken
  Books, 1962.
————. *The Lifetime of a Jew.* New York: Union of American Hebrew
  Congregations, 1950.
Schildkraut, Joseph. *My Father and I.* New York: Viking, 1959.
"Schildkraut as Shylock." *New York Times,* 12 November 1920.
"Schildkraut Plays 'Merchant of Venice.'" *New York Mail,* 12 November 1920.
"Schildkraut Plays Shylock." *New York Clipper,* 17 November 1920.
Schwartz, Maurice. "The Art Era in the Yiddish Theatre." *Jewish Tribune,*
  19 April 1929.
————. "Maurice Schwartz erklert varum er shpilt in vaudeville." *Forverts,*
  11 April 1930.
————. "Shylock in Vaudeville." *Tog* English supplement, 27 April 1930.
"Schwartz First Did Shylock Under Williamsburg Bridge." *New York Herald
  Tribune,* 20 April 1930, VIII, 5.
"Schwartz to Act Iago." *New York Times,* 28 January 1929.
Scolnicov, Hanna, and Peter Holland, eds. *The Play Out of Context: Transferring
  Plays from Culture to Culture.* Cambridge: Cambridge University Press, 1989.
Seidman, Aaron B. "The First Performance of Yiddish Theatre in America."
  Jewish Social Studies 10 (January 1948), 67–70.
Seiger, Marvin. "A History of the Yiddish Theatre in New York City to
  1892." Ph.D. diss., Indiana University, 1960.
Seller, Maxine Schwartz, ed. *Ethnic Theatre in the United States.* Westport, Conn.:
  Greenwood Press, 1983.
Shamay [pseud.]. "Shekspirs lebn un zayn groyser nomen." *Forverts,* 23 April
  1916.
Shapiro, James. *Shakespeare and the Jews.* New York: Columbia University Press,
  1996.
Shattuck, Charles. *Shakespeare on the American Stage.* 2 vols. Washington, D.C.:
  Folger Shakespeare Library, 1976 and 1987.
Shatzky, J. "An akhashveyresh-shpil mit 100 yor tsurik." In *Arkhiv far geshikhte
  fun yidishn teater un drame,* ed. Jacob Shatzky, 159–74. Vilna: YIVO, 1930.
————. "Di ershte geshikhte fun yidishn teater." *Filologishe shriftn* 2 (Vilna,
  1928), 215–64.
Shatzky, Jacob, ed. *Arkhiv far geshikhte fun yidishn teater un drame.* Vilna: YIVO,
  1930.
————. "Goldfadens a statut far a yidisher dramatisher shul in nyu-york, in
  1888," in *Arkhiv far geshikhte fun yidishn teater un drame.*
"Shaylok der id." *Yidishe gazeten,* 15 May 1903.
"Shildkroyt als Shaylok." *Yidishes tageblat,* 26 March 1911.
Shiper, I. *Geshikhte fun yidisher teater — kunst un drame.* 3 vols. Warsaw: Kultur
  Lige, 1923–1928.
Shmeruk, Khone. *Makhazot mikrayim beyidish, 1697–1750.* Jerusalem: Academy
  of Sciences and Humanities, 1979.

A shtendiger oyrekh [pseud.]. "Moris Moskovitsh in der role fun 'Shaylok' af der englisher bine." *Forverts*, 4 November 1919.

Sinsheimer, Hermann. *Shylock: The History of a Character.* 1947. Rpt. New York: Benjamin Blom, 1963.

Skinner, Cornelia Otis. *Madame Sarah.* Boston: Houghton Mifflin, 1967.

Slobin, Mark. *Tenement Songs: The Popular Music of the Jewish Immigrants.* Urbana: University of Illinois Press, 1982.

Soltes, Mordecai. *The Yiddish Press: An Americanizing Agency.* New York: Columbia University Teachers College, 1925.

Sorin, Gerald. "Mutual Contempt, Mutual Benefit: The Strained Encounter Between German and Eastern European Jews in America, 1880–1920." *American Jewish History* 81 (Autumn 1993), 34–59.

———. *A Time for Building: The Third Migration, 1880–1920.* Baltimore: Johns Hopkins University Press, 1992.

Soyer, Daniel. *Jewish Immigrant Associations and American Identity in New York, 1880–1939.* Cambridge, Mass.: Harvard University Press, 1997.

Speaight, Robert. *Shakespeare on the Stage: An Illustrated History of Shakespearian Performance.* London: Collins, 1973.

Sprague, Arthur Colby. *Shakespearian Players and Performances.* Cambridge, Mass.: Harvard University Press, 1953.

Stokes, John, Michael R. Booth, and Susan Bassnett. *Bernhardt, Terry, Duse: The Actress in Her Time.* Cambridge: Cambridge University Press, 1988.

Stříbrný, Zdeněk. *Shakespeare and Eastern Europe.* Oxford Shakespeare Topics, ed. Peter Holland and Stanley Wells. Oxford: Oxford University Press, 2000.

Tashrak [Yisroel-Yoysef Zevin]. *Etikete.* New York: Hebrew Publishing Company, 1912.

Taylor, Gary. *Reinventing Shakespeare: A Cultural History, from the Restoration to the Present.* New York: Weidenfeld & Nicolson, 1989.

Taytlboym, Avrom. *Vilyam Shekspir.* New York: YKUF, 1946.

"The Theatres." *Commercial Advertiser*, 23 February 1901.

Thomashefsky, Bessie. *Mayn lebns-geshikhte.* New York: Varhayt Publishing, 1916.

Thomashefsky, Boris. "Hamlet af der yidisher bine." *Teater velt*, November 1908.

———. *Mayn lebns-geshikhte.* New York: Trio Press, 1937.

"The True Shakespeare's Jew." *American Hebrew*, 15 May 1903.

Tyrrell, Henry. "Jacob Adler — The Bowery Garrick." *Theatre Magazine* 2 (November 1902), 18–9.

Urkowitz, Steven. *Shakespeare's Revision of* King Lear. Princeton: Princeton University Press, 1980.

Valdman, A. "Shekspir tsvishen di dramaturgen." *Varhayt*, 2 May 1916.

"Vaudeville." *New York World*, 20 April 1930.

Vaynshteyn, B. "Di ershte yorn fun yidishn teater in odes un in nyu-york." In

Arkhiv far geshikhte fun yidishn teater un drame, ed. Jacob Shatzky. Vilna: YIVO, 1930.

Vintshevski, Morris. "Shaylok, a idisher id." *Forverts*, 28 December 1901.

"Vos far a min yid iz Shaylok?" *Teater zhurnal* 1 (February 1902).

"Vos Mogulesko denkt vegn Shildkroyt's shpiln." *Forverts*, 9 September 1911.

Watts, Richard, Jr. "Yiddish Art Company Offers Shylock Play." *New York Post*, 7 October 1947.

Weinreich, Max. "Tsu der geshikhte fun der elterer akhashveyresh-shpil." *Filologishe shriftn* 2 (Vilna, 1928), 425–52.

Whitfield, Stephen J. *In Search of American Jewish Culture*. Hanover, N.H.: Brandeis University Press, 1999.

———. "Our American Jewish Heritage: The Hollywood Version." *American Jewish History* 75 (March 1986), 322–40.

Whittaker, Herbert. "Maurice Schwartz, Actor." *Montreal Gazette*, 9 June 1945.

Wilken, Jeanette. "Schwartz an Authentic New 'Shylock.'" *New York Daily News*, 1 October 1947.

Williams, Simon. *German Actors of the Eighteenth and Nineteenth Centuries*. Westport, Conn.: Greenwood Press, 1985.

———. *Shakespeare on the German Stage*. Volume 1: 1586–1914. Cambridge. Cambridge University Press, 1990.

Wilmeth, Don B., and Christopher Bigsby, eds. *The Cambridge History of American Theatre*. Volume 2: 1870–1945. Cambridge: Cambridge University Press, 1999.

Winter, William. *Shakespeare on the Stage*. 1911. Rpt. New York: Benjamin Blom, 1969.

Wolitz, Seth. "The Americanization of Tevye or Boarding the Jewish *Mayflower*." *American Quarterly* 40 (December 1988), 514–36.

Wyszkowski, Yehezkel. "*The American Hebrew*: An Exercise in Ambivalence." *American Jewish History* 76 (March 1987), 340–53.

Yablokoff, Herman. *Arum der velt mit yidish teater*. 2 vols. New York, 1969.

———. *Der Payatz: Around the World With Yiddish Theater*. Trans. Bella Mysell Yablokoff. Silver Spring, Md.: Bartleby Press, 1995.

Yaffe, Richard A. "'Shylock and Daughter' Sets Record Straight." *P. M.*, 6 October 1947.

"Yiddish Art Theatre Gives 'New' Othello." *New York Times*, 4 February 1929.

"Yiddish Duse, About to Make Her Debut on the English Stage in 'Fedora,' Discusses Her Art and Her Ambitions." *New York Times*, 14 May 1905, III, 5.

"The Yiddish Shylock." *New York Times*, 26 May 1903.

"The Yiddish Shylock of Jacob P. Adler." *New York Times*, 16 May 1905.

"Yiddish Shylock Viewed from Ghetto Standpoint." *New York Times*, 31 May 1903.

Yidisher teater in eyrope tsvishn beyde velt-milkhomes. 2 vols. New York: Congress for Jewish Culture, 1968 and 1971.

Young, Boaz. *Mayn lebn in teater.* New York: YKUF, 1950.

Zangwill, Israel. *Ghetto Comedies.* New York: Macmillan, 1923.

Zeifert, Moyshe. "Alts tsulib parnose." *Idishe bine,* 17 December 1909.

——. "Ester Rokhl Kaminski." *Di yidishe gazeten,* 15 August 1909.

——. "Di geshikhte fun idishn teater." In *Di idishe bine,* ed. Khonen Jacob Minikes. New York, 1897.

——. "Der groyser mes." In *Amerike,* ed. Y. Vortsman. New York: Farlag "Natsyonale Bibliotek," 1909.

Zinberg, Israel. *A History of Jewish Literature.* 12 vols. Trans. Bernard Martin. Cincinnati: Hebrew Union College/Ktav, 1975.

Zolotarov, H. "Di tipen fun Shekspir's dramen." *Varhayt,* 7 May 1916.

Zylbercweig, Zalmen. *Leksikon fun yidishn teater.* 6 vols. New York, Warsaw, Mexico City, 1931–1970.

——. "Moris Shvarts zogt 'Shaylok's tokhter' hot groyse idish-natsyonale misye.'" *Morgen zhurnal,* 25 July 1947.

——. "Shekspir af der yidisher bine un literatur." In *100 yor yidish teater,* ed. Charles Klinger (London: Jewish Cultural Society, 1962), 26–32.

——. *Teater mozayik.* New York: Itshe Biderman, 1941.

——. *Di velt fun Yankev Gordin.* Tel Aviv: Elisheva, 1964.

——. *Vos der yidisher aktyor dertseylt.* Vilna: B. Kletzkin, 1928.

Index

Studies in Theatre History and Culture

Actors and American Culture, 1880–1920
  By Benjamin McArthur

The Age and Stage of George L. Fox, 1825–1877: An Expanded Edition
  By Laurence Senelick

Classical Greek Theatre: New Views of an Old Subject
  By Clifford Ashby

Embodied Memory: The Theatre of George Tabori
  By Anat Feinberg

Fangs of Malice: Hypocrisy, Sincerity, and Acting
  By Matthew H. Wikander

Marginal Sights: Staging the Chinese in America
  By James S. Moy

Melodramatic Formations: American Theatre and Society, 1820–1870
  By Bruce A. McConachie

Meyerhold: A Revolution in Theatre
  By Edward Braun

Modern Czech Theatre: Reflector and Conscience of a Nation
  By Jarka M. Burian

Modern Hamlets and Their Soliloquies
  By Mary Z. Maher

Othello and Interpretive Traditions
  By Edward Pechter

Our Moonlight Revels: *A Midsummer Night's Dream* in the Theatre
  By Gary Jay Williams

The Performance of Power: Theatrical Discourse and Politics
  Edited by Sue-Ellen Case and Janelle Reinelt

Performing History: Theatrical Representations of the Past in
Contemporary Theatre
By Freddie Rokem

The Recurrence of Fate: Theatre and Memory in Twentieth-Century Russia
By Spencer Golub

Reflecting the Audience: London Theatregoing, 1840–1880
By Jim Davis and Victor Emeljanow

Shakespeare on the American Yiddish Stage
By Joel Berkowitz

The Show and the Gaze of Theatre: A European Perspective
By Erika Fischer-Lichte

Textual and Theatrical Shakespeare: Questions of Evidence
Edited by Edward Pechter

The Theatrical Event: Dynamics of Performance and Perception
By Willmar Sauter

The Trick of Singularity: *Twelfth Night* and the Performance Editions
By Laurie E. Osborne

Wandering Stars: Russian Emigré Theatre, 1905–1940
Edited by Laurence Senelick